Web Design

VIRTUAL CLASSROOM

About the Author

Laurie started her professional life planning to be an artist, but she discovered computers in 1981 and has been hooked on them ever since. Moving from computer systems management to running computer training centers and then to forming her own computer training and consulting firm (Limehat & Company, Inc.), Laurie has been helping businesses, nonprofit organizations, and individuals make effective use of computers for nearly 20 years. In 1998, she added Web design and Web site hosting to the list of services offered by her company, finally enabling her to combine her creative ability and technical interests. Since 1990, Laurie has trained thousands of students, written hundreds of computer training manuals, and in the last three years has sole authored, cowritten, and contributed to more than 15 nationally published computer books on topics ranging from Microsoft Office to using the Internet to plan a vacation. Her main personal and professional Web site can be found at www.planetlaurie.com, and she can be reached via e-mail at laurie@planetlaurie.com.

Web Design

Virtual Classroom

Laurie Ann Ulrich

Osborne / McGraw-Hill

New York   Chicago   San Francisco
Lisbon   London   Madrid   Mexico City
Milan   New Delhi   San Juan
Seoul   Singapore   Sydney   Toronto

Osborne/**McGraw-Hill**
2600 Tenth Street
Berkeley, California 94710
U.S.A.

To arrange bulk purchase discounts for sales promotions, premiums, or fund-raisers, please contact Osborne/**McGraw-Hill** at the above address. For information on translations or book distributors outside the U.S.A., please see the International Contact Information page immediately following the index of this book.

Web Design Virtual Classroom

Brainsville.com™
The better way to learn.

1234567890 QPD QPD 01987654321

Book p/n 0-07-213110-1 and CD p/n 0-07-213109-8
parts of
ISBN 0-07-213111-X

Publisher	**Acquisitions Coordinator**	**Production Manager**
Brandon A. Nordin	Alissa Larson	epic/Eric Houts
Vice President & Associate Publisher	**Copy Editor**	**Computer and Series Designer**
Scott Rogers	Lunaea Weatherstone	epic/Andrea Reider
Editorial Director	**Proofreader**	**Illustrators**
Roger Stewart	Paul Tyler	Michael Mueller
		Lyssa Sieben-Wald
	Indexer	Beth E. Young
Project Editor	Valerie Robbins	
Patty Mon		**Cover Design**
		Ted Holladay

This book was composed with QuarkXPress™.

Dedication

I dedicate this book to Jasper, whose Web site has astounded me with the positive power of the Internet to give people hope, to improve lives, and to help people who share a common bond find each other and exchange vital information. To some people, Jasper is "only a cat." To me and to my family, he is a wonderful friend—a bright, loving creature who gives and demands affection, winning over everyone with whom he comes in contact. He is a source of unconditional love, complete understanding, and total acceptance, and has been for many years. He can't read (at least, I don't *think* he can), but I hope he knows about all the cats his Web site has helped, and that his site wouldn't exist if it weren't for his bravery and will to survive a terrible illness. His very simple (yet well-designed!) site has had thousands of visitors in just the last year, and I receive e-mail from visitors every day. If you love a cat or know anyone who does, please visit Jasper's Web site: http://www.laurieulrich.com/jasper/.

Contents at a Glance

Contents

Acknowledgments

I'd like to thank Roger Stewart for sharing my vision for this book and giving me the opportunity to write it. I'd also like to thank my editors and the rest of the staff who worked on this book: Alissa Larson, Patty Mon, Lunaea Weatherstone, and Mitch Thomas. Your suggestions and eagle-eyes for detail were invaluable in producing what I hope is a useful and enjoyable book for both experienced and fledgling Web designers.

I must also thank Robert Fuller, my partner in crime, life, work, and everything else. Robert has taught me a great deal about creating Web sites and pages. When I get carried away with the artistic side of things, Robert's respect for the technology and unending desire to do things the right way is an inspiration, and he has helped me turn my frustrated imaginings into functioning pages on many occasions.

Thanks must also go to my mom, Ann Talbot. The ultimate art teacher, she always supported my healthy inclination to color outside of the lines, yet taught me to draw accurately, to paint expressively, and to see the world around me through an artist's eyes.

Introduction

Who Will Enjoy this Book?

You will, if you're a Web designer, want to be a Web designer, or ever thought about being a Web designer. If you're a graphic designer, currently working in the world of print media, you'll enjoy this book because it helps you take what you already know about good design and apply it to the specific needs of the Web. The concepts and ideas I share in this book are intended to enhance the pages you design, giving you some basic rules that won't confine your designs, but will free your creativity by providing a solid design foundation for them.

This book doesn't focus on any particular software product, although the most popular applications are used in illustrations and figures. Certain general techniques and procedures are drawn from the features and commands offered by applications such as Macromedia Dreamweaver, Microsoft FrontPage, Adobe GoLive, Adobe Photoshop, and Macromedia Fireworks. This book is not intended to teach you to use any of these products, but will familiarize you with them and how they work. The general procedures and features covered in this book will enable you to learn these applications more quickly, because you'll be familiar with what they do, how their interface looks and works, and the tools they provide to assist you in designing Web pages and creating graphics for use on the Web.

WHAT MAKES THIS A VIRTUAL CLASSROOM?

The accompanying CD makes this book a "virtual classroom." Instead of just reading about the design topics covered, you can watch and listen to the author (me!) discuss them as helpful visuals appear onscreen, demonstrating software features and design techniques. In addition to a view of my computer screen as I demonstrate features, you'll also see bulleted lists that emphasize and enumerate important points in the discussion.

It's important to note that the CD is not a visual repetition of the book—not everything discussed in the book is covered on the CD, and there are topics broached on the CD that are covered in more detail there than in the book. The goal of the CD is to give you the experience of sitting in on one of my Web design classes, allowing me to elaborate on certain topics that could be better expressed and explained in a full-color, moving medium. Topics in the book that wouldn't be any better explained through sound, color, and motion are not found on the CD, while topics that couldn't be effectively explained through text and black-and-white images *are* found on the CD.

It's entirely possible to learn a great deal from the book without ever watching the CD, and it's also possible to watch the CD and learn a lot without reading too much of the book. I hope, however, that you'll read the book and then watch the CD to enhance what you've absorbed through your reading. This would be the closest match to the hands-on classroom training experience, where I typically discuss a topic and then show it or demonstrate it for the class, inviting the students to work along with me on their computers so that the skills become part of each student's personal experience.

HOW THIS BOOK WORKS

Of course, you know how a book *works*: you open it, and start reading, turning pages as you go. Not too difficult, right? This book, however, has some useful features that you should be aware of:

▶ Tips and sidebars Whenever I thought of something that I'd present as a quick aside during class, I turned it into a tip. Tips relate to the main topic in the nearby text, but are extra bits of helpful information rather than entire topics unto themselves. Sidebars delve a little deeper, discussing larger topics that relate to nearby text.

▶ CD references At the end of chapters containing topics covered on the CD, an "On the Virtual Classroom CD-ROM" notation will appear, directing you to the specific CD lesson that relates to the chapter you've just read.

▶ A handy glossary I thought that by including an alphabetized list of Web and design-related terms, you could learn a little of the lingo, making it easier to become fluent in and comfortable with the Web and the design issues related to it. All the terms in the glossary are found in the book, and many are explained in context within the chapters. I repeated them in the glossary to give you one-stop shopping for the terminology of Web design, graphics, color, and composition.

I hope you enjoy this book, and if you have any specific design questions or quandaries, I invite you to contact me via e-mail at laurie@planetlaurie.com. I answer all reader mail, attempting to do so within 24 to 48 hours of receiving it. I look forward to hearing from you!

 ## WEB DESIGN VIRTUAL CLASSROOM CD

This CD contains an exciting new kind of video-based instruction to help you learn Web design faster. We believe this learning tool is a unique development in the area of computer-based training. The author actually talks to you, right from your computer screen, demonstrating topics she wrote about in the book.

Moving "screencams" and slides accompany her presentation, reinforcing what you're learning.

The technology and design of the presentation were developed by Brainsville.com. The content on the CD-ROM was developed by Osborne/McGraw-Hill, Laurie Ann Ulrich, and Brainsville.com. Patents (pending), copyright, and trademark protections apply to this technology and the name Brainsville.com.

Please read the following directions for usage of the CD-ROM, to ensure that the lessons play as smoothly as possible.

GETTING STARTED

The CD-ROM is optimized to run under Windows 95/98/Me/NT/2000 using the RealPlayer version 8 (or greater), from RealNetworks. However, it will also run fine on most PowerPC Macintoshes with RealPlayer for the Mac. (Note that RealPlayer versions earlier than 8 will not work.) If you don't have the RealPlayer installed, you must install it, either by downloading it from the Internet at www.real.com, or running the Setup program from the CD-ROM. To install from the Web, you should download the latest RealPlayer. You can choose the Basic player, which is free, if you don't want to purchase the full version. You typically have to look around a bit to get to the correct page. You're looking for RealPlayer "Basic."

To install RealPlayer from the CD-ROM follow these steps:

On a Windows PC

1. Insert the CD-ROM in the drive.
2. Use Explorer or My Computer to browse to the CD-ROM.
3. Open the RealPlayer folder and then open the correct folder for your type of computer.
4. Double-click on the setup program there.
5. Follow the setup instructions on screen.

On a Mac

1. Insert the CD-ROM in the drive.
2. Open the RealPlayer folder and then open the folder containing the Mac version of the RealPlayer.

3. Run the Publishing RM8A Installer file.

4. Follow the setup instructions on screen.

RUNNING THE CD IN WINDOWS 95/98/ME/NT/2000

Minimum Requirements

RealPlayer 8 or later

Pentium II P333 (or equivalent)

64M RAM

8X CD ROM

16-bit sound card and speakers

65,000-color video display card (video)

Windows 95, Windows 98, Windows 2000, Windows ME, or Windows NT 4.0 with at least Service Pack 4

Web Design Virtual Classroom CD-ROM can run directly from the CD (see below for running it from the hard drive for better performance if necessary) and should start automatically when you insert the CD in the drive. If the program does not start automatically, your system may not be set up to automatically detect CDs. To change this, you can do the following:

1. Choose Settings, Control Panel, and click the System icon.

2. Click the Device Manager tab in the System Properties dialog box.

3. Double-click the Disk drives icon and locate your CD-ROM drive.

4. Double-click the CD-ROM drive icon and then click the Settings tab in the CD-ROM Properties dialog box. Make sure the "Auto insert notification box" is checked. This specifies that Windows will be notified when you insert a compact disc into the drive.

If you don't care about the auto-start setting for your CD-ROM, and don't mind the manual approach, you can start the lessons manually, this way:

1. Insert the CD-ROM.

2. Double-click the My Computer icon on your Windows desktop.

3. Open the CD-ROM folder.

4. Double-click the jmenu.exe icon in the folder.

5. Follow instructions on the screen to start.

RUNNING ON A MAC

Minimum Requirements

RealPlayer 8 or later

Mac* OS 8.1 or later

32 MB RAM

Virtual Memory turned on, set to 64MB

604 PowerPC* (200 MHz or better)

1. Insert the CD-ROM.

2. Open the CD-ROM folder.

3. Double-click on the ClickToStart icon. If this doesn't work, then open the RealPlayer and from the RealPlayer window open the ClickToStart file. It should begin playing.

4. Follow instructions as described by the author, or read the section below.

THE OPENING SCREEN

When the program autostarts on a PC, you'll see a small window in the middle of your screen with an image of the book. Simply click the book to launch the RealPlayer and start the lessons. On the Mac, you have to start the Virtual Classroom manually as described above.

Regardless of how you start the Virtual Classroom, the RealPlayer window should soon open and the Virtual Classroom introduction should begin running. You click on the links in the lower left region of the RealPlayer window to jump to a given lesson. The author will explain how to use the interface.

The RealPlayer will completely fill a screen that is running at 800x600 resolution. (This is the minimum resolution required to play the lessons). For screens with higher resolution, you can adjust the position of the player on screen, as you like. If the content panel in the RealPlayer is turned on, you'll see a number of entertainment and news stations listed on the left side of the RealPlay window. You can turn those off by going to the program's View menu and choosing Content Pane.

If you are online, you can click on the Brainsville.com logo under the index marks to jump directly to the Brainsville.com Web site for information about the additional hour of instructional material we have available. (See the description in the back of the book, or run the promotional trailer at the end of the Conclusion lesson for more details.)

IMPROVING PLAYBACK

Your Virtual Classroom CD-ROM employs some cutting-edge technologies, requiring that your computer be pretty fast to run the lessons smoothly. For example, each lesson actually runs two videos at the same time—one for the instructor's image and one for the screen cam. Many variables determine a computer's video performance, so we can't give you specific requirements for running the lessons. CPU speed, internal bus speed, amount of RAM, CD-ROM drive transfer rate, video display performance, CD-ROM cache settings and other variables will determine how well the lessons will play. Our advice is to simply try the CD. The disk has been tested on laptops and desktops of various speeds, and in general, we have determined that you'll need at least a Pentium II-class computer running in excess of 300Mhz for decent performance. (If you're doing serious Web-design work, it's likely your machine is at least this fast.)

CLOSE OTHER PROGRAMS

For best performance, make sure you are not running other programs in the background while viewing the CD-based lessons. Rendering the video on your screen takes a lot of computing power, and background programs such as automatic e-mail checking, Web-site updating, or Active Desktop applets (such as scrolling stock tickers) can tax the CPU to the point of slowing the videos.

ADJUST THE SCREEN COLOR DEPTH
TO SPEED UP PERFORMANCE

It's possible the author's lips will be out of synch with his or her voice, just like Web-based videos often look. There are a couple solutions. Start with this one. Lowering the color depth to 16 bit color makes a world of difference with many computers, laptops included. Rarely do people need 24-bit or 32-bit color for their work anyway, and it makes scrolling your screen (in any program) that much slower when running in those higher color depths. Try this:

1. Right click on the desktop and choose Properties.
2. Click the Settings tab.

3. In the Colors section, open the drop-down list box and choose a lower setting. If you are currently running at 24-bit (True Color) color, for example, try 16-bit (High Color). Don't use 256 colors, since video will appear very funky if you do, and you'll be prompted by RealPlayer to increase the color depth anyway.

4. OK the box. With most computers these days, you don't have to restart the computer after making this change. The RealPlayer should run more smoothly now, since your computer's CPU docsn't have to work as hard to paint the video pictures on your screen.

If copying the files to the hard disk didn't help the synch problem, see the section below about copying the CD's files to the hard disk.

TURN OFF SCREEN SAVERS, SCREEN BLANKERS, AND STANDBY OPTIONS

When lessons are playing you're likely to not interact with the keyboard or mouse. Because of this, your computer screen might blank, and in some cases (such as with laptops) the computer might even go into a standby mode. You'll want to prevent these annoyances by turning off your screen saver and by checking the power options settings to ensure they don't kick in while you're viewing the lessons. You make settings for both of these parameters from the Control Panel.

1. Open Control Panel, choose Display, and click on the Screen Saver tab. Choose "None" for the screen saver.

2. Open Control Panel, choose Power Management, and set System Standby, Turn off Monitor, and Turn off Hard Disks to "Never." Then click Save As and save this power setting as "Brainsville Courses." You can return your power settings to their previous state if you like, after you are finished viewing the lessons. Just use the Power Schemes drop-down list and choose one of the factory-supplied settings, such as Home/Office Desk.

COPY THE CD FILES TO THE HARD DISK TO SPEED UP PERFORMANCE

The CD-ROM drive will whir quite a bit when running the lessons from the CD. If your computer or CD-ROM drive is a bit slow, it's possible the author's lips will be out of synch with his or her voice, just like Web-based videos often look. The video might freeze or slow down occasionally, though the audio will typically keep going along just fine. If you don't like the CD constantly whirring, or you are annoyed by out-of-synch video, you may be able to solve either or both problems by copying the CD-ROM's contents to your hard disk and running the lessons from there. To do so:

1. Using My Computer or Explorer, check to see that you have at least 650M free space on your hard disk.

2. Create a new folder on your hard disk (the name doesn't matter) and copy all the contents of the CD-ROM to the new folder (you must preserve the subfolder names and folder organization as it is on the CD-ROM).

3. Once this is done, you can start the program by opening the new folder and double-clicking on the file jmenu.exe. This will automatically start the lessons and run them from the hard disk.

4. (Optional) For convenience, you can create a shortcut to the jmenu.exe file and place it on your desktop. You will then be able to start the program by clicking on the shortcut.

UPDATE YOUR REALPLAYER

The RealPlayer software is updated frequently and posted on the RealNetworks Web site. You can update your software by clicking Help, then Check for Updates, on the RealPlayer window. We strongly suggest you do this from time to time.

MAKE SURE YOUR CD-ROM DRIVE IS SET FOR OPTIMUM PERFORMANCE

CD-ROM drives on IBM PCs can be set to transfer data using the DMA (Direct Memory Access) mode, assuming the drive supports this faster mode. If you are experiencing slow performance and out-of-synch problems, check this setting. These steps are for Windows 98 and Windows ME.

1. Open Control Panel, chose System.

2. Click on the Device Manager tab.

3. Click on the + sign to the left of the CD-ROM drive.

4. Right-click on the CD-ROM drive.

5. Choose Properties.

6. Click the Settings tab.

7. Look to see if the DMA check box is turned on (has a check mark in it).

If selected, this increases the CD-ROM drive access speed. Some drives do not support this option. If the DMA check box remains selected after you restart Windows, then this option is supported by the device.

In Windows 2000, the approach is a little different. You access the drive's settings via Device Manager as above, but click on IDE/ATAPI Controllers. Right-click the IDE channel that your CD-ROM drive is on, choose Properties, and make the settings as appropriate. (Choose the device number, 0 or 1, and check the settings.) Typically it's set to "DMA if available," which is fine. It's not recommended that you change these settings unless you know what you are doing.

TROUBLESHOOTING

This section offers solutions to common problems. (Check www.real.com for much more information about the RealPlayer, which is the software the Virtual Classroom CDs use to play.)

THE CD WILL NOT RUN

If you have followed the instructions above and the program will not work, you may have a defective drive or a defective CD. Be sure the CD is inserted properly in the drive. (Test the drive with other CDs, to see if they run.)

REALPLAYER HANGS AT THE BEGINNING

Sometimes the RealPlayer opens up in a small window and just seems to hang. If you wait a few seconds (perhaps 15 seconds), it will sometimes start up. If not, you may have to restart the computer to get the RealPlayer to start properly again.

THE SCREEN-CAM MOVIE IN A LESSON HANGS

If the author continues to talk, but the accompanying screen-cam seems to be stuck, just click on the lesson index in the lower left region of the RealPlayer window to begin your specific lesson again. If this doesn't help, close the RealPlayer window, and start the Virtual Classroom again.

VOLUME IS TOO LOW OR IS TOTALLY SILENT

1. Check your system volume first. Click on the little speaker icon next to the clock, down in the lower-right-hand corner of the screen. A little slider pops up. Adjust the slider, and make sure the Mute check box is not checked.

2. Next, if you have external speakers on your computer, make sure your speakers are turned on, plugged in, wired up properly, and the volume control on the speakers themselves is turned up.

3. Note that the RealPlayer also has a volume control setting. The setting is reached by clicking on the little speaker icon in the upper-right-hand corner of the RealPlayer window.

4. The next place to look if you're still having trouble is in the Windows volume controls. Double-click on the little speaker by the clock, and it will bring up the Windows Volume Control sliders. Make sure slider for "Wave" is not muted, and it's positioned near the top.

GARBLED OR WEIRD VIDEO IMAGE AND/OR REALPLAYER FREEZES

Many popular video cards use WinDraw drivers instead of DirectDraw drivers. The WinDraw driver incorrectly reports the capability of the video hardware to RealPlayer, causing RealPlayer to think that the video hardware can do things that it cannot. When the video is optimized and the video hardware cannot support the optimization, problems will occur. Problems range from poor quality or garbled video to RealPlayer becoming unresponsive and system freezes. If you experience similar problems, try disabling the Optimized Video setting in RealPlayer.

To disable Optimized Video in RealPlayer:

1. Start RealPlayer.

2. Click the View menu and choose Preferences.

3. Click the Performance tab.

4. Click to clear the "Use optimized video display" check box in the Video card compatibility section.

5. Click OK.

6. Restart your computer.

The following cards are known to have DirectDraw problems. Regardless of the setting in RealPlayer, optimized video is automatically disabled if any of the following card and driver combinations are detected:

ATI Rage II+ PCI, ati_m64

RAGE PRO TURBO AGP 2X (English)

Matrox Millennium G200, AGPMGAXDD32.DLL Matrox

Millennium G200 AGP, mga64.dll

Matrox Millennium G200 AGP, tsirchnl.dll

Matrox Millennium II PowerDesk, MGAXDD32.DLL

Matrox Millennium II PCI, mgapdx64.drv

Diamond Viper V33", vprddle.DLL

NVIDIA GeForce 256 AGP Plus (Dell), NVDD32.DLL

Diamond Viper V330, vprdrvle.drv

Diamond Viper V550, NVDD32.DLL

NVIDIA RIVA TNT2 Ultra, NVDD32.DLL

Hercules Thriller 3D Series (v 0.81.3539), v200032.dll

Diamond Multimedia Systems, Inc.

Stealth II G460 Ver. 1.12\x0d\x0aV, stlthg46.dll

STB Lightspeed 128, with STB Vision 95, stbvisn.drv

Diamond SpeedStar A50 for Windows 98, DMSSA50x.dll

ALL STB cards that use nVidia Riva 182zx:

STB Velocity 128 3D, stbv128.drv

STB Velocity 128 (TV Support), STBV128.DRV

STB Lightspeed 128, without STB Vision 95, stbls128.drv

S3 Inc. Trio64V+, s3_2.drv

Chips And Technologies, Accelerator (new), chipsnd.drv

Cirrus Logic 7548 PCI, cirrusmm.drv

NeoMagic controllers (widely used in Dell laptops):

NeoMagic MagicGraph 128XD, NmgcDD.dll

NeoMagic MagicGraph 128XD, Nmgc.drv

NeoMagic MagicGraph 128 PCI, nmx.drv

NeoMagic MagicMedia 256AV, NmgcDD5.dll

Diamond Stealth II G460, s2g432le.dll

Diamond Stealth II G460, s2g432le.dll

(This last section courtesy RealNetworks' Web site, www.real.com.)

FOR TECHNICAL SUPPORT

Phone Hudson Software at (800) 217-0059

Visit www.real.com (lots of tips there for tweaking RealPlayer performance)

Visit www.brainsville.com

© 2001 The McGraw-Hill Companies

© 2001 Brainsville.com Patents pending

1

What Kind of Web Site Do You Need?

What is a Web site, really? It's a space that a business, nonprofit organization, school, individual, or family can carve out in cyberspace and call their own. Deciding what kind of site you want to design is based on what you want people to do when they visit your site and what's in it for you. People visit Web sites to do a lot of things, including shop, find jobs, get driving directions and maps, look up phone numbers, do research, and quite often, just be entertained. It's important to understand the different types of Web sites there are and what roles they play so you can have a clear picture of yours in mind as you begin the design process.

DEFINING YOUR WEB SITE'S ROLE

The best way to find out what role your Web site will play is to decide what you want from it. The first step in the process of deciding what you want is to identify yourself with respect to the Web site. Are you the designer, working for someone else? If so, it's that person or organization's interests and goals that you need to understand, and you can use a lot of the concepts in this chapter to successfully elicit that information. Not surprisingly, many people who hire Web designers don't know what they want in their Web site, and it becomes the designer's job to help them figure it out.

Are you the owner of the site in addition to being the designer? Then you need to focus on your goals and figure out the best kind of Web site to meet them. Picture the site in your mind, and picture someone visiting it. Don't worry about the specifics of the design and layout yet, just imagine what you want the visitor's time at your site to accomplish. Should they select you to provide a product or service? Should they become informed about some subject? Should they have fun?

BUSINESS WEB SITES

If you run a business, a Web site can be an extension of your advertising efforts, as shown in Figure 1-1. It can be an electronic ad, similar in purpose to a print ad you'd place in a newspaper or magazine. Unlike a print ad, however, a Web site can include all the information you probably have in your brochures and other marketing materials, the things you can't fit into a page-size or smaller ad. It can also contain a lot of things that are often too expensive to include in a print ad or even brochures—including plenty of color and complex images, such as photographs and drawings. Many small businesses have very plain-looking one- and two-color brochures simply because it's too expensive to print in color. The Web is a much cheaper medium than print on many levels.

A Web site that simply markets your business can include information about your company's history, staff photos and profiles, and a mission statement, if you have one. In addition, the site can offer links to professional organizations' Web sites and other places on the Web that your visitors will find interesting or useful.

FIGURE 1-1

A simple marketing Web site tells visitors what you sell and/or what you stand for. Contact information (phone number, e-mail) puts the responsibility for follow-up on the visitor.

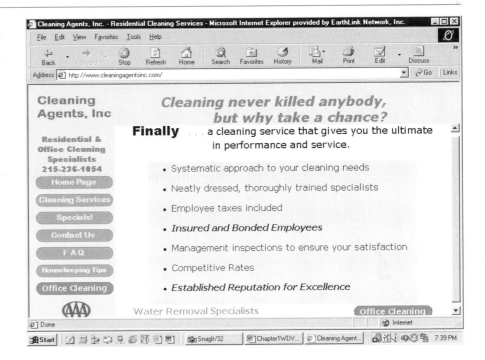

SAVE MONEY BY REACHING MORE PEOPLE In addition to displaying a lot more information (the size of an average computer screen is a lot bigger than even a full-page magazine ad, and your site will probably contain more than one Web page), a Web site is much cheaper than print advertising. You'll pay hundreds of dollars for even a half-page ad in a local paper or circular, and the ad will run for a month at most. A Web site can be had for as little as $35 per year for the Web address and $200 per year (approximately) for Web server space on which to store it, and the site lasts as long as you want it. You're also not restricted to a publication's circulation—your Web site is available to millions of people all over the world.

Business Web sites can also sell things—indirectly by offering an online product catalog and displaying a toll-free number to call to place an order, or directly by allowing visitors to make purchases right through the Web site. A few years ago, it was quite a task to set up a Web site through which

SEE ALSO To find out more about Web sites that market an organization's offerings, see Chapter 2, "The 'We're Here' Web Site."

people could buy things. In the last couple of years, however, it has become much easier to do and no longer requires that the business be set up to accept credit cards. You can simply link your Web site to another site that handles the "shopping cart" aspect of customer shopping and purchasing. The fact that another Web site is handling the purchase is invisible to your site's visitor, and aside from a small per-transaction fee, it's a very inexpensive way to go if you want to sell online. As shown in Figure 1-2, it's opened the door to online entrepreneurs all over the world.

FIGURE 1-2

A new sale is just a few clicks away if your Web site is equipped with a shopping cart.

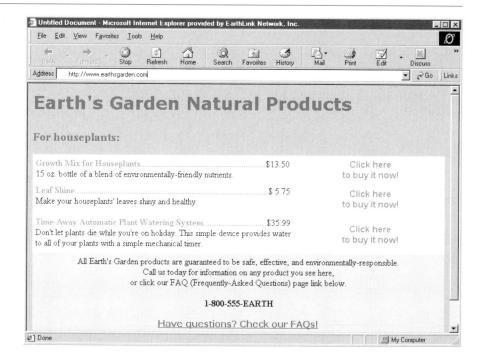

Nonprofit Organization and Educational Sites

If you run or work for a nonprofit organization such as a church, school, or charity, a Web site can be your link to a world full of potential volunteers, students, and donors. As shown in Figure 1-3, rather than being limited to fund-raising and consciousness-raising events, having a Web site expands your ability to share information about your organization's goals and beliefs, including information about the organization—what it does, who it benefits, how it raises and uses funds, and ways for people to participate.

> **SEE ALSO** Chapter 3, "Web Sites that Sell Products and Services," will explain more about your e-commerce options.

> **TIP** A site that sells can also be a site that markets and informs. The same company history, staff information, mission statement, and so on that a marketing site has can and should be part of the picture. Unless your site sells something that can't be obtained anywhere else on the planet, you want to make sure your visitors know why your site is the best place to buy it.

FIGURE 1-3
Generate donations and passion for your cause through your nonprofit organization's Web site.

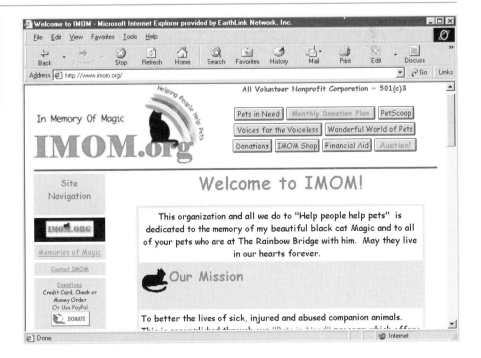

PERSONAL AND FAMILY WEB SITES

What's the difference between "personal" and "family" Web sites? A personal Web site can serve both personal and professional goals, and is devoted to the needs and interests of an individual. A person can create a Web site that includes his or her résumé (which can also be available as a downloadable document for prospective employers and headhunters), lists of professional accomplishments, and descriptions of hobbies. Such a site can be instrumental for job-seekers, as it shows initiative and creativity. A Web site can provide a compelling Internet backdrop to the paper résumé and memories of an interview (see Figure 1-4).

> **TIP** If your organization is a school, your Web site can include course descriptions, schedules, teacher profiles, and a calendar of events. Web sites for children's organizations—pre-K and elementary schools, daycare centers, camps, and after-school activities—can be both fun and informative, and attract families who need their services.

So what does a family Web site do? Among other things, it saves postage on that holiday newsletter with pictures of your kids at camp, the family vacation, or the remodeled kitchen. If you have relatives in several different time zones, making

FIGURE 1-4

Get a job! Post your downloadable résumé on a personal Web site and attract employers or clients.

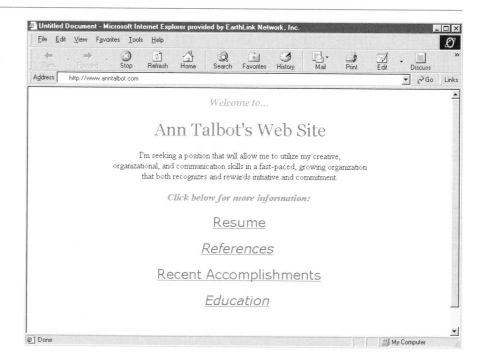

FIGURE 1-5

Let everyone know about the upcoming family reunion or share stories about your ancestors with a family Web site.

phone calls and visits difficult, a family Web site can help everyone stay in touch. As shown in Figure 1-5, family sites include photos of recent events, articles about family members' recent accomplishments, and e-mail addresses to help everyone keep the information flowing. You can even set up a site so that different branches of the family can maintain their own pages within the site, increasing the entire family's enthusiasm and participation.

TIP For a more "personal" slant, some people use their Web site to attract new friends and romantic partners, using it as the ultimate personal ad. This idea is so popular that many online dating services include a place where advertisers can list their personal Web site address.

CHOOSING THE RIGHT TYPE OF SITE FOR YOUR NEEDS

After thinking about all the different types of Web sites there are and the different people and organizations who create and use them, it's time to figure out what kind of site will best meet your needs,

TIP If you're gathering genealogical information, a family Web site can be a great place to post information about your family tree and invite long-lost relatives to get in touch and share what they know about your shared ancestry.

your lifestyle, and your budget. A personal or family Web site is easy, from both a lifestyle and budget perspective. Most ISPs (Internet service providers) offer free Web site space to their subscribers, and many individuals and families take advantage of that, leaving the time it takes to build the site as the only "cost" involved. Your Web address won't be too dazzling, ending up as something like "www.aol.com/members/~smithfamily.htm" or "http://hometown/aol.com/filename.htm" if you're an America Online subscriber. You can update the information on the site as often as you please, and you can choose how elaborate the site should be. If you have little time to devote to the site, keep it simple.

> **SEE ALSO** Find out more about creating e-mail links on your Web pages in Chapter 14, "Creating Hyperlinks to Connect Pages and Sites."

For businesses, nonprofit organizations, and schools, the need to have a real Web address (something.com or something.org for businesses and nonprofits, and something.edu for schools) is much greater, and therefore the cost of registering a *domain name* (the name of your Web site, the word before the .com or the .org) and the cost of storing the site somewhere become a consideration. As stated previously, these costs are small—you can register and store a site (with a Web *host*) for less than $300 per year.

> **SEE ALSO** Find out more about registering a name for your Web site in Chapter 4, "Registering a Domain Name."

> **TIP** If you're a nonprofit organization, you may be able to get a Web hosting company or ISP to donate Web space and a Web designer to donate their artistic assistance. They can deduct the services they provide (or their cash equivalent) from their taxes, and you save much-needed funds.

Businesses, schools, and nonprofit organizations also need to meet a higher standard for their Web sites. Text must be spelled correctly and free from inaccuracies. Product descriptions have to be clear and compelling. Contact information must be current and well placed on the site so people can find it. An important issue to consider is how much time you have to devote to the design and maintenance process. Don't set yourself up to be disappointed or aggravated by planning a Web site that's too complex and that needs frequent updates (such as product pricing, inventory status, shipping information) if you're not in a position to keep up with it. You can hire a webmaster to do these things, but if your organization is small and/or on a tight budget, that might not be a realistic option.

If you want to sell directly from your site, decide how this will dovetail with your current sales efforts. If you have a store, do you want to send people to the Web site to make their purchases or do you make more money on impulse purchases if someone comes into the store to buy something? If the Web site is your only outlet for sales, do you have the time and money to market the site so people know it's there? If not, you might want to reconsider an online-only approach.

> SEE ALSO **Find out more about the webmaster's role in Appendix A, "Web Maintenance and Mastery."**

The key to choosing the right site for your needs is to not bite off more than you can chew. You can always grow your site, increasing its functionality and scope later. Meet the basic needs of your potential visitors now, paving the way to your final goal.

 ON THE VIRTUAL CLASSROOM CD-ROM Accompany the author on a tour of the main types of Web sites: sites that simply advertise a person or organization's presence, sites that sell products directly online, and a variety of ways that individuals, families, and organizations of all types and sizes can use a Web site to share information and ideas, promote their activities, and make money.

2

The "We're Here" Web Site

With all the hype about e-commerce and people making millions through their sites on the Web, it might seem as though a site that simply says, "We're here, this is what we do, this is our phone number, give us a call" is a waste of time. Not so! The very fact that the leading publisher of a certain brightly colored directory has converted most of its advertisements to a Web format is proof that people are turning to the Web to find everything from shoe repair to travel agents. For organizations of all types, as well as individuals with interests or causes to advertise, the "We're Here" site is worth the time and effort you'll put in to make it an effective, attractive, and informative address on the Web.

THE ELECTRONIC ADVERTISEMENT

We've all looked in the phone book to find a store, a service, or a person, and many of us are now using the Web to find those same things. In the next few years, more and more businesses will be listed online, either through their own Web sites or through cyber versions of printed directories. If you or your product, service, interest, or cause needs some publicity, a Web site that lists the same information as one would find in a printed directory can be an instrumental part of your marketing plan. What makes a Web site better than a simple directory listing (or even an ad in a directory)? As shown in Figure 2-1, you can pack more information into the site, create multiple pages within the site, and use color, graphics, sound, and animation to make a much bigger and better impression than a simple listing (such as the one shown here) could ever hope to.

It's not who you are, but who you *were.*

**Call Raven for a FREE
Past Life Regression
Consultation.**

(800) 555-PAST

FIGURE 2-1

When searching the Web, let the consumer find your site, ready and waiting, with all the pertinent information.

What a Very Basic Web Site Gives You

Not all products and services can be sold online. If you're a consultant or provide some other intangible product such as financial management or hypnotherapy, people can't click a "Buy it now!" or "Add to Cart" link, enter a quantity, and then buy two of them with their credit card. They have to call you, you probably have to meet with them—gasp!—in person, and then after discussing their needs and what you can offer, you can provide the service.

TIP You can list your site's address (also known as your URL, which stands for Uniform Resource Locator) with major search sites such as www.yahoo.com and www.altavista.com. Click the "Add a URL" (or similar text) link on their main page to add your site to their index. This is a free way to improve the chances of people finding your site when they search for keywords that are included in your home page text.

Some organizations that do offer a product that could be sold online simply choose not to. Maybe they feel the online sale is just too impersonal, or they don't want people to skip visiting their store where they might see other things they need. Online shopping can expose consumers to products they might not find at the local mall, but at the local mall, shoppers usually goes home with bags full of things they didn't intend to buy. Other vendors don't want to be bothered with selling online—finding and setting up shopping cart software, even if it's provided by another company through another site, can require more time and effort than some people want to devote to a Web site. Even if the desire is there, it's also a lot of work to maintain an accurate product catalog for online sales.

So if you decide to create a basic "We're Here" Web site, what does that get you? A very basic Web site gets you two things: a site that's easy to create and maintain, and a simple (yet compelling) presence on the Internet. Your name, organization name, phone number, e-mail address, mission statement, list of products and services, customer testimonials, and links to sites of related interest are just a few of the things a "We're Here" site can contain, as shown in Figure 2-2. If you're a nonprofit organization, you can pack the site with information that will inform people about your cause and hopefully convince them to participate in some way—by donating time, money, or simply by joining your ranks. If you're a growing business with a tight budget, you're taking advantage of the cheapest advertising venue there is.

> **TIP** Know your audience. If a typical purchaser of the product or service you sell isn't likely to even use the Internet, don't bother to build an online store. A site that tells people you're there is sufficient, and it pays to be online now, even if your particular target audience isn't terribly Web-savvy yet. They will be!

> **SEE ALSO** Chapter 8, "Web Site Layout," gives you plenty of insights and suggestions for setting up a visually pleasing Web page that guides the visitor's eye around the page and through the site's links.

STARTING SMALL WITH PLANS TO GROW

Building a "We're Here" site isn't an end in itself, or at least it doesn't have to be. You can start out with a simple site that gives the basic information about you or your organization, and then add to it over time, as shown in Figure 2-3. Maybe you feel selling online is too much trouble now—you have no one on staff to

FIGURE 2-2

Don't try to pack too much stuff on the home page. You can add links to pages such as "Services" and "Contact Us" to share a lot of information with your site's visitors.

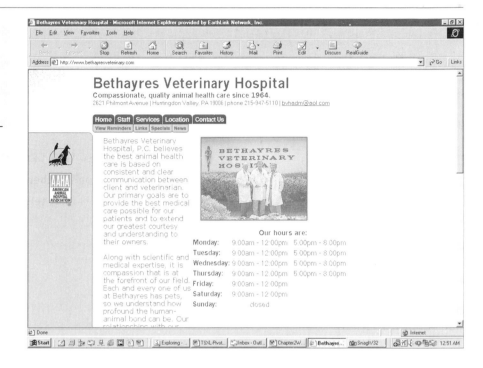

FIGURE 2-3

Even if you start out with a single home page and no additional pages in your site, there's plenty of room for growth by building pages that expand on the information.

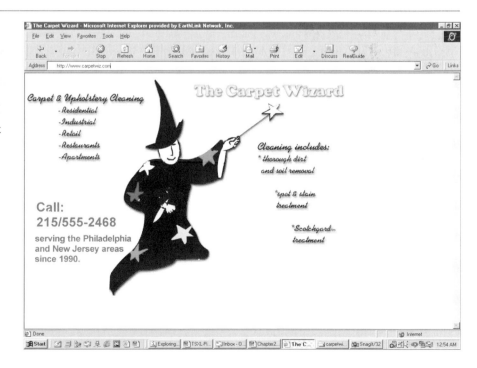

maintain the site, your order processing channel is in need of an overhaul as it is, and another source of sales would be too much to deal with—but it may not always be that way. As your organization grows, you may hire in-house Web talent to maintain a great shopping site. If your organization could never sell directly online (or doesn't sell anything at all), you can always make your site more exciting by adding more pages with more information and/or add multimedia elements to the site—sound, movies, downloadable files—to increase traffic and repeat visits to your site.

There's no specific site layout that paves the way to growth. You can totally revamp your site at any time, adding the extras you're ready to support when the time comes. In fact, it's a good thing to make changes in your site from time to time, if only so that people check back to see what you're up to. You don't want to make major changes on a frequent basis, especially if your site has a lot of pages in it. People get used to navigating a site in a certain way, and are resistant to change and figuring out how to move around in your revamped site. If you do make major changes, keep things like navigation buttons in the same place so people can still find their way.

 ON THE VIRTUAL CLASSROOM CD-ROM Watch as the instructor introduces you to some Web sites that serve as an electronic version of the print ad—promoting their name, telling people where they are, and how to get in touch is the main goal for their site.

3

Web Sites That Sell Products and Services

More exciting than sites that inform, and nearly as popular as sites that entertain, are sites that sell. From famous e-commerce successes like Amazon.com to sites like Priceline.com that help you save money when you shop in person and online for a variety of other vendors' products, shopping online is big business. Every year, more and more people avoid the malls and skip mail order by making purchases through the Web—and the figures continue to climb. If your business sells a product or service, it's understandable that you would want to jump on the bandwagon. With the lure of overnight millionaire status tempting even the most conservative of entrepreneurs, the Web promises (and sometimes delivers) a great sales venue that gives you the ability to offer your wares to people all over the world. If you are currently limited to people who can drive or walk to your store or to the confines of your mailing list, a global reach is a compelling concept.

YOUR E-COMMERCE OPTIONS

The term "e-commerce" really defines what's going on when you sell online. You're engaging in electronic commerce, using the Web to perform sales transactions. You can do this yourself, setting up your own secure server to process credit card transactions with the bank, and installing and running software to process orders from an inventory and shipping perspective. Or you can subcontract the "shopping cart," the software and services that allow people to click on a product, enter a quantity, type in their credit card, billing, and shipping address, and have the sale processed online.

One option is rather heavy in terms of setup and ongoing maintenance. The other costs more per transaction, but doesn't require you to be hardware and e-commerce software savvy. The choice is up to you. What's not negotiable is that the site you create has to be pleasant to look at, easy to use, and provide a sense of security for people who are afraid to use their credit cards online. Imagine a store with dark, winding aisles that lead to dead ends and cash registers that are out of order—would you go back? You want your online store to be the equivalent of the well-lighted, friendly place with smiling cashiers and clearly marked prices. A white background and clean, clear fonts (as shown in Figure 3-1) make even the most alternative shopper feel secure when purchasing from your online store.

RUNNING YOUR OWN ONLINE STORE

If you choose to set up and maintain your own online shopping site, you or a trusted member of your staff should be thoroughly knowledgeable about the process of building an online store. This includes installing and configuring software for handling customer transactions (there are a wide variety of applications available), as well as designing efficient forms to house product images, descriptions, pricing, and shipping information to make it easy for your site's visitors to select and buy the products/services they need. Your forms will also have to con-

Keep your online purchasing
pages bright and easy to read.

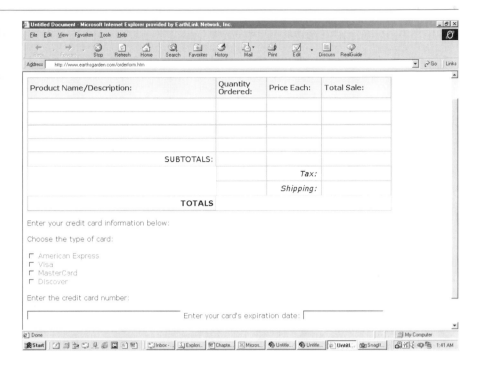

nect to a database of products so that the proper
product image, description, and price appear when
someone chooses a product, and so that when a
purchase is made, the order is pulled from inventory and shipped. The form can include drop-down
lists, check boxes, and text boxes into which visitors will type the specifics of their purchase, as
shown in Figure 3-2. Design the form for someone
who isn't paying attention and doesn't follow
directions—keep the text to a minimum, and keep
it clear and simple. The database that the form
uses will have to be maintained to include new and
discontinued products, reflect price changes, and
check for errors on a regular basis.

If you're going to run your own online store, it will
have to run on a secure Web server, and you'll have
to either maintain one yourself or find a host that

NOTE Unless you're going to let another
company handle your electronic purchase
transactions, you'll need to establish a
merchant account that allows you to
accept credit cards online. You may or
may not be able to use the merchant
account you already have if you currently
accept credit cards in your store or mail-
order business. If you let someone else
do it, your site takes the order, but when
the credit card portion of the transaction
commences, the shopper is invisibly
connected to another Web site where the
credit card information is taken and veri-
fied. You'll be paid, less a transaction fee,
by the provider of this service.

FIGURE 3-2

A typical online order form

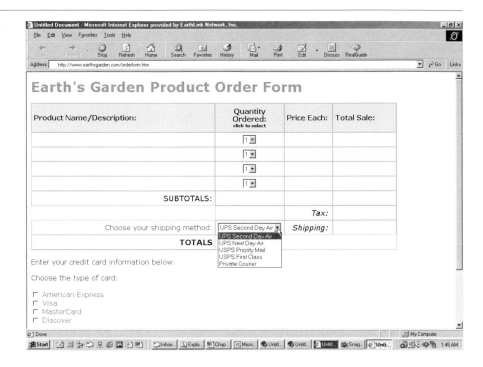

supports e-commerce. To find one, you can search the Web for "e-commerce hosting." You'd be wise to do a little research on the hosting company before signing
on the dotted line, making sure they have the technology in place to handle a lot
of hits on the server and process your customers'
orders flawlessly.

In terms of the site's design, the process of viewing the products and services available should be
easy, and the forms the visitor fills out to make a
purchase should be clear and concise. As conde-
scending as it might sound, you should include as
much hand-holding as possible in your design for
the pages that customers will use. As shown in
Figure 3-3, you don't want to assume any level of
intuition or intelligent assumptions on the part of
your site shoppers. Keep the pages, instructions,
and layout simple, so that there's little or no chance that a visitor doesn't understand what to do in order to make a purchase and complete the transaction.

> **TIP** You can't use the word "secure"
> often enough on a Web site that people
> use to buy products with their credit
> card. Between the media hype and the
> real fraud that exists, people are very
> nervous about online transactions. Make
> sure your site is truly secure, and remind
> buyers of that security at each step in
> the process of making their purchases.

FIGURE 3-3
Keep online instructions as simple as possible.

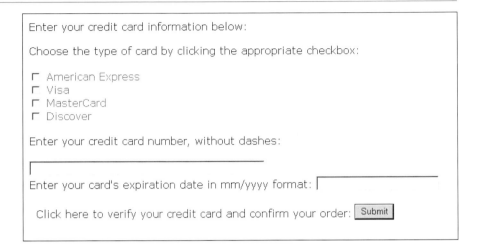

THIRD-PARTY SHOPPING CARTS An alternative to either setting up and maintaining your own online store or using another company to handle your shopping cart transactions is to maintain a more passive shopping site. You can provide order forms on your pages that visitors can print out and fax to a number you provide, and/or call you with their order. How is this any better than mail order? Because your Web site is available to people all over the planet, not just to those lucky enough to be on your mailing list! If you're not sure how you want to go in terms of e-commerce, start small by offering an online catalog of products, but don't literally sell them online. You can work up to that when you're more sure of how you want to go about it.

SUBCONTRACTING THE SHOPPING CART

Just type "shopping cart" into any search site, and an abundance of companies that offer shopping cart software, shopping cart services, and shopping cart advice will appear before your eyes. To match the demand for online stores, entrepreneurs have sprung up all over, offering to handle your shoppers' credit card transactions. Visitors to your site make selections from a list of products and services on your pages, and as soon as they click "Add to Cart" (as shown in Figure 3-4) or "Buy it now!" they're linked to another Web site where the credit card information is gathered and approved. The company handling this portion of the transaction pays you (less a fee for doing the leg-work), along with a recap of each day's (or hour's) transactions so you can set about fulfilling the orders and editing your own inventory database to show the reduction in stock. Once the transaction is completed, visitors are returned to your site, and other than their possibly noticing a change in location on the address bar in their browser window, they'll never know they left.

To incorporate a shopping cart of your own into your site, you have to set up the shopping cart software—the form the shopper will use to buy the products. From a page where you have pictures and/or descriptions of your products, the shopper clicks a link for the product she wants, and that takes her to a form that allows her to select the quantity, color, size, and other specifics. Once her order is correct, the shopper clicks a link to buy the product, and that's where the other Web site kicks in. The interface to that point is in your hands—designing the pages that depict and describe your products, the form where the product's specifics are established, and the instructions for completing the order—it's all up to you. Your

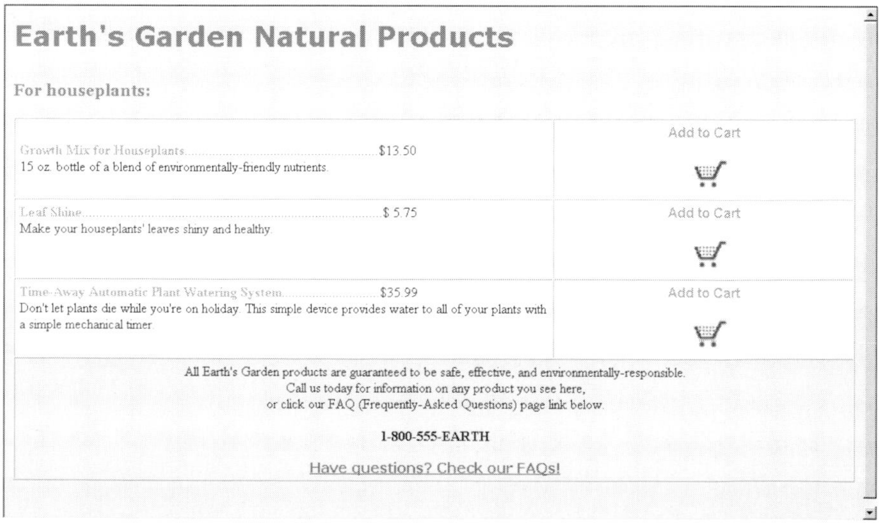

> **SEE ALSO** This isn't intended to frighten you away from setting up your own online store. Many people do it, and are glad to have the control over the system that doing it yourself (or hiring your own people to do it) affords. This book is concerned with how the site should look and work for the visitor, however, not with the specifics of the software and hardware required to set up and maintain the store itself.

FIGURE 3-4

A simple "Add to Cart" link

Earth's Garden Natural Products

For houseplants:

		Add to Cart
Growth Mix for Houseplants...$13.50 15 oz. bottle of a blend of environmentally-friendly nutrients.		🛒
Leaf Shine..$ 5.75 Make your houseplants' leaves shiny and healthy.		🛒
Time-Away Automatic Plant Watering System.......................$35.99 Don't let plants die while you're on holiday. This simple device provides water to all of your plants with a simple mechanical timer.		🛒

All Earth's Garden products are guaranteed to be safe, effective, and environmentally-responsible.
Call us today for information on any product you see here,
or click our FAQ (Frequently-Asked Questions) page link below.

1-800-555-EARTH

Have questions? Check our FAQs!

job as the designer is to entice shoppers to buy, help them select the right product, and guide them comfortably to entering their credit card information.

The pages that showcase your products/services are the ones in which you have the most design freedom. Your online store, even if it's just a part of a much larger Web site, should do what commercials do for the products they peddle—showcase your products in a way that makes the visitor feel good about buying them. They should feel smart, sexy, hip, responsible, prudent, or whatever feeling is appropriate for the products and services you're offering. You can do that with the effective use of color, graphic images, text, and the layout of your pages.

WEB SITE MARKETING POTENTIAL

A lot of people confuse marketing and sales and think they're the same thing. They're related, but they're distinct activities, with distinct skills and distinct outcomes. If you market a product, you're making people aware of it, enticing them to find out more so when the sales process begins, they're primed to buy. Therefore, just because you have a site that sells your products, it doesn't mean you have a site that markets your products.

This book is filled with advice on making your Web site attractive and effective. You'll also learn a lot about ways to create certain impressions and evoke specific feelings through your use of text, color, and graphic images. That's part of the marketing process, but not the most important part. You have to market your site before people will

SEE ALSO Chapter 14, "Creating Hyperlinks to Connect Pages and Sites," will help you understand how to set up the connections to your shopping cart host's site.

TIP When you're designing product pages, it's a good idea to get someone's objective opinion of your design before you go online with it. Ask a friend or colleague who'll tell you the truth to look at the pages and give adjectives for how the site makes them feel. If you're selling insurance, for example, they should feel safe and secure, and a responsible, conservative feeling should be invoked by your pages. If you're selling party supplies or toys, a fun, frivolous, lighthearted feeling should pervade your product pages and the rest of your site as well.

SEE ALSO For more information on using color to make a statement, read Chapter 11, "Working with Color on the Web." You'll also learn some valuable tips for using tables, a great tool for building online catalog pages, in Chapter 12, "Structuring Web Pages with Tables, Frames, and Layers."

visit it, and they can't buy anything if they don't stop by to shop.

Marketing your Web site includes all the typical stuff you have hopefully been doing to market your business, your organization, and/or yourself. You've got business cards, brochures, an ad in the local yellow pages or some other useful and well-circulated directory, you belong to chambers of commerce, you talk about you, your company, or your cause whenever you get a chance. In all of that, also include prominent mention of your Web site. Your business cards need to be revamped to include your e-mail address and your Web site's URL. Make the site address stand out. Hopefully, you've chosen a domain name that's easy to remember and spell, and you want it to be on every piece of marketing collateral you have.

> TIP Don't forget your voicemail or answering machine's outgoing message. Instead of "I'm either on the phone or away from my desk, leave a message at the tone," followed by a beep, consider listing alternate contact methods such as your e-mail address (which hopefully includes your domain name) and the address of your Web site. "We can't take your call now, but if you leave a message, we'll call you back. You can also reach us via e-mail at _____, and check out our Web site at www.domainname.com!" People who call often may get tired of listening to the whole spiel, but if you get a lot of phone traffic, it's a great way to inform people of your Web presence.

Other effective Web site marketing techniques include participating in newsgroups, mailing lists (where people send e-mails to a group of subscribers on an evolving list of topics), and forums. Choose a group that will have members who can make use of your services and/or are likely to refer others to you. For example, if you're a chiropractor and you sell vitamins and herbal products through your practice and on your Web site, join a forum on sports training, physical therapy, or alternative medicine. Think about where your customers would be if they were joining such groups, and get involved. To find newsgroups, lists, and forums, type some keywords (such as "vitamins," "healing," "herbs," or "holistic," using our chiropractor example) into a search site and you'll probably find more groups than you possibly have time to join.

Getting your site found when people search for those same keywords is also very important. If you sell widgets, you want your site to come up in the list of sites when someone does a search for "widgets," right? Right. How do you make that happen? Try one or more of these ideas:

▶ Add meta tags to your Web page source code, as shown in Figure 3-5. Meta tags can include a list of keywords that will help a search engine relate your

FIGURE 3-5

An example of using meta tags to help your site be found by a search engine

```
<html>
<head>
<title>Welcome to PlanetLaurie...</title>
<meta http-equiv="content-type" content="text/html;charset=iso-8859-1">
        <title>Welcome to PlanetLaurie...</title>
        <meta name="keywords" content="web design, training, web books,
html, designing web graphics, Laurie Ulrich, , web safe colors, web design
training, learning dreamweaver, learning dreamweaver and fireworks,
microsoft office, templates, dreamweaver, fireworks, photoshop, animal
rights">
        <meta name="description" content="PlanetLaurie, providing help and
tips for web designers and general computer users">
```

site to a visitor's search criteria. Yes, you'll need to know a little HTML, but you can borrow the code from another site and simply replace their keywords with yours. Then paste the code into yours, and you're done.

▶ Submit your URL to major search sites. Choose popular search sites that you and other people you know use on a regular basis. Most of the major search sites, such as www.yahoo.com, www.excite.com, and www.altavista.com, have an "Add a URL" or similarly worded link somewhere on their site, as shown in Figure 3-6. Click it and follow the instructions to submit your

TIP Some search sites make you choose a category for your site when you go to add your URL to their index. When you do this, think from your customers' perspective and put yourself where they would be most likely to look for you. If you're not sure, ask a couple of your customers: "If you had to look for me in a directory, which section or category would you look in first?"

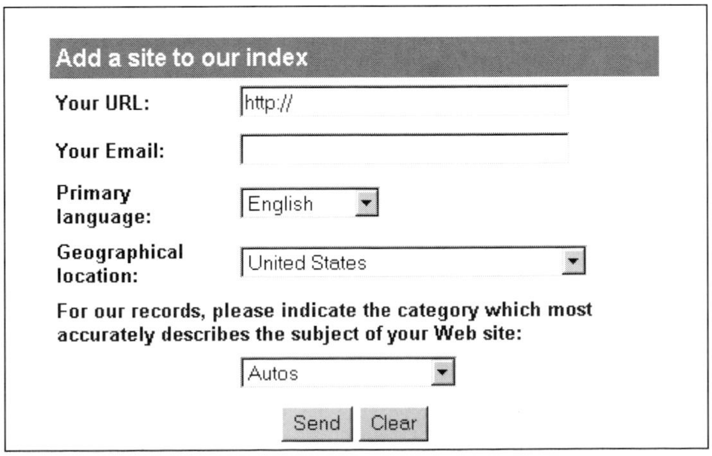

FIGURE 3-6

Adding your URL to a search site is simple.

Add a site to our index

Your URL:	http://
Your Email:	
Primary language:	English
Geographical location:	United States

For our records, please indicate the category which most accurately describes the subject of your Web site:

Autos

Send   Clear

site's URL, improving the chances that someone can find your site by searching for your name or keywords that are included in your home page text and meta tags.

▶ Pay to have yourself listed. There are a lot of companies that charge a fee (the fees vary; most are in the $200 per year range) to make sure your URL is listed with as many major and minor search sites as possible, increasing the frequency with which your site is listed when someone does a search, and making sure your site appears as close to the top of that list as possible.

> **SEE ALSO** **Yikes! HTML? Don't be threatened. If you're interested in setting up meta tags for your Web site or understanding all that stuff you see when you choose View | Source from within the Internet Explorer window, or View | Page Source if you're using Netscape, check out Appendix A, "HTML Basics."**

AFFILIATE MARKETING DEFINED

Just what is *affiliate marketing*? Breaking down the term, it means marketing through an affiliate, someone with whom you have some sort of relationship. Now, this doesn't mean having your mother tell all her friends about your Web

FIGURE 3-7

Your affiliate link can be a banner ad, or a discreet text link.

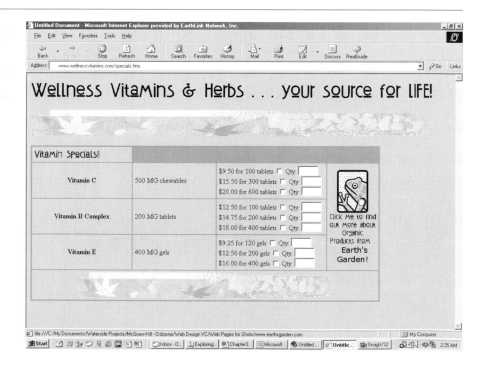

site. Rather, it means forming relationships (of a business nature) with other Web sites that are visited by people who could use your products and services as well. Figure 3-7 shows information available through a link on a site pertaining to a related topic.

Imagine again that you're a chiropractor. You sell vitamins and herbs through your Web site, as well as advertising your practice itself. Potential affiliates might be bookstores, Web sites that sell fitness equipment, athletic equipment suppliers, and even doctors. Bookstores? Sure. Picture someone who is searching a bookstore Web site for books on vitamins or alternative medicine. When the list of books appears, so does a banner ad with your Web site on it. They've expressed an interest in something you sell, so they're directed to your site. Doctors? Maybe. Some doctors are interested in helping their patients employ alternative healthcare to maintain their health or deal with problems that traditional medicine hasn't been able to help. If such a doctor has a Web site, he or she would be a good candidate to set up a link from his or her site to yours. Think about people, businesses, and other organizations that sell products or offer information related to what you're offering. These are all potential affiliates.

Put yourself in your customer's shoes. Find Web sites that offer products, services, or information that your potential customers would need and/or enjoy. Contact the owner of the site, and find out if they will include a link from their site to yours. Some affiliate agreements are done on a handshake. Others require contracts be signed. Some sites want you to provide the artwork if the link will be a graphic. Others want complete artistic control and you have no say in how the link to your site will look. The deal you strike depends on the terms with which you're most comfortable, and should include no more time and effort than can be justified by the realistic expectation for increased traffic to your site through theirs.

TIP In the same way you design your site's pages to evoke the appropriate feelings from your visitors, make sure the link to your site from the affiliate's site doesn't clash with your image. If, for example, you've carefully cultivated a respectable, conservative site, don't allow a brash and circus-like banner ad to be the introduction visitors have to your site from the affiliate's page.

Some affiliate agreements include a commission program. Say, for example, you have an ad on someone else's site. If a visitor clicks that ad and ends up at your site where he or she makes a purchase, you agree to pay the other site's owner a commission for that sale. Some agreements pay on the click (known as a *click-through*); others pay only when a sale results from the link from their site to yours. Obviously, you want a reciprocal arrangement if commissions or click-through fees are involved. If you're going to pay for sales at your site that originated at theirs, you want to be paid if someone goes to their site from yours and buys something. Of course, that requires that they have an ad at your site and that their site actually sells something. There are software programs that both affiliates can run to monitor the clicks and sales, enabling you to document the traffic that came to your site via theirs, and vice versa. Don't ever enter into an agreement that involves paying commissions or

> **TIP** There are a lot of books on the market and Web sites devoted to informing people about the money to be made and exposure to be gained through affiliate marketing. Do a search for the words "affiliate marketing" on the Web. You'll find a host of resources to get you up to speed on the process of finding affiliates, hammering out mutually beneficial contracts, and monitoring the clicks to and from your site as well as the commissions you pay and are paid.

click-through fees if there isn't some auditing system in place. You don't want a potentially beneficial relationship to deteriorate through one or both parties being suspicious about payments and reporting.

 ON THE VIRTUAL CLASSROOM CD-ROM Take a tour of some Web sites that sell products online, and listen as the instructor gives you a sense of what's going on behind the scenes when you click that "Add to Cart" button.

4

Registering a Domain Name

Your domain name, also known as your URL (which stands for Uniform Resource Locator), is your identity on the Web. It's your address, so people can find you, and it's also the first impression people get—of you, your organization, and your Web site. Choosing and registering a domain name is a very important step in the process of building a Web site. Of course, you can build all of your pages and have them all set and ready to go before you even have a domain, but you won't have anywhere to put them. When you register a domain, you normally associate it with a particular Web server (by a numerical designation that uniquely identifies the server). Your domain, on that specific server, then becomes the physical location of your Web site.

CHOOSING THE RIGHT DOMAIN NAME

What's the "right" domain name? It's a name that's easy to spell, easy to remember, and that makes the right statement about your Web site. When people first started registering domain names, the field was wide open—you could pretty much have any name you wanted. After a few years of people gobbling up domain names, however, the field is getting a little tight. People's personal names, last names (for actual families or for family-named companies), business names, and organization names and acronyms are becoming harder and harder to register without having to tinker with them, adding "e-" in front of them or registering the .net version of the domain because the .com is already taken. For example, a client of mine, Lensco Products, wanted to register lensco.com, but couldn't get it. They had to go with lensco-products.com—a little longer, but still workable. I myself wanted laurie.com, but that was taken, so I registered laurieulrich.com. Then I realized that was hard to spell because people leave the L out of my last name a lot. So now I also have planetlaurie.com, the somewhat tongue-in-cheek reaction to getting tired of the whole domain name selection process.

> **TIP** Work for a law firm or other long-named organization? If the company's official name is something like Smith, Jones, Brown, White, and Gladstone, a good URL might be sjbwg.com, or just smithjones.com if (a) that's not taken already and (b) Brown, White, and Gladstone don't mind being left out. Domain names that are initials don't have to spell a pronounceable word; just don't choose one that's so long it looks like a word from a foreign language. No one will ever remember it, much less be able to type it without errors!

THE DOMAIN EXTENSION DEBATE

What happens if the name you want is taken in the .com version of the domain, but the .net and .org versions are available? And what's this .ws extension? The .ws extension stands for Web site, and it's been promoted within the pool of available domain extensions because so many names in the .com versions are unavailable. It isn't widely recognized yet, so for the sake of increasing your domain's recognition factor, you're still probably better off trying to find a .com or .net name rather than resorting to .ws.

The .tv extension is also a new addition to the pool of extensions available to anyone and will probably surpass .ws in popularity because of the psychological connection to television. If you're in the entertainment field in any way, a .tv extension can be a good choice, in addition to or even instead of the .com version of your preferred domain name. Bear in mind, however, that there is no real connection between this extension and the television industry. A small country named Tuvalu had the .tv extension, and sold it for $50 million dollars—quite a boon to the economy of this tiny island nation with a population of only 11,000 people. Figure 4-1 shows a registration site and the list of available extensions, including .ws and .tv.

A common debate these days is whether to bother registering other extensions for a domain name if .com is already taken. It's really up to you, but realize that .com is the extension most people think of first. If they remember your company name and that it was also your domain name, they'll type the name with a .com at the end when they go to find the site online. If they come up dry, they may think your site is not operational, rather than trying the company name with other extensions.

> **TIP** If you're lucky enough to find a domain name that's available in both the .com and .net versions, register both. It'll cost you a little more, but you won't have to worry about someone registering the .net version and stealing your domain name thunder.

FIGURE 4-1

Choose from several different extensions for your domain name when you check availability.

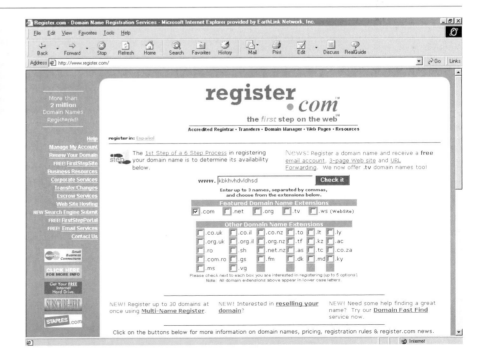

> **BUT ARE YOU REALLY NONPROFIT?**   A few years ago, you had to prove you were an actual nonprofit organization in order to register a .org domain name, and although those rules are no longer enforced, I don't recommend using the .org version of the name unless you're truly nonprofit. It's rather misleading to the public to use it for personal sites and commercial business sites. If you want to register the .org version of your name or company name, that's fine—it prevents the confusion that often results when two different organizations register the same name with different extensions. It's a little shifty, however, to develop a .org site if you're not really a charity or some other not-for-profit entity.

SHOULD YOU ADD AN E?

It's a common scene in the last year or so, when domain names have become such a hot commodity. A person sits down in front of his or her computer, full of hope and excitement, and goes to a domain registration site to register a name, sure that no one else has thought of it. The person types it in, clicks the button to check availability, and much to the person's shock and horror, the name is taken, perhaps in all of the possible extensions or maybe just the .com. In any case, hopes are dashed, and excitement crushed.

Some sites automatically offer alternative names, based on the one you asked for, as sort of domain consolation prizes. A few of the options are actually useful, but most of them are silly. When I did a search to see if laurie.com was taken, a suggested alternative was, unbelievably, easylaurie.com (see Figure 4-2). Obviously, I didn't take that one. Who would?

If, however, there's a reasonable variation on the name you wanted, go for it. Try adding "e-" to the beginning of the name, or "online" to the end of it, as in "e-company.com" or "companyonline.com." Try abbreviations, try leaving the "inc" off the name, or try adding it if the domain name without it is taken.

CHECKING NAME AVAILABILITY

To see if the name you want is available, go to any one of the many domain registration sites. Three popular ones are:

FIGURE 4-2

Among the really ridiculous suggested alternatives may be the cure for your Someone Took My Domain blues.

▶ www.networksolutions.com

▶ www.register.com

▶ www.domainbank.com

The process of checking on the availability of a name is basically the same at any of the sites. You type the domain you want, and then choose the extensions you want to check (see Figure 4-3). You can also type the domain name with the .com or other extension on it and search for that. After you click the Go or Search button, a few seconds pass and then the verdict is in—the name is either taken or available. If the extension version you asked for is taken, the site may tell you if the other extensions of the same name are taken as well.

> **TIP** Curious about the two-letter extensions you see on some Web addresses? They indicate the country the site owner lives in. Some of them are obvious, such as .uk for United Kingdom or .ca for Canada. These extensions are normally preceded by .co for commercial.

So Who Has the Domain You Wanted?

Most domain registration sites offer what's known as a Whois search. This search displays the name of the person or organization who registered a particular domain

FIGURE 4-3
Click the Go button to verify
the availability of the domain
name you want.

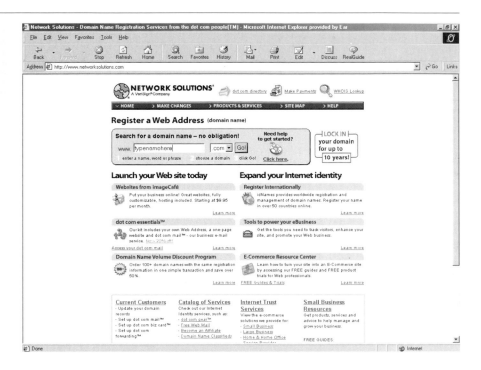

FIGURE 4-3
Click the Go button to verify the availability of the domain name you want.

name. It includes a name, address, e-mail address, and often a phone number (see Figure 4-4). You'll normally see a disclaimer below it, indicating that it is provided for information purposes only, and that it is assumed that you won't abuse the access to this data by calling the person or harassing him in any way. You can contact him, though, if you want to offer to buy the domain name. People have made millions selling domain names, and some registration sites even have a page devoted to the process of reselling domains.

REGISTERING A WEB ADDRESS

Once you've found an available domain that you like, it's time to register it. The registration site will guide you through this process. They have a vested interest in helping you set up your name through their site, because although they don't make money on the site registration directly, the longer you're at their site, the more time you spend looking at all the advertisements that pop up on the screen (see Figure 4-5). Don't get me wrong—you will be paying for your domain name, but that money

FIGURE 4-4

Check out the name and e-mail address of the person who grabbed that great domain while you weren't looking.

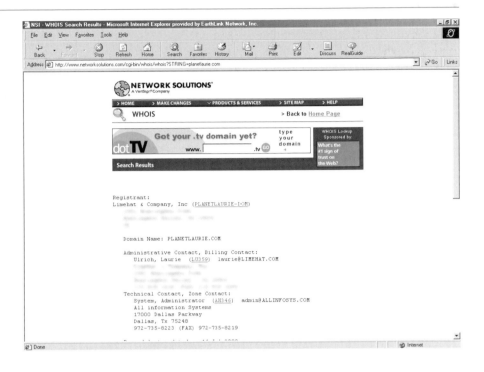

FIGURE 4-5

You'll see ads for all sorts of Web-related products and services as you follow the steps in registering your domain name.

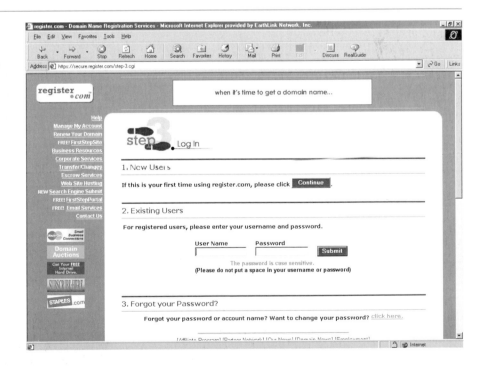

goes to the InterNIC, the Internet's administrative body. The registration site makes money by selling ad space on their site and through affiliate agreements with those advertisers.

Most sites follow the availability-checking step with a link/button that says Click Here to Register or words to that effect. You're taken to a screen where you can enter your billing, technical, and administrative contact information (see Figure 4-6). This is also where you enter information about your Web server, such as its physical location (usually identified by a DNS number, a four-segment number that identifies the actual location of the server). If you don't have a server selected, you can usually *park* your domain with the registration site, and it's usually free. This means that your domain name will be reserved for you, but it won't have any real cyberspace until you set up a Web server of your own or

> **TIP** As your Whois information will be available to anyone with a computer and a modem, you might consider using a P.O. box for your address and an unlisted phone number that can't be traced back to an address for your contact information.

> **SEE ALSO** Appendix A covers the topics of Web page testing and uploading pages to a Web server. You should also check the glossary, a resource for complete definitions of all terms used in this book and in discussions of the Internet and Web in general.

FIGURE 4-6

Enter your name and address and, if applicable, the name of your organization.

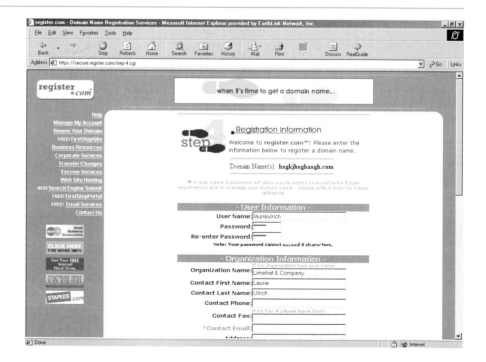

PARK NOW, TRANSFER LATER If you elected to park your domain at first and then you find a Web host or set up your own server later, you need to go back to the registration site to make the transfer. Look for a domain management or administration link that you can click to fill out a form that includes your domain name and the DNS information for the server to which it should be transferred. It may take as long as a week for the transfer to happen, but after the transfer is complete, your site will be stored on a Web server, and you can start uploading Web pages to that site as soon as they're designed and tested.

rent space on someone else's. If you have a Web server for your site, enter the information requested.

After this last setup step, you're normally taken to a screen where you enter your credit card information to pay for the registration (see Figure 4-7). When you register a domain, it belongs to you for either one year or two years. You can also register for longer periods of five or ten years.

FIGURE 4-7

After your credit card and billing information are approved, you're the proud owner of a new Web address!

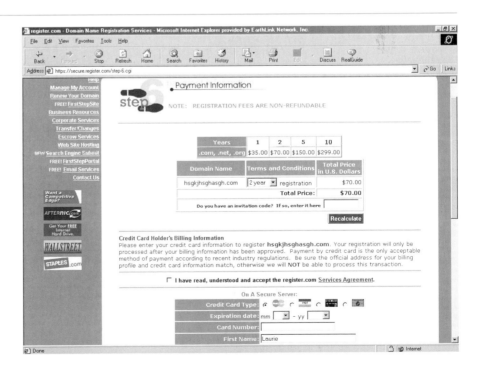

ON THE VIRTUAL CLASSROOM CD-ROM Sit back and watch as the instructor shows you how a domain name is chosen. You'll see the process of registering a domain name and hear some valuable tips for selecting a name for your Web site that's both relevant and memorable.

5

Storyboarding Your Site

Fail to plan, and you plan to fail, as the saying goes.

As annoying as a well-deserved "I told you so," this old adage

is also especially true when it comes to Web site design. Before

you sit down in front of the computer and start designing your

pages, you need to take your visions of your individual pages

and how they work together as a cohesive site, and put them

on paper or onscreen so that you can review and revamp them.

A good technique for doing this is called *storyboarding*—the

drawing of pictures that illustrate the way the site you have in

mind will look and function.

You may have seen storyboards for television and movies. They're the way a director or production designer puts his or her vision out there for the rest of the crew to see, enabling everyone involved to share that vision and begin working on making it happen. When a show is storyboarded, each scene is depicted to indicate where the actors will be, what camera angles will be used, even the general lighting and set design that will be utilized. Your Web site storyboards will depict the way your pages will look, where the text and graphics will be placed, and the colors and layout you'll employ. They will also include notes about the functionality—hyperlinks between pages and to other sites, animation, sound, and forms that visitors will fill out.

> **TALKING TO YOURSELF** Although you may be alone in the Web design process, the value of storyboarding is not diminished—if anything, the objective "voice" of your visions onscreen or on paper is even more important when there's no one else there to say, "No, I don't like that, but how about this?" The storyboard becomes your sounding board, and it's a step in the design process that I don't recommend skipping.

SKETCHING YOUR IDEAS

Storyboards are, traditionally, drawings or sketches of a process, be it scenes in a play or pages in a Web site. The words "drawing" and "sketching" frighten some people, especially those who'll tell you that they "can't even draw stick figures." No one's talking about creating art, though, so don't worry. By drawing or sketching your ideas, I mean to scribble them—draw simple boxes that represent your site's pages, and start jotting down the headings and making a quick representation of the graphics you intend to use inside them—we're talking simple here. After those simple page sketches are created, you'll draw lines connecting the pages, showing which ones will be connected by hyperlinks. By drawing lines that point away from your collection of pages, you can indicate links to the outside world. Jot down the URLs of the sites these external links will point to.

So you just sit down and start drawing pictures of your Web site and its pages? Yes, that's all there is to it. It's a simple process, no more complex and no less essential than creating an outline before writing a report or a story. To create these sketches, you can stick with paper and pencil, or you can create computerized images, using any of a variety of simple programs. I like working on paper, if only because I don't have to think at all about the vehicle for creating the sketches—it's just a pencil in my hand, with my mind and the site I have pictured orchestrating the whole process.

CHOOSING A STORYBOARDING MEDIUM

If you really hate to draw, and despite my protests that this doesn't require any drawing ability whatsoever, you want to use the computer to create your storyboards, more power to you. You can use something as simple and accessible as Paint (see Figure 5-1), one of Windows' Accessories (click Start | Programs | Accessories | Paint), or a more powerful illustration program such as CorelDRAW or Adobe Illustrator. You can also use PowerPoint or Word, utilizing the freeform and flowchart symbol drawing tools available in the AutoShapes menu on the Drawing toolbar. Again, though, you'll have to think about the drawing program's

FIGURE 5-1

Use something simple—like Paint—so you don't have to be concerned with anything other than getting your ideas onscreen.

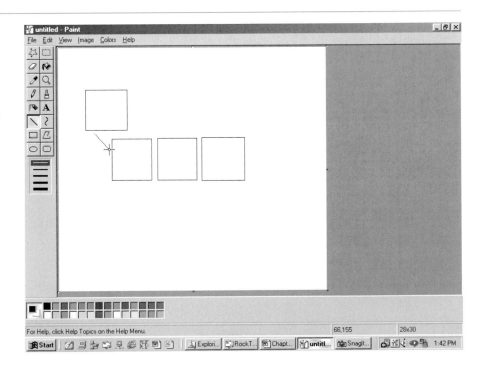

tools, and that may slow down your drawing process unless you're very proficient with the software.

If you want quick and easy, stick with paper and pencil (see Figure 5-2). You can use graph paper if you want to keep your lines straight and have 90-degree angles on your boxes' corners (though that's not important to the process). Paper's a nice choice because you can store it anywhere and take it with you with a minimum of fuss. Also, other than a strong wind or fire, there's not much chance of the paper malfunctioning. I also like paper because I can crumple it up and throw it on the floor if I hate it, and then if I change my mind, I can pick it up, smooth it out, and start drawing on it again.

> **TIP** Think about when and where you'll be storyboarding, and remember that it's an ongoing process. Paper and pencil are very transportable. However, if you're working with a partner on the project, you may have to use the computer to facilitate sharing your ideas if your partner is not always in the room with you. If you create a computerized storyboard, you can both mark it up with your ideas and then agree on the final version.

BUILDING THE LEVEL OF STORYBOARD DETAIL

Your storyboard should start with a simple series of boxes, one for each page in your site (not counting other people's pages to which your pages' links might point, although you can depict them as small boxes on the periphery of your

FIGURE 5-2

A simple drawing on paper gets the Luddite Movement's seal of approval.

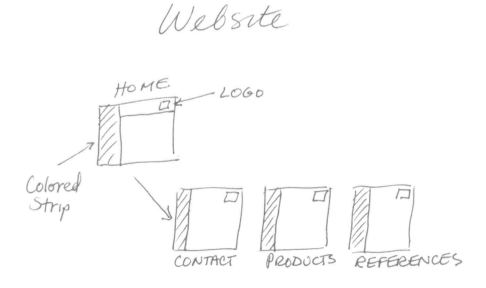

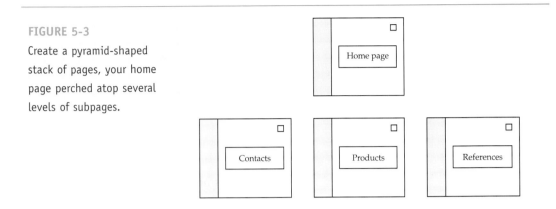

FIGURE 5-3

Create a pyramid-shaped stack of pages, your home page perched atop several levels of subpages.

drawing). You can draw the boxes that represent your pages in the shape of a pyramid, with the home page at the top (as shown in Figure 5-3), or as a long row of pages on the same level (as in Figure 5-4). The configuration you choose will simply reflect how you see your pages hierarchically or whether you even see a hierarchy among them. Regardless of the configuration, each box should be accompanied by the name of the page and should contain the main heading that will appear on that page. You don't have to write or type all the text that will appear on each page, but it's helpful to have a bullet list next to the box that includes all the topics the page will include, as well as some indication of where paragraph text will go on the page and what it will cover. You can also draw little shapes to indicate graphics you'll be inserting. Make notes next to the boxes with the names of any graphic files you've already accumulated or ideas for where to find them or who's going to make them (if you aren't the graphic artist in addition to being the Web designer, that is). This part of the storyboarding process is a precursor to the next step in the design process, which is gathering your content. Even if you don't have any of your content gathered yet, this is another good reason to storyboard your site—it gets you thinking about where you're going to find (or how you're going to create) the content you have in mind.

FIGURE 5-4

If your pages are just a series of equals, you can storyboard them as a series of boxes on one level.

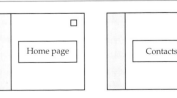
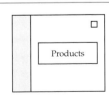
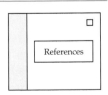

As you begin to put your ideas on paper or onscreen, you'll be amazed at how much detail you start to include. You don't want to completely compose any of your pages on the storyboards, though, so resist that temptation. These images are merely intended to help you organize your thoughts and create tangible evidence of your ideas to help you deal with them objectively or to facilitate teamwork in a partnership or team design environment. By the time your storyboards are complete, a complete stranger, with no prior sense of your Web site vision, should be able to see where you're going and what your site will look like, just by looking at the storyboards, as shown in Figure 5-5.

DEVELOPING A SITE FLOWCHART

Flowcharting software, and applications such as Microsoft PowerPoint that contain organization charting tools, can be used to create an image of your site's hierarchy and to show the relationship between pages and the flow from one page to another (see Figure 5-6). Any application that offers the ability to draw shapes with text in them, and to connect those shapes with lines or arrows, will also do the trick.

The site flowchart can be in addition to your sketched storyboards, or it can serve as the storyboards themselves. If you're using an application such as FrontPage or

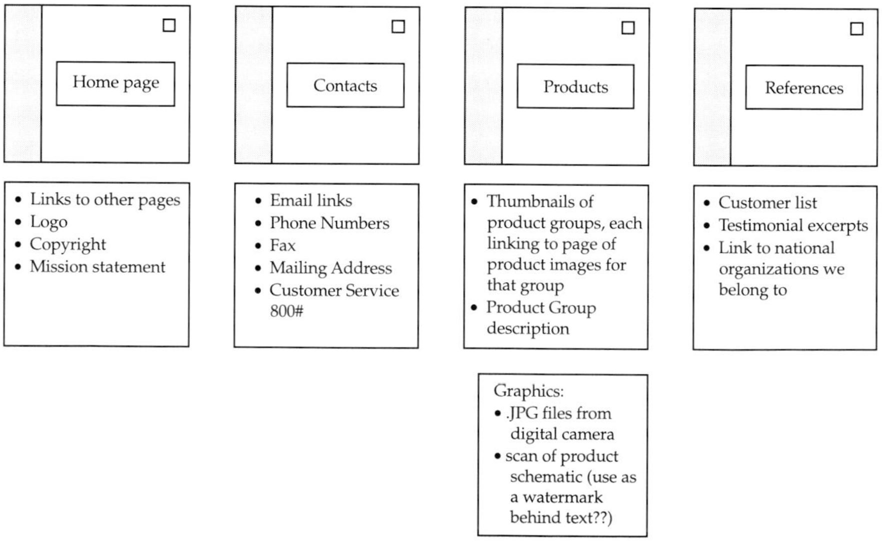

FIGURE 5-5

Using the computer for your storyboards makes it easier to keep lists of topics and to insert notes as reminders.

Home page
- Links to other pages
- Logo
- Copyright
- Mission statement

Contacts
- Email links
- Phone Numbers
- Fax
- Mailing Address
- Customer Service 800#

Products
- Thumbnails of product groups, each linking to page of product images for that group
- Product Group description

Graphics:
- .JPG files from digital camera
- scan of product schematic (use as a watermark behind text??)

References
- Customer list
- Testimonial excerpts
- Link to national organizations we belong to

FIGURE 5-6

Use shapes such as arrows
and symbols that represent
decisions and storage devices
to depict the flow, function,
and content of your site.

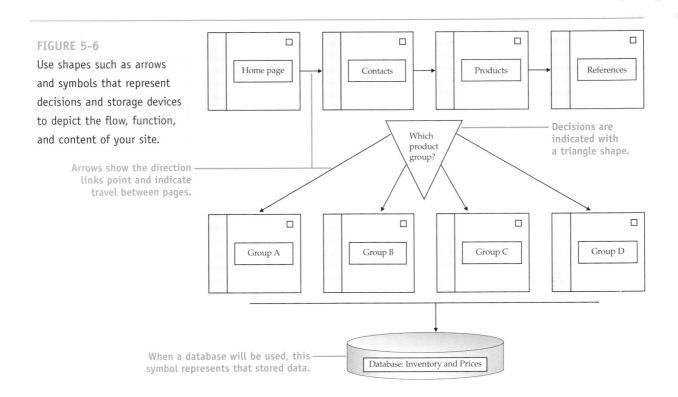

Arrows show the direction
links point and indicate
travel between pages.

Decisions are
indicated with
a triangle shape.

When a database will be used, this
symbol represents that stored data.

Dreamweaver to create your site, you'll be
repeating the flowchart/organization chart–
creation process when you actually start building
your site and setting up its pages. The storyboarding process that helps you plan and develop the
site's page hierarchy will help prepare you for the
site-creation process in the Web design software
of your choice.

TIP When you're planning and storyboarding your site, imagine you're the
visitor. Think about what information
you'll be providing through your pages,
what decisions you'll be asking visitors
to make, what tools you'll use to compel
them to read, to buy, to act—whatever
you want them to do. It's important to
maintain the visitor's perspective in all
of your design decisions, and the storyboarding process is a great place to start.

ON THE VIRTUAL CLASSROOM CD-ROM Using sketches, computer-generated drawings, and bona fide flow-charting software, the instructor demonstrates the process of storyboarding a Web site.

Gathering Your Web Content

Pictures and text, text and pictures—in the visual world of the Web, you rarely see one without the other. Whether your Web page is virtually all text, all pictures, or a smattering of both, it's a good idea to have that content gathered and organized before you sit down to start building your pages. Why? Because the very process of gathering the content forces you to think about it—where it will go, how it will be used, if it works with your overall plan for the Web site—and that alone is a significant benefit. Beyond this, and probably the most compelling reason to gather your content before you start creating your pages, is the time you'll save. Imagine yourself sitting at the computer, facing the Web design tool of your choice, and you want to insert a picture. Where is it? Oh, right. You still need to scan it. Now, where'd that photo get to? To avoid that scramble for content that contributes to the inefficient stop-and-go process of Web design, get your text and graphics organized now.

COLLATING YOUR TEXT CONTENT

I'm not talking about your simple headings here. Those you can just type in without much preparation other than deciding on the precise wording and making sure everything's spelled correctly. No, I'm talking about paragraph text—articles, stories, mission statements—any text that already exists somewhere or that needs to be created so that all you have to do is paste it into the Web page, between paragraph tags if you're working in HTML or inside a frame or table cell. If you're designing someone else's Web site, it's all the more important to get text from them, because you probably don't want to be responsible for the accuracy and content of any information you post to their site. It's their job to provide that for you unless the text in question is advertising or marketing copy they've asked you to create.

If you're designing your own Web pages, you'll want to take the time now to find and/or write the articles, stories, and longer paragraphs of text and store them as text files. If you're writing them, you can use any word processor, even the Notepad program that comes with Windows. If the articles or stories already exist, find them. Search the Web, dig through your disks, or have someone e-mail the items to you, but get your hands on them now.

Once you have the text content, organize it. Store the text files—document files, e-mail messages and attachments, files you've downloaded from the Web—in a folder on your local hard drive along with your Web pages. Give the files names that make it easy to spot the one you want when you're about to insert the text into your Web page. If, for example, the text is your client's company history, call the file "company history." Keep the names simple and relevant.

Of course, you won't be inserting these actual files into your Web pages. You'll be opening them in their native applications—Word or Notepad, for example—and copying the text to the Clipboard (CTRL-C or Edit | Copy). Next, you'll position your cursor on the Web page at the spot where the text should appear, and paste it (CTRL-V or Edit | Paste). The text will appear in your Web page in the Normal paragraph style, regardless of any formatting that was applied to the text through word processing software (see Figure 6-1).

FIGURE 6-1

Even if it was formatted else-where, your pasted text appears in the Normal style.

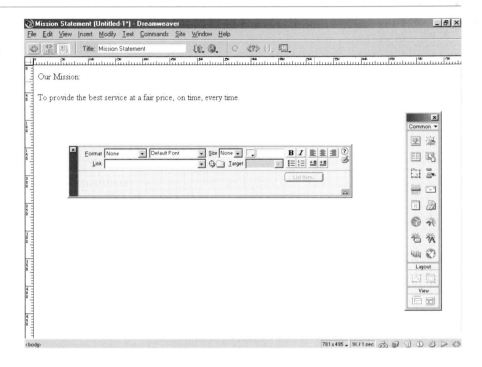

GRAPHIC FILE FORMAT CONSIDERATIONS

The first thing to know about graphic files for the Web is that the formats you may have used for print work (BMP, TIF, EPS, and others) are not appropriate. The only graphic formats you can use for the Web are:

▶ **GIF** This stands for Graphic Interchange Format, and is pronounced like "gift" without the T.

▶ **JPG** Pronounced "jay-peg," and named for the Joint Photographic Expert Group which created it (but you probably don't care about that).

▶ **PNG** Pronounced "ping," this stands for Portable Network Graphics, and is meant to describe the format's portability and viability for use on the Web.

TIP Be sure to proof the text in its native application before you use it in a Web page. This means running the spell checker, cleaning up spacing and punctuation problems, and making sure the text is accurate and grammatical. Of course, it helps if the text is intelligently written and a pleasure to read, but that's not always possible! The main goal is to have the text cleaned up and ready for use on the Web page so you don't have to worry about the content. Once the text is in your Web page, you want to be able to focus solely on placement, alignment, and formatting.

Why are these three types the only formats that are acceptable? Because they're the only ones that Web browsers (such as Internet Explorer and Netscape) display properly. These file formats are bitmap file formats, which means that each pixel of the image stores its own color values—literally, each bit of the picture is mapped. Think of it like the comics, where you can see the dots that make up the images. Groups of colored dots create the appearance of a single color or pattern. Bitmap images are groups of pixels which, when viewed as a group, display an image such as a photograph or drawing. If you zoom in on them, as shown in Figure 6-2, you can see the pixels that make up the image. Viewed onscreen in a normal size, however, you can't really tell how the image is constructed.

The key to Web graphics doesn't end with using the right file formats. Successful use of graphics on the Web requires that you pay close attention to the size of the files as well. The larger a file is—not the image dimensions, but the file size—the longer it takes to download. You obviously don't want your site's visitors drumming their fingers on the desk as they wait for your images to appear onscreen. You want the images to pop right up, especially if they contain information the visitor needs or if the images serve as hyperlinks that you want visitors to click to navigate your site.

FIGURE 6-2

Zoom in on a bitmap graphic (such as this GIF file) to see the pixels that make up an image.

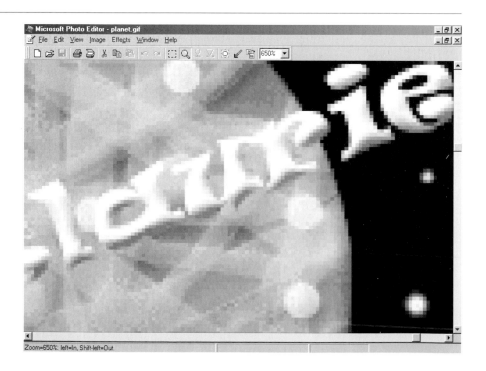

How do you control file size? By reducing the pixel size of your images. For example, if you scan a photograph (as shown in Figure 6-3), go ahead and scan it at 300 pixels per inch, to give yourself more detail to work with in editing the image. After retouching and editing the image, however, reduce the resolution to 72 pixels per inch so that the file size is smaller and will load faster on the Web. You can scan, edit, and adjust the resolution of the image through an application such as Adobe Photoshop or Corel PHOTO-PAINT.

Beyond the scanning resolution, reducing the height and width of the image to the smallest acceptable size will also help keep file sizes down. This doesn't mean your pictures need to be the size of postage stamps—if you need a 5" by 7" image on your Web page, so be it—just be prepared to save it at the lowest pixel per inch setting you can, so that the image doesn't take forever to load. If you're thinking that this will compromise important image clarity, remember that no one

> **TIP** Pixels per inch refers to the pixel resolution of the image. You may also hear or read the term "dots per inch," but this reference comes from the print world. Its use when referring to graphics for the Web is inaccurate, although it is used by people and some software applications, if only to provide a common frame of reference—the "dots" are actually pixels.

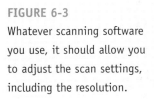

FIGURE 6-3

Whatever scanning software you use, it should allow you to adjust the scan settings, including the resolution.

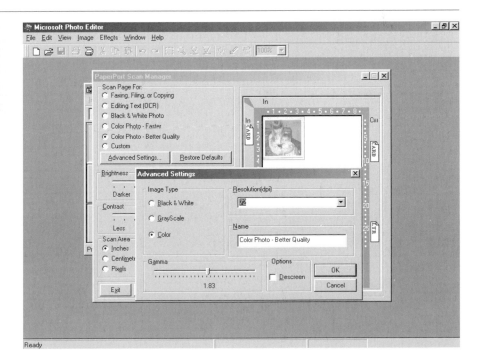

expects Web images to be crystal clear and most monitors don't display clear, crisp images anyway. Your goal is to use images that are clear enough for recognition, and that contain colors that complement your Web page.

FINDING AND SCANNING GRAPHIC IMAGES

The graphic images you'll be using should also be stored in a folder (perhaps one called "Images") along with your other site content. In order to have graphics to store, however, you have to find them. Sometimes this is a simple process—the pictures already exist and all you have to do is scan them, or maybe they were taken with a digital camera, so they're on your computer already and all you have to do is move the graphic files to the folder you've designated for Web page images.

If you don't have images ready to scan or sitting there in your digital camera waiting to be loaded on your computer, you have to do a little searching. If the images you need are intended to depict products for sale through your Web site, you have to take pictures of those products. If you need "atmosphere" pictures—images to convey a mood or visually suggest an action on the part of the site's visitor—you can take advantage of several different sources for photographs, drawings, and clip art.

> **TIP** When saving a scanned image or an image you created yourself, you can choose to save it as *interlaced* or *progressive*, two terms that mean the same thing—that the image will appear quickly, but achieve its final clearest state slowly. If you want visitors to know that an image is there and you want them to be willing to wait for it or be immediately able to use it (as a link, for example), the fact that it comes up choppy and/or fuzzy doesn't matter. Within anywhere from five seconds to a full minute (depending on the file size), the image will clear up and appear in its complete state. The visitor will have been able to use the image as a link or discern its basic content already, and won't feel as impatient waiting for the image to completely compose.

THE WEB

There are many Web sites that offer free images that can be used in your Web pages. Most of them will tell you if the images are copyrighted or if they're free to use (in addition to being free of cost), and if they are copyrighted, what you have to do in order to legally use them. To find these sites, use your favorite search site, such as yahoo.com or hotbot.com, and type "free graphics and photographs" or similar keywords in the search box, as shown in Figure 6-4. Once you get to the

FIGURE 6-4

Search for sites that offer low- or no-cost images that are legal to use on your Web site.

site and view the images it has to offer, the site will usually offer a Download button next to each image or provide instructions for copying the file to your local drive. Typically, this involves right-clicking the image and choosing Save Picture As from the resulting shortcut menu, which opens the Save Picture dialog box. The downside of mining the Web for images? Everyone else in need of graphic images is mining the same supply, and people start to recognize images that get used a lot. Try to find obscure images you've never seen before, and chances are your site's visitors won't have seen them either.

CD-ROMs

For sale at virtually every office supply store under the sun, hundreds of photographs, drawings, and clip art images are available on CD-ROMs. The only cost is the cost of the CD-ROM (usually less

TIP While it's easy enough to take images you see at other Web sites (I won't tell you how if you don't know already), it's illegal to do so without permission. Copyright infringement is not only illegal, it's wrong, so don't do it. If there's an image in use at someone else's Web site and you absolutely *must* have it, contact the site's webmaster and ask what you need to do. They may say to go ahead and use it (perhaps they got it for free and it wasn't copyrighted), or they may tell you that you can use it if you cite the artist/photographer's name under the picture. In any case, don't take without asking.

than $20), and they're free of copyright limitations, so you can use them as you please. The downside? Everyone who shops at the store where you got the CD could have bought one too and therefore could be familiar with the images. Also, the images on these CDs tend to be very generic and not terribly creative. Lots of sunsets and seascapes, children with rosy cheeks on playground swings. You may have to comb through 200 images to find one that's not too cute or too predictable.

SOFTWARE

If you have software programs that allow you to insert images into their documents, that software probably comes with clip art images. The images are legal to use in your Web pages (no copyright issues), and you already paid for them when you bought the software. Microsoft Publisher and CorelDRAW are two applications that come with a lot of their own art, so if you have them, you have a plentiful supply of images. The downside? Everyone who has the software has seen and used the images. I've seen people go to a Web site and say, "Hey! I have that picture in my Microsoft Clip Gallery!" If you use these images, use them sparingly and don't use them in key locations.

YOUR OWN IMAGES

Need a picture of people eating in a restaurant? Take a picture yourself, using a digital camera (to save yourself the time and effort of developing and scanning the image or sending the film out to be put on CD). You'll be able to control the type of restaurant (casual, formal, Chinese, Italian), and while you probably can't pose the patrons or adjust the lighting, you can choose to take the picture at a busy time to show a restaurant full of people or focus on a couple at an out-of-the-way table if your goal is to show that the restaurant is romantic. Of course, as your picture includes people, you'll want to get their permission to use them in the image. If that's not possible, consider using "stunt patrons"—the restaurant staff or your friends—so that the permission issue is eliminated.

If you have drawing capability, draw the image you need, and then scan your drawing. If you're well versed in the use of any illustration software (such as CorelDRAW or Adobe Illustrator), use it to create computer-generated images. The downside? The time and effort. Only you know if the time and effort are worth it, and if you have the skills to do it. If you do, the results will be unique and can set your Web site apart from the competition.

CAPTURING IMAGES WITH A SCANNER

For images that you have in print (traditionally developed photographs, hand-drawn pictures, printed artwork), the only way to get them into your Web pages is to scan them. By scanning them, you make an electronic copy of the image and that copy can be saved in .GIF, .JPG, or .PNG format.

If you have a scanner, it came with software that you hopefully installed and can use to scan images. If you've installed that software (thereby telling your computer which scanner you have and alerting scan-friendly software that the scanner's there and how to talk to it) and you also have applications such as Adobe Photoshop or Microsoft Photo Editor, you can use the application to scan the image. A typical scanning session goes as follows, with only slight variations depending on your scanner and the software you use to scan and save the image.

> **TIP** However you choose to obtain your graphics, make sure they're right for your Web pages—that they have the right tone, and that they're relevant to the site's content. Don't throw graphics onto a page just for the sake of having them. If your site includes a list of customer service numbers, it's nice to have a picture of a smiling person wearing a phone headset alongside the numbers. It's nice to have it, but not essential.

To Scan AN IMAGE:

1 Open the lid of your scanner and place the image on the plate (the big piece of glass), face down. Don't worry about which direction the image is facing—you'll be able to turn it the other way before scanning if you find out it's upside down.

2 Open your scanning software or an application that offers an Import or Acquire command for scanning. In Photoshop, the command is File | Import | Twain, as shown in Figure 6-5. This opens a scanning program (the software that came with your scanner) within the Photoshop workspace.

3 Choose the type of image you're scanning—a black and white photo or drawing, a color photo, or text (see Figure 6-6).

4 Adjust the scan settings so that you're scanning the image at the desired resolution. As mentioned earlier, you can scan the image at 300 pixels per inch, but you'll want to reduce it to 72 pixels per inch later, after any retouching you do.

5 Click the Preview button. This tells the scanner to take a look at what's on the plate and display it in the scanning program's workspace. You'll be able to tell after the

FIGURE 6-5

Preparing to import an image

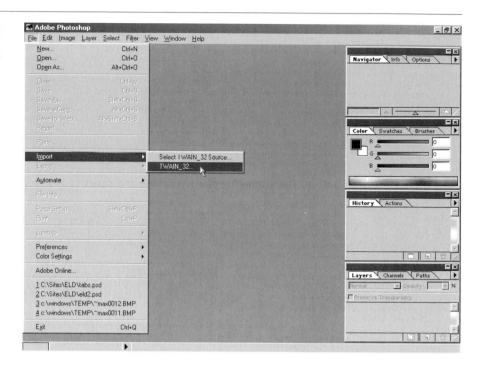

FIGURE 6-6

Choose the type of image you
want to scan.

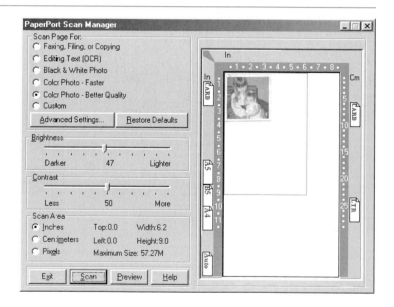

preview if you have the image facing the wrong way. If you do have to turn it around, click Preview again to take a fresh look at the scanning plate—chances are you haven't placed the image in exactly the same spot on the plate.

6 Using your mouse, adjust the size and placement of the box that defines the area to be scanned, as shown in Figure 6-7. You need to do this even if you're scanning the entire image area, and you definitely need to do this if you're just scanning a portion of the image.

7 Click the Scan button. The scanner copies the image and saves it as a temporary file.

8 If you're using an application such as Adobe Photoshop, the image appears in a new document window, ready for you to save it. If you're using a scanning program, select the software you want to use for retouching and saving the image.

9 Retouch the image as needed, and save it in an appropriate format.

Once saved, your scanned image can be re-edited as needed. Among other things, you can increase or decrease the image size and adjust colors, brightness, and sharpness. Depending on the power of the software you're using to edit the image, you can even apply *filters* that mimic artistic effects such as watercolor, textures,

FIGURE 6-7

Use the four-headed arrow to move the box.

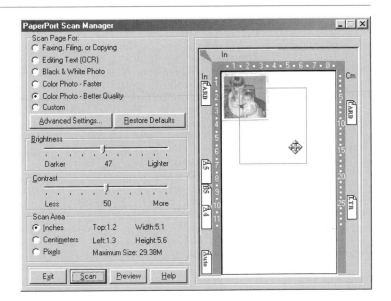

FIGURE 6-8

If your image is blurry, you can sharpen it, or if you need less detail, apply the Blur filter.

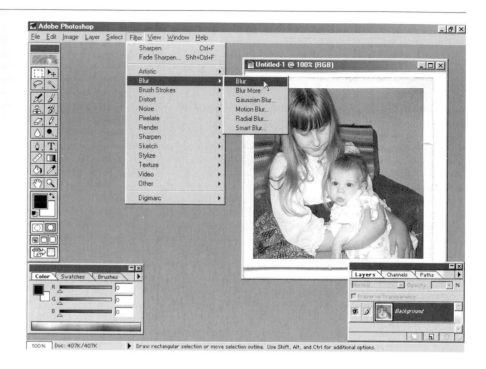

or motion (see Figure 6-8). Tinkering with your image enables you to take a simple, even boring image and turn it into something creative and eye-catching.

USING PHOTOGRAPHS

Photographs are compelling as Web site content—people often react to them much more strongly than they do to clip art images and simple graphics, simply because they're "real." Photographs can be retouched and artistically altered to change the reality they originally depicted, making them powerful tools in conveying a Web site's message. Because they're so important, it's essential that they look as good as possible, load as quickly as possible, and are used effectively.

First, photographs should be saved in .JPG format rather than .GIF. Why? Because the .JPG format stores more information about the image, and therefore maintains a higher level of image detail, which is understandably important for photographs. JPG files can be saved in what's known as *progressive* format, which means that they'll

> **TIP** Older versions of Internet Explorer don't support progressive JPG files, but the number of people using older versions shrinks every day, so it's not really something you need to worry about.

FIGURE 6-9
A progressive JPG appears quickly (in a blurry state) to let the visitor know what's coming.

compose slowly—appearing blurry and choppy at first (see Figure 6-9), and then becoming clearer as the image loads in the browser window. JPGs that are not stored in progressive format will not appear until the image is completely ready to display—this can be a liability because visitors may not wait for the image to appear. Progressive JPGs appear immediately, and improve right before the visitor's eye—increasing the chance that the visitor will hang around to see the final version.

> **TIP** When images are saved in .GIF or .JPG format, they're compressed. JPG files are known as *lossy*, meaning they lose some detail in the compression process. The loss, however, is virtually undetectable. GIF files are considered *lossless*, which means they don't lose content. This isn't really a reason to use them for photos, however, because the .GIF format stores less image information to begin with.

WORKING WITH LINE ART AND LOGOS

Images that consist of lines and shapes are best saved in .GIF format. Logos, borders, cartoon-like clip art, and simple shapes (such as the buttons shown in Figure 6-10) all fall under the line art category when it comes to Web graphics. You can save

FIGURE 6-10

Simple shapes work well as GIFs.

them in .JPG format, but it's not necessary because the less complex nature of a logo or drawing doesn't require the extra color information the .JPG format stores.

The .GIF format doesn't survive the resizing process well when you drag its handles to make it bigger or smaller, as shown in Figure 6-11, so do your resizing through graphic illustration software such as Adobe Photoshop, Corel PHOTO-PAINT, or Microsoft Photo Editor. Using the software to tinker with image size means you'll have a dialog box to work with, entering pixel and/or inch dimensions (see Figure 6-12). This approach also allows you to control the image proportions, as you'll find a Constrain Proportions (or similar) option that you can turn on so that if you increase the width of the image, the height adjusts automatically, and the image retains its *aspect ratio*, or ratio of width to height.

FIGURE 6-11

When you increase the size of an image with your mouse, the edges can get choppy, and you'll lose clarity overall.

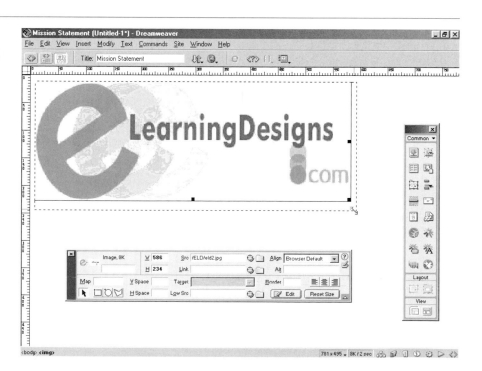

FIGURE 6-12

Resizing an image through graphic illustration software nets much better results.

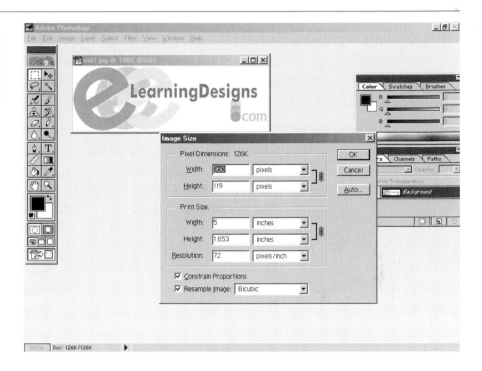

FINE-TUNING YOUR GRAPHIC IMAGES

Beyond resizing them, once you've found and locally stored the images you want to use, you may decide you need to edit them—clean up a photograph, smooth the edges of a curved shape in a piece of line art, or add text to an image. Any of these "tweaks" can be performed through the same software you use to resize an image. The tools may vary between applications, but for basic image manipulation, any graphic illustration program you have will allow you to edit the image, remove parts of it, or add new content.

Imagine that one of your images is a photograph of your business—your storefront or an office building. Imagine further that, sadly, when the picture was taken, the photographer didn't notice there was a big mud puddle in the grass by the front door or that the trash hadn't been picked up yet, and there's an ugly bin in the picture. Rather than taking a new picture on a dry day after the trash has been picked up, retouch the one you have. Using a program such as Adobe Photoshop or Corel PHOTO-PAINT, you can remove unwanted content, replacing it with more appealing fill, such as grass to fill in the mud puddle, or a clean sidewalk and curb where the trash bin was. You can even get rid of people in a group photo, which is convenient when you've had some staff changes but still want to use that great picture from the awards dinner.

Your retouching options include painting over imperfections—scratches on the photograph, red eye, creases, smudges, or even content that was actually part of the picture—tufts of hair that should have been combed into submission, inappropriate lettering on a worker's T-shirt, or peeling paint.

If painting over something isn't feasible (you need to get rid of a person or a large plot of dead grass, for example), you can copy content from one part of the photograph to another. Is there a wall behind the group of people? Copy a clean section of the wall and paste it over the person you want to get rid of. Of course, this works best if the unwanted person is in the back row, against the wall. To get rid of the plot of dead grass, copy some of the healthy, green grass and paste it over the dead spots, as shown in Figure 6-13. In Photoshop, you can use the Rubber Stamp tool to pick up a section of the photograph and then stamp it over another part.

To clean up imperfections or get rid of hard edges where you've pasted a block of something over something else, most retouching programs offer a Smudge tool or reasonable facsimile, as shown in Figure 6-14. This type of tool allows you to

FIGURE 6-13

Pick up the green grass and stamp it on top of the dead spots to create the illusion of a healthy, perfect lawn.

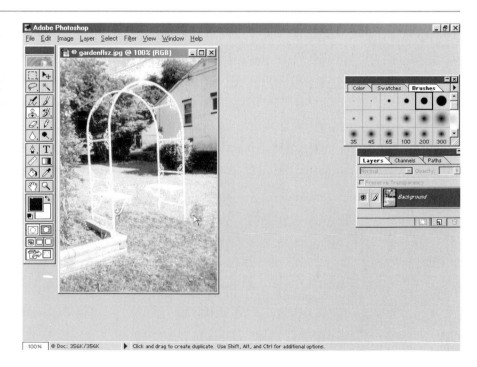

FIGURE 6-14

Smooth over a spot or imper-
fection in your picture.

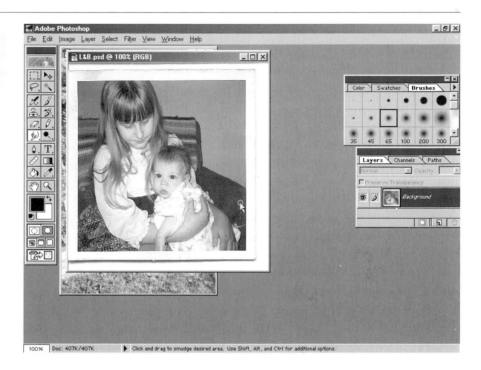

blend the edges of adjoining areas and smooth out flaws. While these edits would
be visible in a large, crisp printout of your photograph, the Web provides the perfect environment for viewing these tweaked images—there's rarely quite enough
detail or clarity to spot the pasted grass or the blocked-out guy from marketing
who doesn't work for you anymore.

 ON THE VIRTUAL CLASSROOM CD-ROM **Figuring out what will be on
your page is a big part of making your page a reality. Join the instructor as
she demonstrates the importance of planning a successful Web design project.**

 ON THE VIRTUAL CLASSROOM CD-ROM **The way you store your Web
page files and images is key to successfully designing a site, uploading it to
a Web server, and maintaining the site as time goes by. The author will
demonstrate and discuss the need for a simple and logical filing system for
your pages-in-progress.**

7

Evaluating Web Design Software and Tools

By now you know the kind of Web sites you can create, the steps to take in registering a domain for your site, how to gather content for the Web pages, the right size and type of graphic files to use, and the quickest ways to format text. What more can you possibly need? How about some advice on what bells and whistles your site can employ and some examples of the software that enables you to create them? Even if you already have the software you intend to use, it's worth checking out the options, if only so you have choices as your Web design skills increase and your goals and standards are raised to match your ability.

WHAT'S POSSIBLE ON THE WEB

The best way to find out what's possible on the Web is to look around and see what's being done. Explore the Web, visiting as many different Web sites and different types of sites as you can. It's really a great way to find out what you like and what works for people with sites similar to yours (or the one you're planning). You can also read Web industry magazines and newsletters to find out what's happening, but some of the emerging technologies you might read about aren't necessarily right for you or the site you have in mind. For example, there's a lot you can do with multimedia—sound, movies, and so on—but if the site you're designing is for people buying auto parts or selecting a cemetery plot, you might want to avoid anything that will slow down the buyer who needs a carburetor *now* or that might offend someone who has no interest in being entertained. In short, what's possible may not be what's appropriate.

As you consider which Web features—animated GIFs, movies, streaming video, sound, forms, shopping carts, and so on—you want to integrate into your site, think about your audience. What will the likely visitors to your site want to see? Do they need to be dazzled? Will they think the bells and whistles are cool, or will they resent the time it takes for their Internet dial-up connection to load the page content? You know your audience best—take what you know about them and make your feature decisions based on that. If you're designing a site for someone else, find out all you can about their site's typical visitor or the type of people they're looking to attract. Some things to consider:

▶ Visitors who are connecting to the Internet from home are still predominantly modem users. Despite the availability of cable modems and DSL connections for the home, most people are dialing in to the Internet at a whopping 56.6 Kbps (kilobytes per second), and usually a lot slower than that, just due to Internet traffic and the modem they happen to get when they dial into their ISP. Why is this important? Because even if your target audience is techno-savvy and will appreciate lots of sound and motion on a Web site, they may get bored waiting for the pages to load. Just because a visitor might appreciate more "cutting edge" Web page features doesn't mean he or she has the budget for a faster Internet connection.

▶ If your market is made up of corporate users—perhaps you sell a product or service that's most often used by businesses—and most of your visitors will be connecting from the office, you can feel safer using movies, video, sound, and other features that are slow via modem. Why? Because most companies have a faster Internet connection than home users, and the pages will compose faster, even with the extra page components.

▶ Give your audience options. If your page will open with a movie (created with a product such as Macromedia Flash, to be discussed later), give users a link to click that allows them to bypass the movie and go right to the meat of your site (see Figure 7-1). This is useful for people who have a dial-up connection to the Internet and for people who've been to your site before and don't need to see the movie again.

> **TIP** If your Web site will be of interest to business users but isn't businesslike in nature (say, an entertainment site of some sort), be aware that many companies use a variety of tools to prevent their staff from accessing unapproved Web sites. If the site you're designing could fall into the "not during business hours" category, assume most of your visitors will be connecting from home via modem.

▶ Sound and video are great, and if you've decided they're right for your audience, more power to you. Be prepared, however, to change the sounds and video offerings frequently. For the same reason you probably own more than one CD or

FIGURE 7-1

Add a "Skip the Flash movie" or similarly worded link to your opening page to give people a choice.

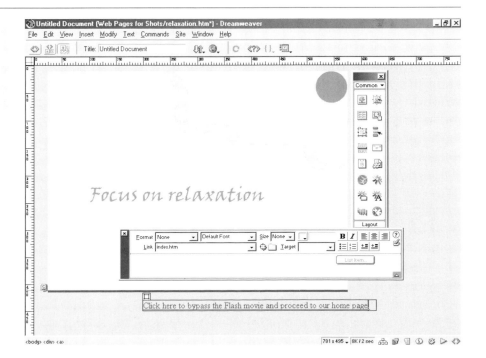

FIGURE 7-2

People can save download time by choosing not to click the link that starts your video.

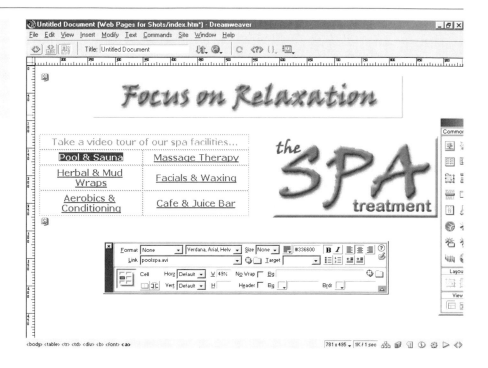

videotape, your audience doesn't want to hear the same sounds and video every time they visit your site. When you do add video to a Web page, it's a good idea to make viewing it optional—give people a link to click if they want to run the video (as shown in Figure 7-2), rather than having it start spontaneously. That way, if visitors have already seen it or don't have a fast Internet connection, they're not held hostage by the video, forced to wait for it to download and then watch it. If that happens, they're likely to click the Stop button and leave your site all together. You don't want them to do that, right?

TIP **If viewing your video is key to experiencing your Web site, don't forget to make it clear which link starts the video, and offer the ability to download the software needed to view the video. You can do this by including a link that downloads the program directly or a link that connects visitors to a site where they can download the program from its manufacturer.**

WHAT ARE MY PRODUCT CHOICES?

When it comes to Web page design software, the choices are about as plentiful as they are for most other major software categories—word processors, spreadsheets, databases, graphic illustration/design—but there are three major players:

Dreamweaver from Macromedia, FrontPage from Microsoft, and GoLive from Adobe. All three programs give you the ability to create Web *sites*, cohesive, connected groups of related pages. All three programs give you a WYSIWYG environment through which you create the Web pages, and all three also give you a way to view the HTML code that is being created behind the scenes (see Figure 7-3 for an example). This means that those who are HTML-savvy can edit their code, and for those users learning or just curious about HTML, there's a way to see how what one does in the WYSIWYG environment turns into HTML code.

With regard to the peripheral Web design applications—software used to create movies, record and edit sound, retouch photographs, and create graphic images—the choices are equally

> **TIP** The term WYSIWYG (which stands for What You See Is What You Get) wasn't invented by or for Web design software. Windows and Windows-based software really brought the term into the average computer user's lexicon about ten years ago, with the release of software that showed you onscreen how your documents would look when printed. It has a lot of meaning in the Web design arena, however, because it represents one of two approaches to Web design—through a WYSIWYG application or through writing raw HTML code using a text editing program. The pros and cons of these two approaches (as well as working in both environments) are discussed later in this chapter.

FIGURE 7-3

Dreamweaver gives you a split-screen view of your Web page, enabling you to see your page content and its underlying HTML code at the same time.

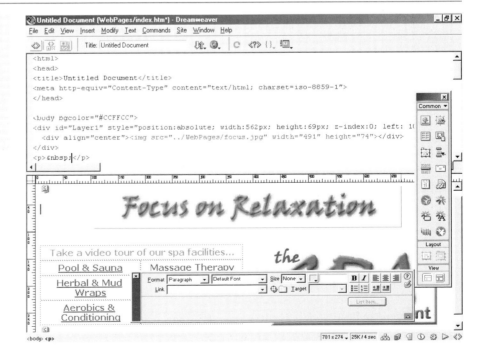

abundant, but again, there are a handful of products that lead the pack in terms of popularity and functionality:

▶ **Movies** For creating Web-based movies, the most popular program is Macromedia Flash (shown in Figure 7-4). With a fairly friendly interface and a great deal of power, Flash gives you the ability to create hundreds of frames on several layers. You then populate those frames with existing graphic content (photos, clip art, drawings) and make them move and change shape.

▶ **Sound** When it comes to recording and editing sound, there isn't a clear winner. Many Web designers use the sound software that came with their computer (provided by the manufacturer of the sound card and/or speakers). For short bursts of sound (or sounds that will be looped), you can use the recording software (Sound Recorder) that comes with Windows 95/98/Millennium, found in the Accessories list on the Start menu. The Sound Recorder window (shown in Figure 7-5) allows you to record sound through your computer's microphone, using simple tools that resemble the controls on a tape recorder or VCR. If your sound needs exceed these options, you can search the Web for

FIGURE 7-4

Use Macromedia Flash to make graphics, shapes, and text move and "speak" through event-synchronized sounds.

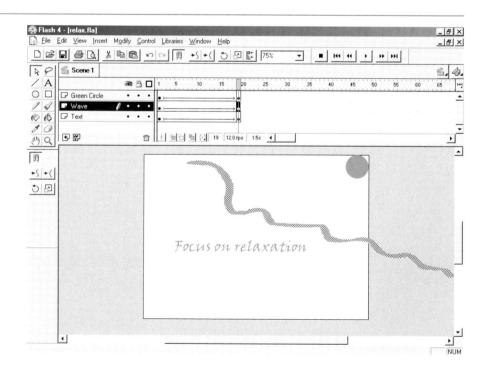

FIGURE 7-5

The Sound Recorder window resembles the controls on a tape recorder or VCR.

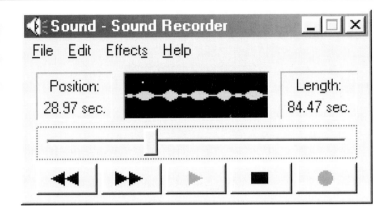

"Sound Recording and Editing." The process of acquiring software online is covered in more detail later in this chapter.

▶ **Images** With regard to retouching photographs and creating Web graphics, Adobe has the market locked up with Photoshop and ImageReady. Photoshop gives you an arsenal of tools for scanning, editing, and retouching drawings, clip art, and photographs (see Figure 7-6). ImagcRcady, which comes with Photoshop, has the same set of tools you'll find in Photoshop for creating and

FIGURE 7-6

Paint over imperfections in a photo and create original artwork as well with Adobe Photoshop.

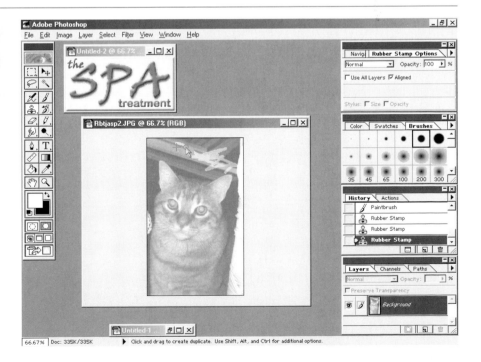

editing images, but also allows you to create rollover images (graphics that change in relation to your mouse movements) and animations from the simple to the fairly complex (see Figure 7-7). When it comes to animation, however, ImageReady is no rival for Flash (not that it ever intended to be), although the concept of creating frames and filling them with graphic content is found in both products.

In all of the above categories—Web design, movies and animation, sound recording/editing, and graphic creation/retouching—there are hundreds of shareware and some freeware applications to be found online, in software stores, and through software catalogs. If finding an inexpensive alternative to some of the big sellers discussed earlier in this section is important to you, these shareware and freeware alternatives are worth checking out.

> **TIP** If you're looking for a job in the Web design field, it pays to master the major players. This means learning Dreamweaver, FrontPage, Flash, and Photoshop like the back of your hand. If you're planning on working as a free-lance Web designer, the choice is up to you, but again, you're likely to find clients that know or expect you to know the products that get the most press.

FIGURE 7-7

Create a series of frames in ImageReady and save your creation as an animated GIF file.

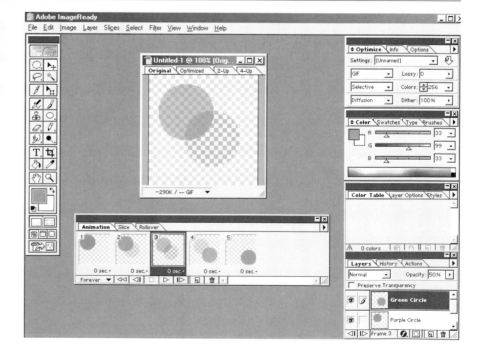

COMPARING DESIGN ENVIRONMENTS

When it comes to Web design—the composition of Web pages through the typing of text, insertion of graphics and multimedia objects, and the creation of tables and layers to set up page layout—you have two choices for building your pages. You can build them in a WYSIWYG application such as Dreamweaver, FrontPage, or GoLive, or you can create them in a text editor (such as Notepad, which comes with Windows, or a more powerful editor such as TextPad from Helios Software), typing HTML code directly. The WYSIWYG applications create HTML code, but insulate the designer from the code itself. You can get at the code if you want to, but conceivably, you don't ever have to see it or "deal with" it, the latter being the attitude of someone who knows nothing about HTML and prefers to keep it that way.

WORKING IN A WYSIWYG ENVIRONMENT

The words What You See Is What You Get are basically true when it comes to Web design in a WYSIWYG environment. To illustrate this statement, take a look at the Dreamweaver application window, as shown in Figure 7-8. Text is typed onscreen, and is formatted through a floating palette (the Properties Inspector), which offers tools for changing the font, size, and color of the text. Graphics are inserted by clicking a button on another floating palette (the Objects palette), and using the Properties Inspector, you can change the alignment of text or graphics.

> **TIP** While it's entirely possible to design an attractive Web page without ever typing a single character of HTML code, I don't recommend remaining in a WYSIWYG vacuum if you really want to be an accomplished Web designer. It's helpful to at least understand the structure of the HTML language and be able to perform minor edits in the HTML code your WYSIWYG application creates. Certainly, it's best if you can master HTML (and that's not too difficult, as the language and its "grammar" are very simple). Even if you prefer to work in a WYSIWYG environment, it's great if you can create a Web page in a pure HTML environment, if only to cover you in case you ever have to do some design or editing work and don't have access to Dreamweaver or a similar product at the time.

Tables and layers help you position your text and graphics and create your page layout, and you can use your mouse to resize the layers, tables, and individual table cells, shown in Figure 7-9. When you type text or insert a graphic, it will generally look through a browser as it looks onscreen in the design application

FIGURE 7-8

WYSIWYG applications provide onscreen toolbar buttons and palettes to insert and format Web content.

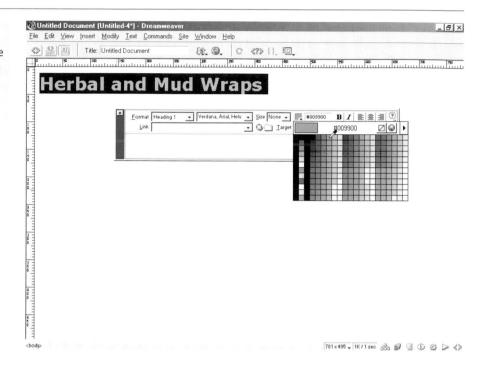

FIGURE 7-9

Drag a table or table cell walls to resize them horizontally or vertically.

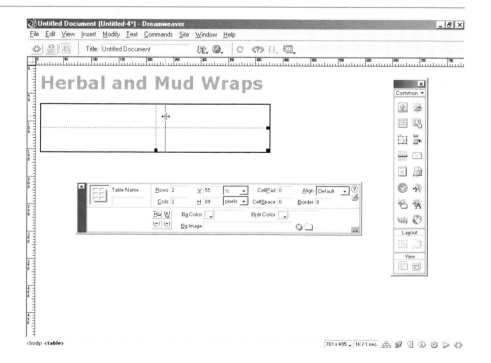

(Dreamweaver, FrontPage, GoLive). Where things get a little dicey is in the placement of layers, the sizing of tables and the cells within them (including nested tables), and the size of the page when it's viewed on monitors set at different resolutions.

To keep track of your Web page in progress and how it will look online, WYSIWYG applications provide a command for previewing your Web page in a browser (as shown in Figure 7-10). You needn't be online to do this, as you're looking at a local copy of your Web page. This saves you uploading your page and graphics to the Web just to see how the browsers will interpret your Web's underlying HTML code. As browsers vary in terms of how they display the same Web pages, it's a good idea to test your pages in both Internet Explorer and Netscape, the two most commonly used Web browsers.

WRITING HTML CODE

HTML code might look a little scary if you don't know anything about it and just give it a quick glance. Go to any Web site online and choose View | Page Source (in Netscape) or View | Source (in Internet Explorer) to see the HTML code that

FIGURE 7-10

As you work on your pages, preview them through a browser to make sure your content and layout will work online.

FIGURE 7-11

Don't let the complex look of HTML code scare you off; it's a simple, English-based language that anyone can learn.

```
herbal.htm - Notepad                                              _ □ ×
File   Edit   Search   Help
<html>
<head>
<title>Untitled Document</title>
<meta http-equiv="Content-Type" content="text/html; charset=iso-8859-1">
</head>

<body bgcolor="#FFFFCC">
<h1><font face="Verdana, Arial, Helvetica, sans-serif" color="#009900">Herbal
  and Mud Wraps </font></h1>
<table width="55%" border="0" cellspacing="0" cellpadding="5" height="89">
 <tr>
   <td colspan="2">
     <div align="center"><font face="Verdana, Arial, Helvetica, sans-serif">Find
       out more about our 100% Organic Treatments!</font></div>
   </td>
 </tr>
 <tr>
   <td width="51%" height="42"><font face="Verdana, Arial, Helvetica, sans-serif"><a
href="seascrub.htm">Sea
     Scrub Mud Bath</a></font></td>
   <td width="49%" height="42"><font face="Verdana, Arial, Helvetica, sans-serif"><a
href="herbskin.htm">Herbal
     Skin Conditioning Wraps</a></font></td>
```

creates the page you're looking at (see Figure 7-11). It might look complicated, and it may be difficult, at first, to see how the programming code you're seeing results in the Web page you were just viewing. Once you understand just a little about the way HTML works, however, you won't be scared anymore.

Creating a Web page by writing (well, typing) HTML code requires the use of a text editor, such as Notepad (one of the Windows Accessories) or a more powerful editor such as TextPad. To construct HTML code, you type the HTML *tags* (the words and abbreviations inside the greater-than and less-than symbols, such as <body> to indicate body text), and type the *attribute* settings (such as color="red") for the various components of your Web page. The tags are responsible for creating Web page content, and the attributes define the appearance of that content. Of course, this is just the foundation of an HTML document—HMTL does much, much more—but with an understanding of common tags and attributes, you can create a simple Web page by writing HTML code, and you can certainly begin to edit code on existing pages. Figures 7-12 and 7-13 show a simple Web page and its corresponding HTML code.

So how do you decide which environment is best to work in? If you know both tools (a WYSIWYG application and HTML) equally well, it boils down to preference.

FIGURE 7-12

Using either a WYSIWYG environment or a text editor to write HTML code, a simple page can be constructed quickly.

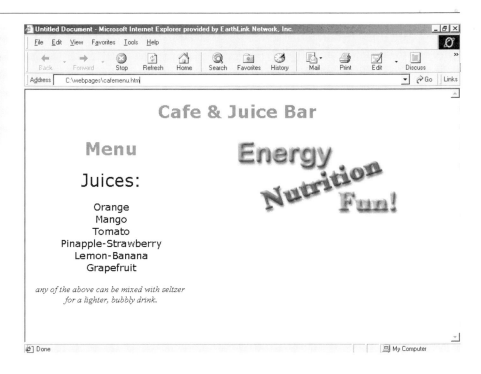

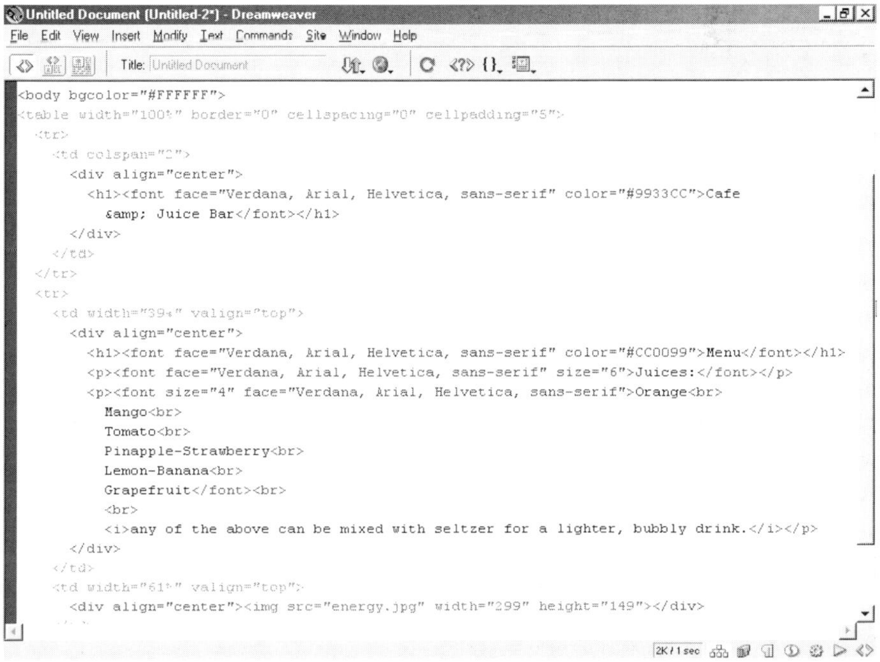

FIGURE 7-13

You can see how a Web page is constructed by viewing the HTML code for a simple page containing text and graphics in a table.

If you don't know HTML, you'll probably prefer to continue working in a WYSIWYG environment, dabbling in the HTML code only when it's required. If you learned HTML before the WYSIWYG applications developed into the friendly and functional tools they now are, you'll probably stick with what you know. I don't mean to sound wishy-washy, but it really is a matter of what you know and what you feel most comfortable using.

The most effective combination for most people is to enter text and insert graphics and other elements (movies, sound) through the WYSIWYG environment, and use HTML for fine-tuning—adjusting table widths and heights, changing the URL that a link points to, and adjusting colors, positions, and dimensions of Web content. This isn't to say that anyone who favors one environment to the exclusion of the other won't be a successful or effective Web designer. On the contrary, people do much better when they're using tools they know and like.

BUILDING YOUR SOFTWARE LIBRARY

It's a good idea to try software before you commit to it as a tool in your Web design kit. Some of the available tools come with Windows (Notepad, Sound Recorder), and others come with other popular software (FrontPage came with certain editions of Office 2000). These programs that ride in on the coattails of other software applications certainly have an advantage in terms of being selected as the tools of choice, simply because they don't require any effort to obtain them. To counter this, the manufacturers of competing products offer demonstration versions of their software that you can download through their Web sites. Demo software is generally crippled in some way (perhaps you can't print or can't change the default settings) or it's set to stop working after a certain number of days on your computer or after a certain number of uses. Try these manufacturers' sites (Macromedia's site is shown in Figure 7-14) to find out more about downloading demo software:

▶ www.macromedia.com

▶ www.adobe.com

▶ www.microsoft.com

FIGURE 7-14

The Macromedia site allows you to download demo versions of Dreamweaver and Flash, in the hopes that after trying them, you'll want to buy them.

To peruse the available shareware and freeware applications (you might find a great text editing program or an application that helps you make animations), go to the Web. Sites such as www.tucows.com (shown in Figure 7-15) and www.hotfiles.com provide descriptions, ratings, and pricing for hundreds of programs, and you can search their database to narrow the list to products in the category you need.

> **TIP** Another piece of software that every Web designer needs is an FTP (File Transfer Protocol) program. You need FTP software to connect to your Web server and upload your Web page files and content (graphics, sound, and movie files). You can search the Web for inexpensive (and sometimes free) FTP programs and download them easily. WS_FTP Pro, FTP Commander, and CuteFTP are some popular choices.

CHOOSING AN HTML TEXT EDITOR

You might be perfectly happy with the text editor that comes with Windows—it's called Notepad, and you'll find it in the Accessories list on the Start menu. It allows you to type text and save it in HTML format, turning your text into HTML code. Sounds like all you need, right?

FIGURE 7-15

Search for a text editor or animation program, and choose one that's priced right and rated well.

Well, sort of. It's kind of a case of ignorance being bliss. If you never try a text editor that gives you some of the following features (found in Helios's TextPad, a popular text editor), you'll continue to be happy with Notepad:

▶ **Bookmarks** Mark sections of the HTML code for quick access, saving you scrolling around to find specific points in the document (see Figure 7-16). After bookmarking a section of the HTML, you can go back to it by pressing the F2 key, which takes you from bookmark to bookmark until you find the one you wanted. As you're likely to only bookmark a few spots in your document, this means you normally find the spot you're looking for in just a few presses of the F2 key.

▶ **Match Bracket** A maddening aspect of HTML is its absolute rigidity. Browsers can't intuitively interpret HTML code—the code must be clean and accurate. The most common error is mismatched brackets around HTML tags. If there aren't matching sets of brackets on all of your tags, the page may not display properly through a Web browser, because the HTML won't be properly interpreted. The Match Bracket command in TextPad (see Figure 7-17) finds missing brackets for you so you don't spend hours combing through code to find the missing < or >.

FIGURE 7-16

Bookmark important sections and then hop between them with a simple keystroke.

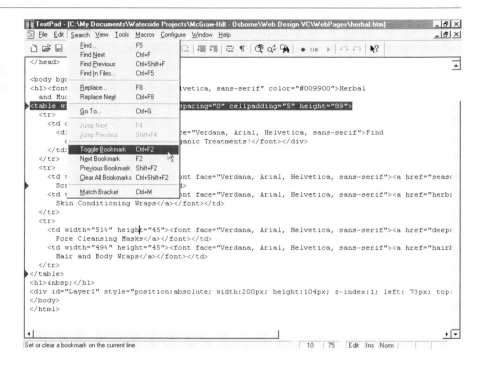

FIGURE 7-17

TextPad helps you find mismatched brackets.

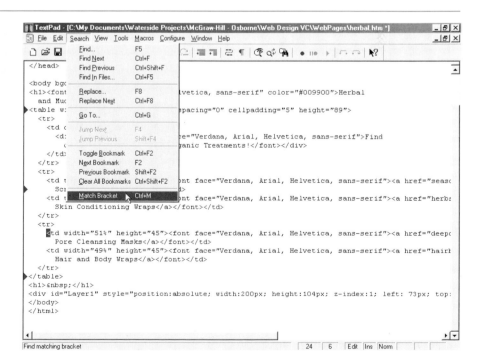

▶ **Compare Files** Have two pages that are virtually identical? How about the same page, one on floppy disk and one on your hard drive, and you're not sure which is the one you want to upload to the Web server? Use the Compare Files command to find differences between two HTML files.

▶ **Macros** If you're familiar with the time and labor savings that macros provide in applications such as Microsoft Word, the idea of creating macros in a text editor will not be foreign to you. Even if you've never heard the word "macro" before, you'll instantly see the benefit of creating and using them in a text editor used for writing HTML code. A macro is a program you create by recording a series of steps. For example, you can record yourself entering the HTML code for a three-column by three-row table centered on the Web page (shown in Figure 7-18). By recording yourself doing this once, you eliminate the need to ever again type all the requisite code. To invoke the macro and perform its steps (creating the centered 3x3 table) in the future, all you'll need to do is choose User Macro from the Macros menu and select the one you want to play. Any coding tasks that take time, have a significant margin for error, or you think you'll do more than once are worth turning into macros.

FIGURE 7-18

Would you rather type all of this or make two menu choices to insert it automatically? That's what I thought you'd say.

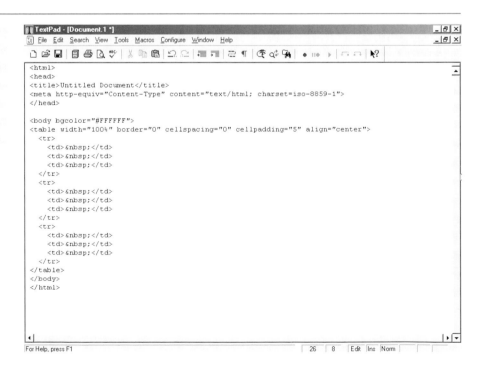

8

Web Site Layout

Good taste is not always innate, and the abundance
of uninspired, ineffective Web sites is proof enough of that
fact. Another culprit is simply not knowing some basic rules
for designing any visual two-dimensional space, whether it's
a brochure, a business card, or a Web page. This chapter intends
to put you on the road to fully understanding the concepts of
good composition and to mastering the ability to not only spot
but create Web sites that are both visually appealing and useful
to their visitors.

The Keys to Good Composition

If your Web page has good composition, it is pleasing to look at, and the items on the page—text and graphics—are distributed so that no one item overwhelms or eclipses another visually. The ingredients that create a good composition covered throughout the chapters in this book are:

▶ In Chapter 10, "Adding Graphic Content," you'll learn to choose a background graphic that doesn't render text illegible and make pictures fade into the background unnoticed (see Figure 8-1). It's also worth noting that a background color or image isn't always needed—it's not like a white background is some sort of sin or that you've wasted a design opportunity by not applying a color or image to your page.

▶ Also covered in Chapter 10 for effective Web design: selecting graphics that load quickly, that include or are placed near text that explains them, and that convey your site's message clearly.

▶ Chapter 9, "Adding Text Content," talks about the importance of using fonts that don't fight with one another. Your Web pages will be easier on the eye if you keep fonts clear and large enough to be read, avoiding the use of too

FIGURE 8-1

If your page requires a background, choose a subtle image or a solid color that complements other site colors.

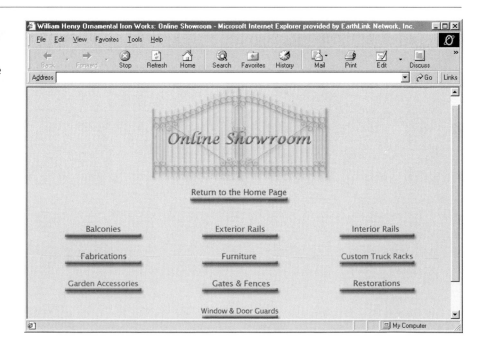

many different fonts on a single page (see Figure 8-2), and keeping fonts the same throughout a Web site.

▶ Mentioned throughout the book, because of its importance: maintaining an overall look for your site that matches the tone of your business, product, service, cause, or you as a person.

So good composition can be said to be well chosen and have well-placed content. Good composition isn't the sole property of one style or of people who think they have the aforementioned good taste. There are plenty of sites that I would redesign if I were hired to do so, but that doesn't mean they aren't well designed to begin with, or that they violate the four basic components of good site composition:

> TIP Not sure what works for a business or person like you? Check out the competition's sites. You can take what works for them and make it better, and toss the stuff you don't like. This sort of reconnaissance mission is a good way to check out the overall layout of other sites, providing food for thought and a clear vision of what you want and don't want.

▶ **Consistency** This component refers to the reliable placement of content on every page of the site. If your logo is in the upper-right corner of one page, put it in the

FIGURE 8-2

Stick with one or two fonts per page, choosing carefully from the serif, sans serif, and artistic font groups.

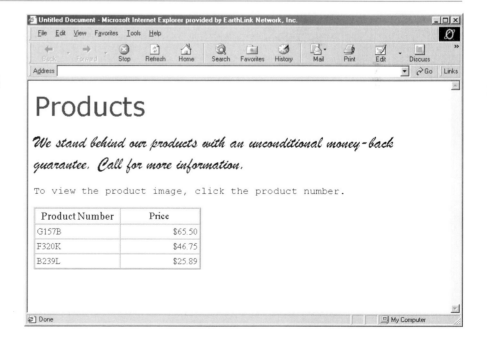

same place on the other pages. Every page of your site can be new and different, but some things should be in the same place so people feel comfortable.

▶ **Alignment** When choosing horizontal and vertical alignment settings for your text and graphics, keep them consistent (there's that word again!) throughout the pages of your site.

▶ **Position** Have a caption under a picture? Place it so there's no doubt to which picture the text pertains. Your page shouldn't be a conceptual puzzle for visitors to solve. Position is also important in terms of balance. Place objects on the page so that symmetry (or an effective, purposeful lack thereof) is achieved.

▶ **Repetition** Sounds like consistency again, but it's not. Repetition helps people retain information. Repeat concepts, use the same pictures and colors throughout your pages when related information is conveyed. Repetition helps people retain information. See what I mean?

As you move through the remainder of this chapter, each of the basic components of a well-designed site will be explained in greater detail, and you'll see several examples of both good and bad design, at least from a composition perspective. You may not agree with all the examples—a site I like may repel you, or vice versa. Should that happen, don't assume that you don't "get" the idea of composition, or that the design concepts described here are incorrect. Rather, chalk up any disagreements to the fact that much of this area is subjective, like art—one person's treasure is another person's trash. There are basic tenets of design that are universally accepted, but the way they're employed is entirely up to the designer, and the success of the design is up to each person who views it.

CONSISTENCY

When designing the layout for a single page, such as a flyer, for example, or a Web page that will have no subpages, you need only worry about the layout of that one page. There's no need to think about how your layout might be implemented on related pages that have different content. If, on the other hand, you're designing a Web page that will have related subpages to which the first (or home) page links, your layout decisions must take those subpages into account. Why? Because on a well-designed Web site, the related pages must *look* related. Unless your site boasts something like, "Every page designed by a different person!", visitors expect cohesiveness and consistency throughout the site. They may not be aware that they're expecting this, but if every page is vastly different from the last, their comprehension of site content, retention of information read, and desire to come back are diminished.

How do you achieve this consistency? As you're designing your site's home or main page, keep the content of the subpages in mind. Your main page can be different from the subpages, but some key items should be in the same place on the home and subpages:

▶ Navigation buttons

▶ The organization's logo or name

▶ Links such as "E-mail" or "Contact Us"

If you keep these elements in the same place on every page, visitors are freed to concentrate on your content. They won't have to worry about getting back to a particular page or where to find connections to other pages and sites. Figures 8-3 and 8-4 show two pages from the same site. Note that on both pages, the navigation buttons are in the same place and other page elements are also in the same place, are the same size, and look similar.

Don't assume that consistent equals boring. It doesn't. You can be as creative in your layout and content as you like. Just don't send your visitors on the equivalent of a scavenger hunt every time they go to a new page in your site. Give them something to rely on, something they can count on being in the same place on every page. If you do, they'll enjoy their stay and come back often.

> TIP Chapter 12, "Structuring Web Pages with Tables, Frames, and Layers," will show you some great Web page elements that make it much easier to take your layout vision and turn it into a Web reality. These elements will be implemented throughout this chapter's examples, and you can refer to Chapter 12 for the how-to information you need.

ALIGNMENT

If you've ever used a word processing application, such as Microsoft Word, Corel WordPerfect, or even WordPad, the bare-bones word processing accessory that comes with Windows, you've aligned text. By default, all text you type into a word processor is aligned to the left side of the page. The same is true for text on a Web page. If you type your page content into a WYSIWYG application

FIGURE 8-3

Consistency helps you, too, by making it faster and easier to develop subpages.

FIGURE 8-4

Don't reinvent the wheel with every new page in the site.

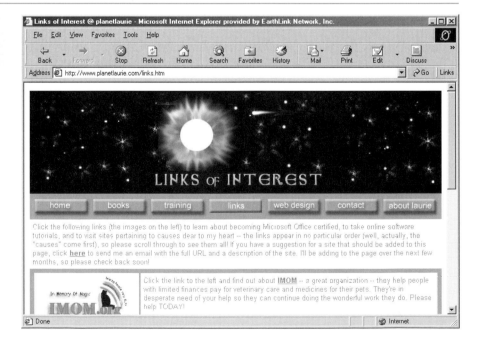

such as Macromedia Dreamweaver or Adobe GoLive, the text is left-aligned (see Figure 8-5). If you create your page using HTML code directly, the body text is aligned to the left unless you enter alternative alignment instructions. So even if you've never altered your document's alignment, you've been working with aligned text.

It's quite likely, however, that you have tinkered with the alignment of your text at some time. You've probably seen the benefit of centering a page title or section heading, or right-aligning a column of numbers in a tabbed list or table. These deviations from the default left-alignment of the main document draw attention to the text that is aligned differently than the rest of the text. That's a good thing when it comes to titles or headings, as shown in Figure 8-6. Right-aligning numbers makes sense so that the decimal places line up, especially when the numbers represent currency, which should always have two numbers to the right of the decimal point.

Alignment, therefore, is more than aesthetics; it's part of the information-delivery process. If you want something to stand out, if you want to herald a change of

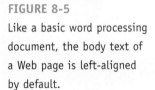

FIGURE 8-5

Like a basic word processing document, the body text of a Web page is left-aligned by default.

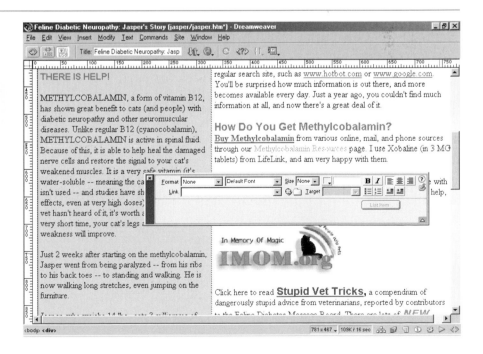

FIGURE 8-6

Even if nothing else varies between heading and paragraph text, aligning it differently than the paragraph text makes it stand out.

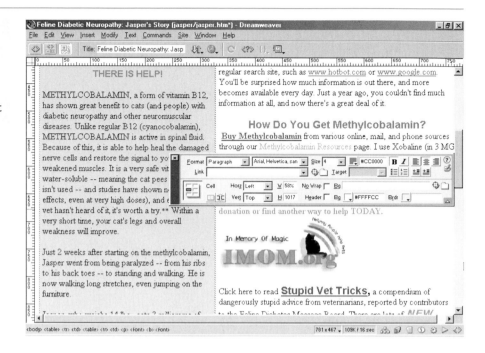

topic or the beginning of a new section within your Web page, it's a good idea to vary something about your heading. The heading can (and should) be made larger than the paragraph text, and to make it stand out further, changing its alignment is a good idea. If you want someone to be able to read a column of numbers easily, don't make them squint at the screen to figure out a phone number or distinguish between numbers in the case of currency. Figure 8-7 shows the benefit of altering the alignment of both text and numbers.

So it's a good idea to vary alignment when doing so will draw attention to one text element over another. But is it good to vary alignment throughout a page? No, not when it comes to paragraph text, captions under pictures, columns of link text, or a variety of headings on the same page. If you're centering your headings, center all of them. If most

TIP Don't use right-alignment on a Web page, other than within table cells well away from the right side of the page. To do so risks that some users won't see the right-aligned text, as it can get lost for users with lower-resolution settings on their monitors. If, for example, you're designing for the average user with an 800 x 600 monitor setting, people with 640 x 480 resolution may have to scroll to the right to see the entire page, and right-aligned content can be missed entirely.

FIGURE 8-7

Changing the alignment of Web page content can make it easier to read.

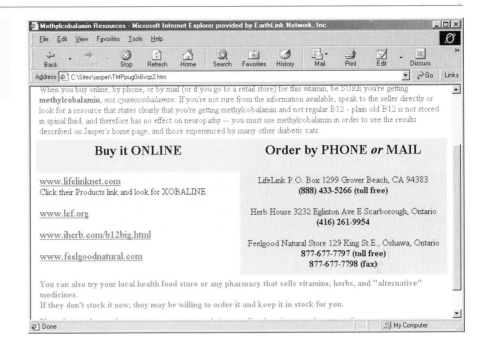

of your pictures are left-aligned within the table cells or layers that house them, left-align all of them.

This may seem like an overly regimented, all-or-nothing approach to design, but it's not. Keeping your alignment consistent throughout your pages will make it easier for your site visitors to read the site content, and gives your layout, no matter how creative and imaginative, a clean look. Figure 8-8 shows a page with consistent alignment throughout, and Figure 8-9 shows the same page with a variety of alignments applied to page elements. You decide.

> **TIP** Don't center paragraph text—it makes it too hard to read the text as the word-wrap doesn't flow naturally.

POSITION

Ever walked into a room full of people, not knowing anyone, and had no idea who was with whom and which people knew which other people? Mingling in such an environment is tricky. Until people start making introductions, giving you a frame of reference for themselves—"Hi, I'm Bob, and this is my wife, Nancy!"—you might not feel comfortable starting conversations. Not paying

FIGURE 8-8

The visitor's eye can comfortably read paragraph text, and easily spot headings and important links.

Images centered within the cells

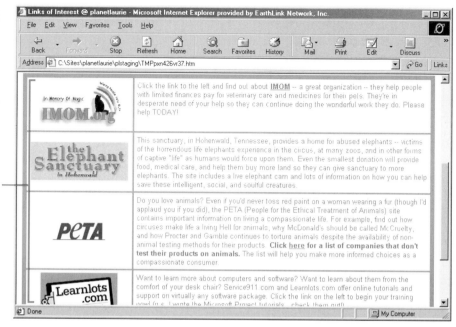

FIGURE 8-9

The centered paragraph text is very hard to read.

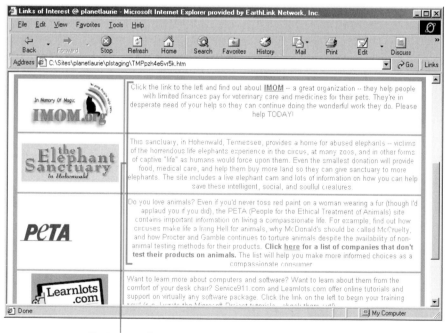

Text centered in paragraphs

attention to the placement of and relationship between objects on your Web pages can give your visitors the same uneasy feeling.

Your Web page content, typically made up of text and pictures, is usually related somehow. This picture goes with this text, this heading pertains to this text and the picture that goes with it. If your placement of these objects doesn't make these relationships clear, your site's information may be missed. Links won't be clicked, pictures won't be explained, text won't be read. Imagine receiving your morning paper in pieces—each article, picture, and headline cut out and handed to you in a pile—and then trying to catch up on the news. It would be nearly impossible. As shown in Figure 8-10, if pictures and their captions (and headings and their related text) aren't placed close together, it's not clear what's going on.

Web page design tools (such as Dreamweaver, GoLive, or HTML) don't give you total freedom to place things anywhere you want them. It is simple to place a caption directly under or alongside a picture, however, and to make sure a heading and the text to which it relates are close enough to eliminate confusion. For example, instead of pressing ENTER to move to the next line below a picture, press SHIFT-ENTER to create a line break instead of a paragraph break. The distance between

FIGURE 8-10

Too much distance between a picture and its caption can leave visitors wondering about the meaning of a picture, or where to find information about it.

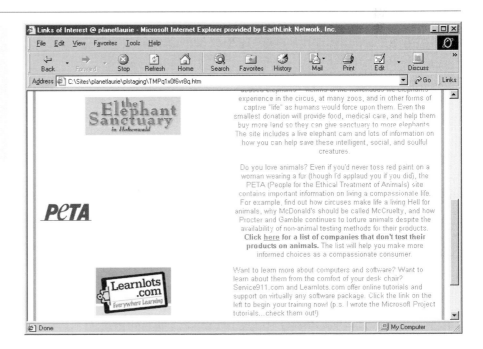

the picture and the caption will be smaller, making it clear that the text and the picture go together. Figure 8-11 shows a picture and text that describes it, nestled neatly in a table cell.

Position is also important in terms of balance. Just as it's important to match the related text and graphic elements on your Web page, it's important to place those pairs and groups of related content—and standalone elements as well—so they don't overwhelm each other.

There's a trick to checking your page for proper balance, and it will sound silly, but try it anyway. Sit back from the page onscreen, and squint at it. Squint? Yes, because you don't want to be concerned with reading or interpreting elements onscreen—you're looking at the size and visual weight of the elements on your page. Does one item stand out and draw your attention away from everything else? Is there an object that overwhelms the items near it? Unless that object is the most important thing on the page, you don't want it to be so dominant. Of course, you don't have to go through this exercise for every page you design. It's just a handy technique to use if you're not sure if you've achieved the right balance on the page.

FIGURE 8-11

Closeness is good in all relationships, especially on a Web page.

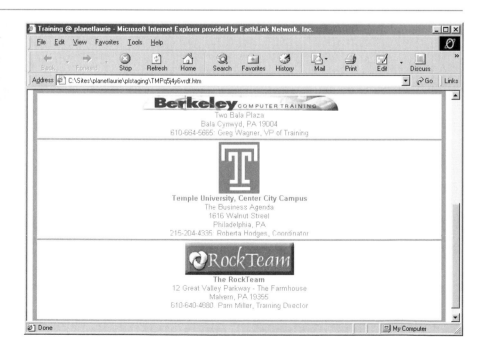

REPETITION

Repeat after me: it's important to repeat important information. Some information is absorbed the minute it's shared, assuming the person hearing or reading it is fascinated by the information and has been looking high and low to find it. Once it's been found, the person will absorb and retain that information like there's no tomorrow.

On the other hand, if information is unsolicited, the recipient may easily forget it. If the person visiting your site isn't in hot pursuit of the information you have to share, he or she may read it, think, "That's nice," and move on, forgetting what's been read. You can do a few things to prevent this:

▶ Keep your site visually interesting.

▶ Make sure all of your text is well written, clear, and concise.

▶ Repeat important information—be it conveyed through text or images—throughout your site.

The first two techniques are obvious. If visitors open a page that looks dull, they'll move on before reading anything. If you manage to get their attention, but the text is poorly written and hard to follow, they'll be off to someone else's site in no time. If you manage to get and keep their attention, you want to make sure they retain the important messages your site conveys. How? By making sure that company and product names, keywords, statistics, phone numbers—anything you want your visitors to remember—are repeated throughout the site, preferably on every page.

Now, this doesn't mean that you should flood your site's pages with robotic repetitions of names and numbers. This would conflict with your goal of keeping a visitor's attention through well-written content. Rather, the repetition can be subtle and artfully placed. Some ideas:

▶ Use your company's logo as a background graphic. Assuming the image is light-colored and doesn't compete with page content (see Figure 8-12), this can be an effective way to remind people where they are.

> **TIP** Chapter 10, "Adding Graphic Content," discusses the creation and use of *watermarks,* which are images with low color saturation, used behind text and other images.

FIGURE 8-12
Take your company logo, reduce its opacity so that it's faded to subtle shades of its original colors, and use it as a background graphic.

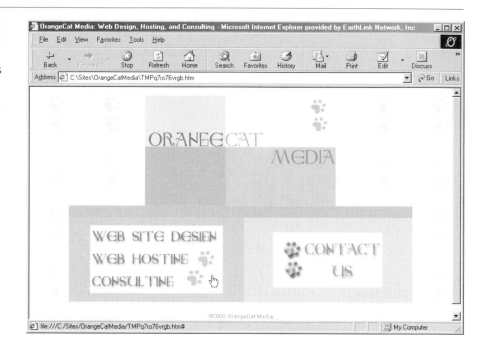

▶ Place your company logo on every page. No, you don't want a huge logo image on every page, but a small copy of the logo in the same place on every page helps identify your site and makes sure your visitors remember the image. See Figure 8-13, where the logo tops the page.

▶ Make sure a link that returns visitors to the home page (or to a page that is pivotal to experiencing the Web site) is on every page of your site, and that it's placed so that no one has to go looking for it, as shown in Figure 8-14. Make sure it's in the same spot on every page.

I CAN'T GET YOU OUT OF MY HEAD **Repetition requires some finesse. You don't want people to be conscious of your repeating text and images, but you want to make an impression. Like the jingle you hear once in a commercial and end up humming all day, you want the important pieces of information from your site to stick with your site visitors. When they're ready to make a purchase, write a check for a donation, join a forum, or subscribe to your newsletter, they remember you and return to your site.**

FIGURE 8-13

Embed the image of your logo in your site visitor's mind by repeating it on every page.

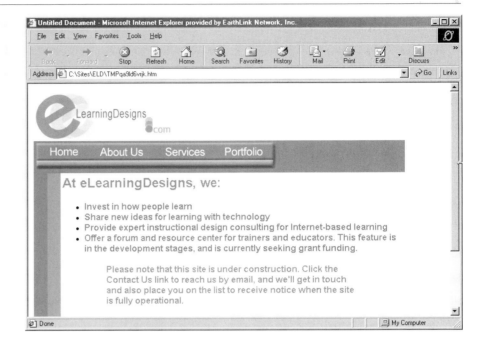

FIGURE 8-14

Knowing that home is just a click away is very soothing to site visitors.

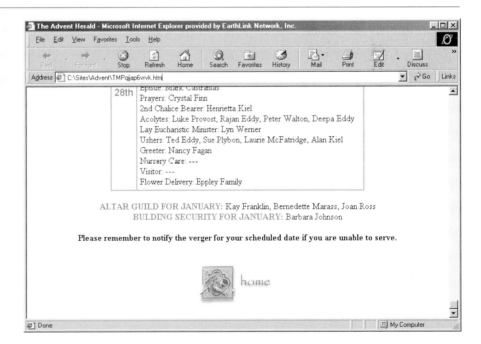

FIGURE 8-15

In marketing, the "Nine Times Rule" says that a prospect must see your materials nine times before he or she will respond.

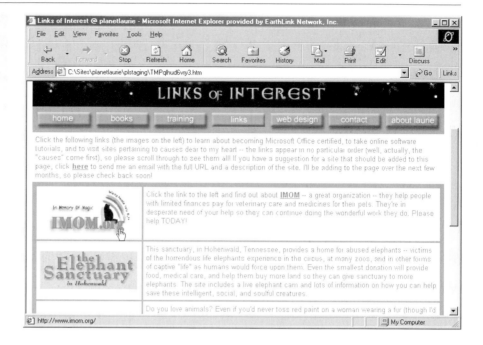

▶ Does your site support a cause or an organization with a slogan or concise mission statement? Repeat it whenever you can do so subtly and in relevant ways (see Figure 8-15). For example, if your site contains information about making donations to charitable causes, use the logos for those charities whenever you refer to them—you'll ingrain the images in your visitor's mind.

DESIGNING AN EFFECTIVE PAGE LAYOUT

Effective is a subjective term. Something is considered to be effective if it achieves its goal, and in the case of a Web page, effectiveness means that the page has the effect or result you wanted it to have. If your Web page is supposed to sell something—a product, an organization, an idea—the page is effective if your visitors are sold. If your Web page is supposed to tell people how to find you, and someone comes into your store and says they found you online, your page was effective. Figure 8-16 shows a page that is intended to advertise an event, and it does so quite effectively. The event is described, the date and time is clearly shown, and information for purchasing tickets, finding the location, and even reviews of previous similar events are just a click away. The tone of the page matches the nature

FIGURE 8-16

Imagine the needs of visitors to your site, thinking of what they'd want to know, see, and understand.

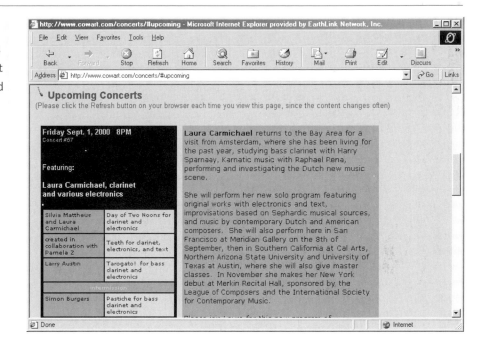

of the event, and the visitor's eye is able to move quickly over the page so all the pertinent information is easily absorbed.

The tools you'll find most useful in setting up your page layout can be created easily in all the major WYIWYG Web design applications (such as Dreamweaver, GoLive, and FrontPage):

▶ **Tables** A series of columns and rows with resizable cells, tables give structure to your page and allow you to position text and graphics consistently throughout the entire page (see Figure 8-17). Many of the challenges of effective alignment and positioning are solved through the use of tables (see Chapter 12, "Structuring Web Pages with Tables, Frames, and Layers").

▶ **Frames** Though not as effective as tables, frames do allow you to create regions on your page, sizing and formatting them as desired. As

TIP **The visitor's window size and screen resolution may result in your frames being automatically resized, and the visitor may need to scroll within the frame to see all of your page content.**

FIGURE 8-17

Tables allow you to create absolute symmetry, or to simply control the flow of text and position of graphics.

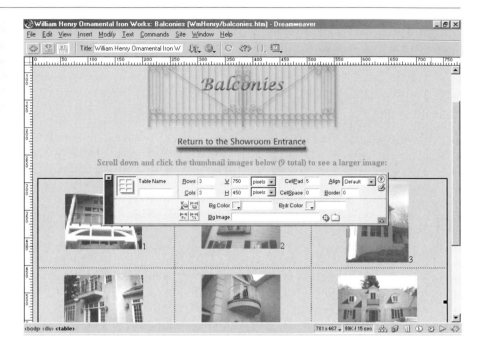

you'll discover in Chapter 12, there are some drawbacks to frames, but there are situations for which they're the perfect layout tool (see Figure 8-18).

▶ Layers Like free-floating table cells, layers allow you to position blocks of text, graphics, or combinations thereof anywhere on the page, even making them overlap. Older browsers don't display layers, though, so what sounds like the perfect layout tool may not be. As time goes by, more people are using the latest versions of browser software, and layers will become something you can use in your page design and know most people will be able to see them. Figure 8-19 shows a page that has several layers on it.

USING THE SAME LAYOUT THROUGHOUT A WEB SITE

Once you've found the right layout for your site's pages—normally applied first to the home or main page—you can use that same page layout for your other pages. This will do two things:

FIGURE 8-18

You can set up an intricate layout for text and graphics with frames.

Frames can be sized to fit an image or headline.

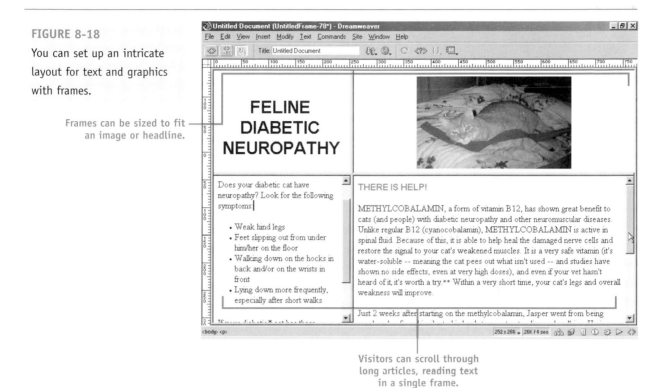

Visitors can scroll through long articles, reading text in a single frame.

FIGURE 8-19

Need to confine text to a specific block and place it "just so"? Several layers may be your answer.

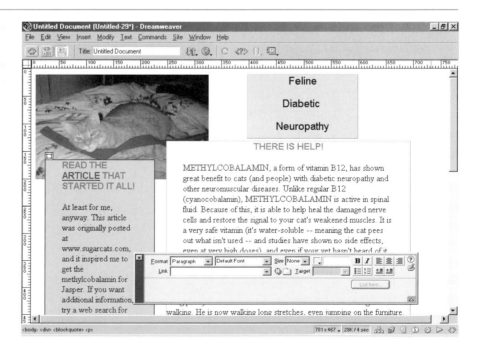

▶ Allow you to achieve the consistency that any good Web site requires.

▶ Develop subpages quickly, because the layout is already set up. All you need to do is insert the text and graphics that vary with each page.

To use the layout from one page in another page, you can save any page as a template, and then base future pages on that template. Using Dreamweaver as an example, you can use the File | Save As command and choose to save the open page as a template. This will make the page available for use as the basis of future pages. Any content that is in the template, such as tables, layers, frames, text, or graphics, will automatically be part of any page created with that template.

To use a template to start a new Web page (again, using Dreamweaver as an example), choose File | New From Template. Pages saved as templates appear, as shown in Figure 8-20, and you can choose the onc you want to use as the foundation of your new page.

> TIP If you've already saved a page as an HTML document (for use on the Web), you can still resave it as a template. This results in two versions of the file— one that's a Web page, and one that's a template to be used in creating new Web pages.

For a site to have consistency throughout, of course, you'll want to use the same template for all the pages. You may have two or three similar templates—similar in terms of layout, background, common text, or graphic content—and use them throughout a large site to accommodate a variety of page types. It's a good idea to give your template files relevant names so you can easily tell one from another.

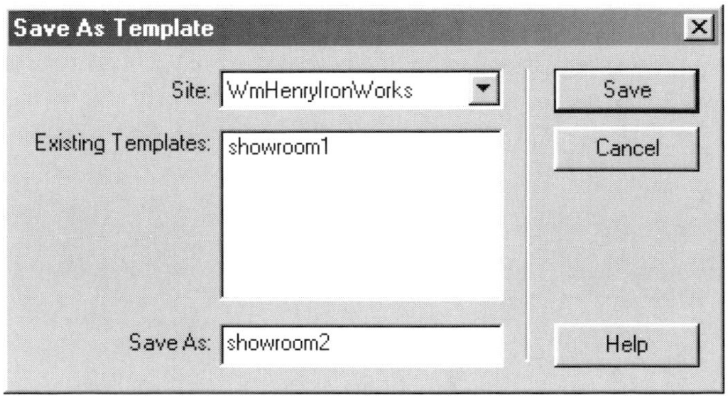

FIGURE 8-20

Any document can be a template. Choose a template that will provide the layout and basic content you want in your new Web page.

For example, "Template1" isn't as useful or illustrative a name as "3colwithnav" (for a template that provides three columns and navigation buttons) or "layers-wback" (for a template that gives you a series of layers and a background graphic). If the template will be used within a particular site and won't be used in developing pages for other sites, you can give it a name that's more relevant to a specific site.

You'll come up with your own relevant naming conventions. Just remember that files used for the Web should not have any spaces in their names. They should also be as short as possible to save you time and typos inserting them as you design a page, set up links, and edit your HTML code.

9

Adding Text Content

They say a picture's worth a thousand words, and while that may be true, I'll take a thousand words any day. This chapter will introduce you to the world of text on the Web—the design considerations, how Web design tools deal with it and allow you to work with it, and how to make sure your words have the impact you want, expressing the message you intend.

UNDERSTANDING THE ROLE OF TEXT IN A WEB PAGE

Text. Who can live without it? If someone said you could never use text in a Web page, you might be nearly as upset as if someone said you couldn't talk on the phone again. Without the spoken word, the phone is pretty useless. Without text, most Web designers would be unable to build a single page.

Obviously, the major role of text on a Web page is the same as its role in any other format: to share information. Text tells people the name of your Web page, describes you or your services and products, indicates where to click to buy something, and shows how to move to another page or Web site for more information. Text is very important in a Web page, as important as text in a book, a letter, or a printed advertisement.

The fact that text is as important in a Web page as it is in printed medium might be surprising, considering all the other tools a Web designer has at his or her disposal, including graphics, sound, and animation. You would think text would be eclipsed by the intensely visual photograph, the arresting movie, or the memorable sound, but it's not.

If you've worked with text in terms of desktop publishing, graphic design, or simple word processing, you may think you know a lot about it. You're probably right. You probably know the names of at least 50 different fonts, can tell me how big 36-point text is, and what it means to kern text. Does this knowledge prepare you for dealing with text on the Web? Well, sort of.

Text on the Web must meet the requirements and limitations of Web browsers, and must be formatted according to the tags and attributes of HTML code, even if you're designing your pages with a WYSIWYG application such as Dreamweaver or FrontPage. You'll have to learn a new measurement system, new names for colors, and understand which fonts will fly online and which ones won't.

INSERTING WEB PAGE TEXT

Adding text to a Web page is as simple as typing a letter. Just click on the page where you want the text to appear, and type. By default, the size of your text will be the same as the default set in your Web browser software, and it will follow the formatting of paragraph text—usually the equivalent of Times New Roman, 12-point text.

If you use a WYSIWYG design application, you can edit the text just as you would in a word processor: click among the characters and use the DELETE and/or BACK-SPACE keys to edit the text. You can highlight and delete or replace the text as you would in Microsoft Word or any other word processing application. Figure 9-1 shows paragraph text in a Web page being designed using Microsoft FrontPage.

If, on the other hand, you're creating your Web page through direct use of HTML code, you can type and edit the text easily enough, but it won't appear onscreen as it will online. You'll have to preview it in a browser window to see how it'll look. Figure 9-2 shows the split-screen Design and Code view in Dreamweaver. You can see the HTML code and the text as it will appear when viewed on the Web.

BUILDING HEADING TEXT

Headings are important words, phrases, or sentences that you want to stand out on the Web page. Rather than applying several formats, such as font, size, and alignment, it's much easier to apply a heading *style*, or group of formats, in one step. You can do this in both the WYSIWYG and HTML text environments.

FIGURE 9-1

You can type text quickly and easily in a WYSIWYG environment.

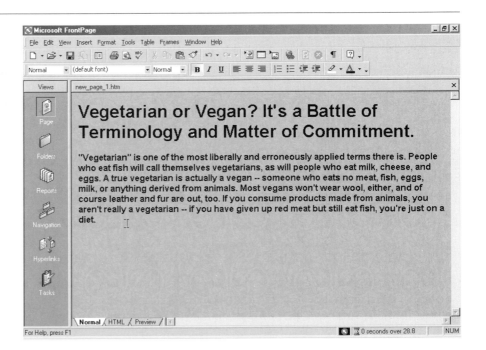

FIGURE 9-2

Body text appears in the default font of your text editor when you create a Web page in HTML.

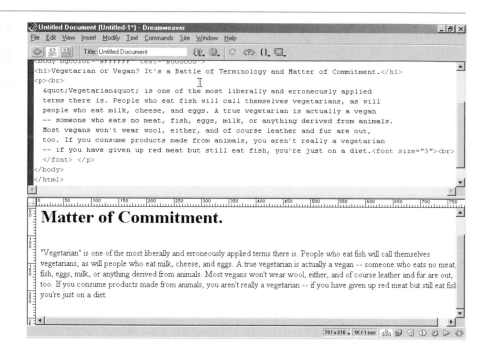

To apply a heading style in a WYSIWYG application such as Dreamweaver, select the text you want to turn into a heading, and use the Properties Inspector palette to apply a Heading style, as shown in Figure 9-3. The text will be formatted automatically, increasing in size and changing to a different font.

If you're using FrontPage, you can apply a style by choosing Format | Style, and choosing an H1, H2, or H3 (Heading 1, Heading 2, and Heading 3) style. There are six heading levels to choose from. As soon as you pick one, click OK and the style is applied to any selected text. Figure 9-4 shows the Style dialog box with the H1 style selected.

For HTML developers, the <h1> tag (accompanied by the closing </h1> tag after the heading text) will turn the text into Heading 1 text. You can apply h2, h3, and so on, using the <h2>, <h3>, etc., tags. Figure 9-5 shows a heading formatted in HTML.

BUILDING PARAGRAPH TEXT

Text that exceeds a single line is considered to be a paragraph, although any text, even a single word, that ends with your pressing the ENTER key (which inserts a paragraph break) is technically a paragraph. When it comes to your

FIGURE 9-3

Apply a Heading style to your text in Dreamweaver.

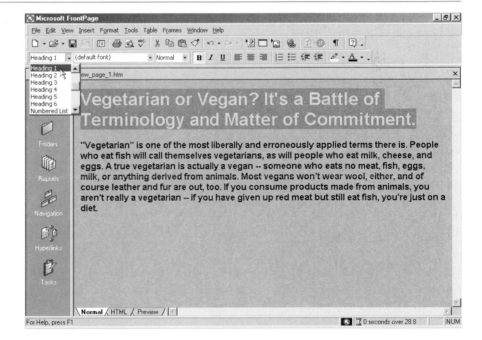

FIGURE 9-4

Preview a style through the Style dialog box and then apply it to selected text in FrontPage.

FIGURE 9-5

You can easily control where the heading style starts and stops with `<h#>` tags in HTML.

```
<html>
<head>
<title>Untitled Document</title>
<meta http-equiv="Content-Type" content="text/html; charset=iso-8859-1">
</head>

<body bgcolor="#FFFFFF" text="#000000">
<h1>Vegetarian or Vegan? It's a Battle of Terminology and Matter of Commitment.</h1>
<p><br>
    &quot;Vegetarian&quot; is one of the most liberally and erroneously applied
    terms there is. People who eat fish will call themselves vegetarians, as will
    people who eat milk, cheese, and eggs. A true vegetarian is actually a vegan
    -- someone who eats no meat, fish, eggs, milk, or anything derived from animals.
    Most vegans won't wear wool, either, and of course leather and fur are out,
    too. If you consume products made from animals, you aren't really a vegetarian
    -- if you have given up red meat but still eat fish, you're just on a diet.<font size="3"><br>
    </font> </p>
</body>
</html>
```

Web page, however, it's important to pay attention to the needs of blocks of text—several lines of text pertaining to a single topic—which make up the traditional paragraph.

Why is paragraph text important? Because it takes up significant real estate on your Web page, it conveys information, and it needs to be legible and effective in both appearance and content. You want it to catch the visitor's eye, but you also want it to be easy to read. In terms of design, the achievement of these goals can be in conflict. On the one hand, giving text a bright color makes it eye-catching. On the other hand, bright red text is harder to read if that text is more than a couple of words. Your eye will definitely be drawn to yellow text on a bright blue field, but you don't want to read an article in that color scheme.

So paragraph text needs to stand out, but not blind the visitor. Use dark colors (like black or navy) on a light background. If your pages have a black back-ground, use white or very light blue text, not yellow, for long stretches of text. The best way to test the legibility of text is to read it yourself. If you end up blink-ing and your eyes feel tired after reading a paragraph or two, tone down your color scheme and keep testing. Ask other people to test the page and to give you their honest opinion. If the information is important, it's worth the effort to make sure your text is legible.

Some other things you can do to make text stand out:

▶ **Indent paragraphs.** Use the `<blockquote>` tag (don't forget the closing `</blockquote>` tag) before a paragraph to indent it on both the left and right. This is a good technique for a single paragraph within a long article, or for a longer paragraph among shorter ones. If you're using a WYSIWYG application to design your page, you can apply left and right indents using toolbar buttons and menu commands. Figure 9-6 shows the Indent buttons in the Dreamweaver application's Properties Inspector.

▶ **Apply exciting formats to the first letter or word.** Like the big "O" in fairy tales that started "Once upon a time," you can draw attention to a paragraph by formatting the first letter or phrase in the paragraph, as shown in Figure 9-7. This draws the viewer's eye to the paragraph, but the bright or large text doesn't last for the whole paragraph, so their eyes aren't irritated by the effect.

▶ **Vary the color, but only slightly.** If most of your text is black, make an important paragraph navy blue or dark purple. The subtle color difference

---

FIGURE 9-6

If you're working in HTML, add the `<blockquote>` tags around text you want to indent.

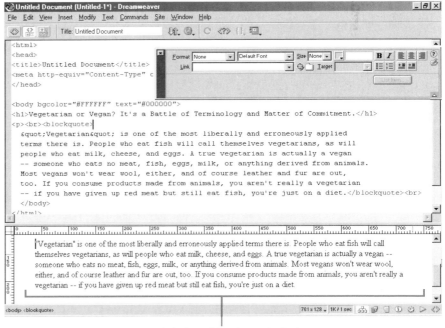

Text is indented by about 50 pixels on both sides of the paragraph thanks to the `<blockquote>` tag.

FIGURE 9-7

Start big and bright, but quickly return to text that's easy on the eyes.

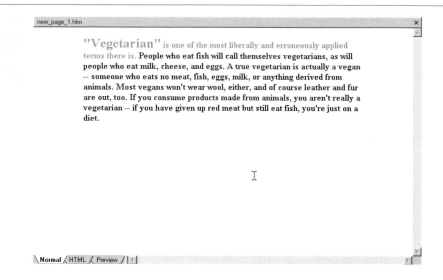

new_page_1.htm

"Vegetarian" is one of the most liberally and erroneously applied terms there is. People who eat fish will call themselves vegetarians, as will people who eat milk, cheese, and eggs. A true vegetarian is actually a vegan -- someone who eats no meat, fish, eggs, milk, or anything derived from animals. Most vegans won't wear wool, either, and of course leather and fur are out, too. If you consume products made from animals, you aren't really a vegetarian -- if you have given up red meat but still eat fish, you're just on a diet.

\ Normal ⟋ HTML ⟋ Preview ⟋

is enough to draw attention, but the color change isn't drastic or hard to read.

▶ **Position the text near a picture.** Put the paragraph in a table, with a graphic next to it. The picture will grab the viewer's attention, and their eye will naturally wander over to the text you want them to read. It helps if the picture is relevant to the text, too. Photographs and realistic images are much more effective than abstract art or geometric shapes and designs, because the content is easily recognizable. As shown here, a picture of a chicken accompanies text regarding a diet free of eggs, thus making the visual association between the text and the graphic. The visitor's eye will be drawn to the chicken image, and then they'll read the text.

"Vegetarian" is one of the most liberally and erroneously applied terms there is. People who eat fish will call themselves vegetarians, as will people who eat milk, cheese, and eggs. A true vegetarian is actually a vegan -- someone who eats no meat, fish, eggs, milk, or anything derived from animals. Most vegans won't wear wool, either, and of course leather and fur are out, too. If you consume products made from animals, you aren't really a vegetarian -- if you have given up red meat but still eat fish, you're just on a diet.

WRAPPING IT ALL UP

As important as making sure your text is read is making sure it wraps properly. Text *wrap* is the automatic flow from one line to the next when there is more text than will fit across the width of the page. As you approach the right margin of the page (or a table cell, layer, or frame), the text wraps down to the next line as soon as a word that won't fit between the previous word and the margin is typed. This wrapping will continue until you press the ENTER key to insert a paragraph break, or SHIFT-ENTER to insert a line break.

When typing a paragraph, never force a break (line or paragraph) unless you want to start a new paragraph. Why? Because if you change the width of the page, cell, layer, or frame, the text won't flow normally. In Figure 9-8, the first paragraph was typed without any forced breaks along the right margin. The second paragraph includes forced line breaks, and after the table cell was narrowed, undesirable gaps appeared where the breaks were inserted.

PARAGRAPH AND LINE BREAKS DEFINED

For many people new to Web design, there is some confusion over the difference between line and paragraph breaks. The difference is that a line break doesn't end a paragraph—it simply breaks a line and forces the text after the break onto the next line of the same paragraph. A paragraph break ends the paragraph, and

FIGURE 9-8

Let text wrap naturally so that the text will always flow properly from line to line, even when the text area is resized.

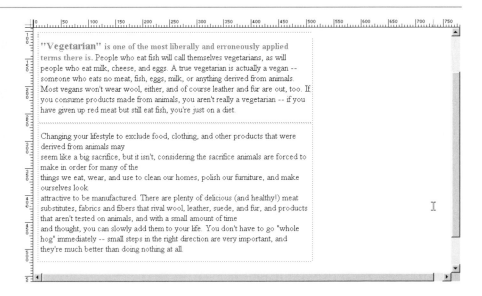

FIGURE 9-9

A paragraph break literally breaks one paragraph into two, and a larger amount of vertical space is inserted between them.

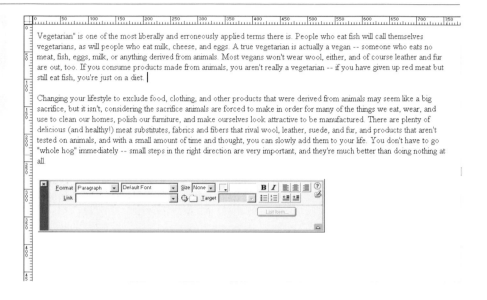

starts a new one on what is the visual equivalent of two lines below the end of the previous paragraph (see Figure 9-9). The other difference is that if you insert a line break, you cannot apply different alignment or indent settings to the text before and after the break. If you insert a paragraph break, you can apply different alignments and indents to the text in the two paragraphs separated by the break.

BREAKING THE HTML CODE

As you type your Web page text and insert breaks, HTML line and paragraph break tags are created. Paragraph breaks are represented by the `<p>` opening tag at the beginning of a paragraph, and the `</p>` closing tag following it. If you insert a line break, a lone `<br>` tag is inserted, as shown in Figure 9-10, which includes both kinds of breaks in the sample HTML code.

UNDERSTANDING THE WEB'S FONT LIMITATIONS

The Web—and in this context I mean Web browsers—supports only a handful of fonts in your paragraph text. As shown in this illustration, the basic fonts are clean and clear, and you've probably seen them before in word processing documents and certainly on Web sites you've visited. Because browsers support such a small group of fonts, it's a good idea to stick to

Arial

Helvetica

Times New Roman

Verdana

FIGURE 9-10

If you want to get rid of a paragraph break, be sure to remove both the opening and closing paragraph tags.

```
<p><font color="#CC0000"><font color="#000000">Vegetarian&quot; </font></font><font
color="#000000">is
    one of the most liberally and erroneously applied terms there is. People who
    eat fish will call themselves vegetarians, as will people who eat milk, cheese,
    and eggs. A true vegetarian is actually a vegan -- someone who eats no meat,
    fish, eggs, milk, or anything derived from animals. Most vegans won't wear wool,
    either, and of course leather and fur are out, too. If you consume products
    made from animals, you aren't really a vegetarian -- if you have given up red
    meat but still eat fish, you're just on a diet.</font> </p>
<p>Changing your lifestyle to exclude food, clothing, and other products that
    were derived from animals may seem like a big sacrifice, but it isn't, considering
    the sacrifice animals are forced to make in order for many of the things we
    eat, wear, and use to clean our homes, polish our furniture, and make ourselves
    look attractive to be manufactured. <br>
There are plenty of delicious (and healthy!) meat substitutes, fabrics and fibers that rival
wool, leather, suede, and fur, and products that aren't tested on animals, and with a small
amount of time and thought, you can slowly add them to your life. You don't have to go &quot;
whole hog&quot; immediately -- small steps in the right direction are very important,
and they're much better than doing nothing at all.</p>
```

these basic fonts when typing paragraphs, as well as headings—by using these fonts you know your site text will look the same to every visitor.

If you want to use more exotic fonts, create a graphic through an application such as Adobe Photoshop or Macromedia Fireworks. The graphic will appear as text on the Web page, but the browser won't be dealing directly with the text; it will simply be displaying a graphic that's legible. Figure 9-11 shows such a graphic, containing text in a font that most Web browsers won't support.

FORMATTING TEXT

The process of changing the appearance of text is known as *formatting*. If you use a word processor, you're probably accustomed to the process of applying fonts, changing font sizes, even changing text color. These same formatting options are available to you when dealing with text on your Web page.

If you're designing a Web page through a WYSIWYG application (such as Dreamweaver or FrontPage), the formatting is done through a series of formatting tools—dialog boxes, toolbar buttons, keyboard shortcuts—and you see your formatting applied to selected text immediately. Figure 9-12 shows a selected string of text and the FrontPage tools available to format it.

> **TIP** Serif? Sans serif? Huh? If these terms are new to you, think of angels. Yes, angels. The term *serif* comes from the Latin *seraphim,* meaning angel. Serif fonts have flourishes on the ends of letters, similar to an angel's wings. An example of a serif font is Times New Roman. *Sans serif* fonts have no flourishes, and the term itself means, literally, *without serif.* Arial is a sans serif font, and so are Helvetica and Verdana.

FIGURE 9-11

Keep graphics containing text small—you don't want people waiting forever to read important text because the graphic takes too long to load.

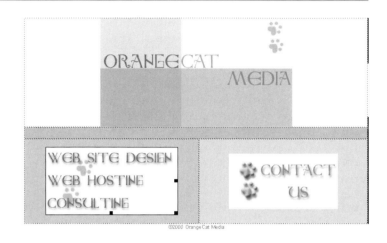

FIGURE 9-12

The process of formatting Web text in a WYSIWYG environment is a lot like word processing.

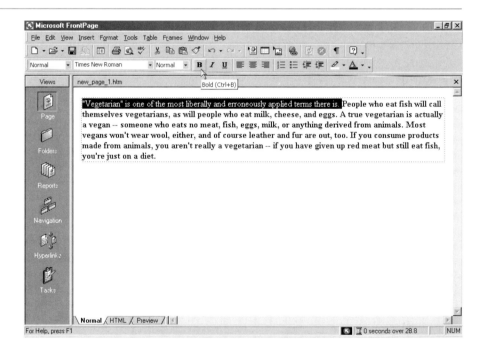

HTML users will have to stop and preview their pages to see the effects of their formatting. That formatting is applied through a series of tags and attributes, which is part of the HTML code. As shown in Figure 9-13, the tags that assign fonts, sizes, and colors to text appear surrounding the text within the HTML code.

FIGURE 9-13

The font, size, and color of the text appear in quotes.

```
<html>
<head>
<title>Untitled Document</title>
<meta http-equiv="Content-Type" content="text/html; charset=iso-8859-1">
</head>
<p align="left"><font color="#000099"><b><font face="Arial, Helvetica, sans-serif">Changing
  your lifestyle to exclude food, clothing, and other products that were derived
  from animals may seem like a big sacrifice, but it isn't, considering the sacrifice
  animals are forced to make in order for many of the things we eat, wear, and
  use to clean our homes, polish our furniture, and make ourselves look attractive
  to be manufactured. <br>
  There are plenty of delicious (and healthy!) meat substitutes, fabrics and fibers
  that rival wool, leather, suede, and fur, and products that aren't tested on
  animals, and with a small amount of time and thought, you can slowly add them
  to your life. You don't have to go &quot;whole hog&quot; immediately -- small
  steps in the right direction are very important, and they're much better than
  doing nothing at all.</font></b></font></p>
<p> 
<p><br>
```

SIZING TEXT

While the process of applying text formats in a Web design application such as Dreamweaver is very similar to formatting text in a word processor, one significant difference is found in the sizing of text. Rather than using a points system, a series of sizes from -7 to +7 is available, and size 3 is set to match the default font size as established through your default Web browser.

This probably sounds confusing, but hang on. Think of it this way. If your default font is set to 12-point Arial (set, for example, through Internet Explorer, which you may have established as your default Web browser), size 3 text will be the equivalent of 12 points. This further means that size 4 text will be 14 points, and size -2 text will be 10 points. No, this system wasn't designed to confuse you, even though it may until you get used to it. As shown here, the Dreamweaver Properties Inspector palette displays a list of sizes available for a block of selected text.

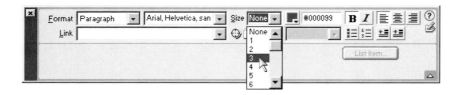

Why did they abandon the commonly used and understood point system for Web text? Because the size of text is dictated by the viewer's screen resolution. A system based on points that translate to inches would have no use online. If one person is viewing a Web page at 800 x 600 pixel resolution, the text will appear larger than for someone viewing that same text, formatted in the same font, if his or her screen resolution is set to 1024 x 768. The key when choosing a font size for Web text is to make sure it's legible, and to establish that through previewing it in a variety of resolutions. You don't want people at higher resolutions to be squinting at tiny text, nor do you want to waste space on text that's too large when viewed at 800 x 600.

ALIGNING AND POSITIONING TEXT

Text, whether on the page, in a table cell, or in a frame or layer, is left-aligned by default. As you type text, or even if you paste it from another source, it aligns to the left side of the page, cell, frame, or layer. You can alter this alignment by choosing center or right alignment. This can be done from within a WYSIWYG application or through the use of font attributes in HTML. Figure 9-14 shows the Dreamweaver interface, with the Properties Inspector's alignment buttons, as well as the HTML code generated when center alignment was applied to selected text.

Of course, all of this refers only to the horizontal alignment of text. You can also adjust the vertical alignment within table cells, changing from the default middle alignment to top or bottom. Figure 9-15 shows the Dreamweaver Properties Inspector, and the vertical alignment choices available.

FIGURE 9-14

You can choose from left, center, or right alignment for your Web page text.

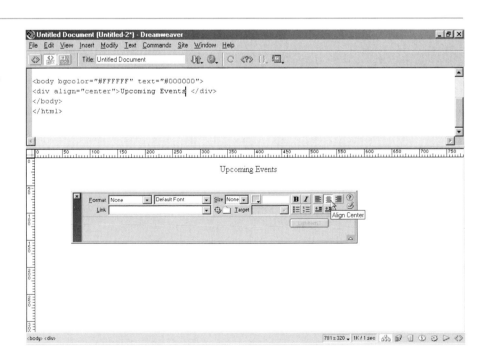

FIGURE 9-15

If you want your table cell text to start at the top of the cell, choose top alignment.

WORKING WITH TEXT COLOR

The color of your text has a lot of impact on how legible it is, whether or not it gets noticed, and how the reader should feel about the text and its message. For example, if your text is bright red, a traditionally eye-catching color, it will be noticed and it will make the reader feel tense. Red is an action color, and it makes people move fast. It's a hot color, as opposed to a cool color like blue or most shades of green.

The legibility factor of any color is based on the color behind it. If your page is white, colors such as yellow and pastel shades of blue, green, or pink won't be very easy to read. Conversely, those same colors are easy to read on a black or dark blue background. You're the best judge (assuming you're not color-blind) of what works—if you squint or blink in horror at the colors you've chosen, it's time to go back to the drawing board.

> **TIP** Fifteen percent of the male population is color-blind, and will see green and red as gray. If green and red are next to each other (say, red text on a green background), the text will be difficult, if not impossible, to read because it will look like gray on gray. Avoid using these colors together, and avoid using them separately on a gray background. By the way, about 5 percent of the female population is also color-blind, so in a mixed group of 100 visitors to your site, approximately 20 of them may not be able to appreciate some or all of your color selections.

WEB-SAFE COLORS

So far, I've been talking about "red" and "green" and "blue"—common names for basic colors. These are also names for Web-safe colors, and many shades of them are also among those that are okay for use on the Web. There are 256 shades of Web-safe colors, to be exact, and most current illustration/graphic design applications offer a palette of Web-safe colors for you to work with so you can create and edit images for use on the Web. Figure 9-16

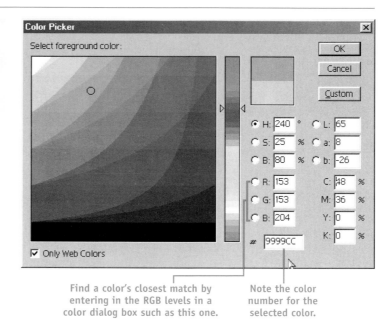

Find a color's closest match by
entering in the RGB levels in a
color dialog box such as this one.

Note the color
number for the
selected color.

shows the Web-safe color palette (in the Color Picker) offered through Adobe
Photoshop when you have chosen to work in RGB (red, green, blue) mode and see
only Web colors. Other color values, such as HSB (hue, saturation, and brightness), are also shown in this dialog box.

Web design applications such as Dreamweaver and FrontPage offer only Web-safe
colors in their palettes, and you can apply the colors easily to graphics, backgrounds (for pages, tables, layers, or frames), and of course text. As shown here,
the Dreamweaver color well displays Web-safe colors and an eyedropper for making your selection. A shade of blue has been applied to selected text.

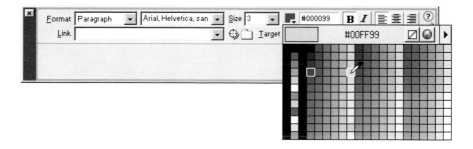

APPLYING COLOR TO TEXT

Changing the color of text is simple, and the technique depends on the tool you're using to design your Web page. If you're working in a WYSIWYG environment, you'll make your selection from a dialog box and/or palette, as shown in Figure 9-17, which shows a color dialog box available through FrontPage. You'll also be able to enter color numbers (if you've been given a number by a client, for example), and in the figure, the number appears in three comma-separated segments.

If you're designing in HTML directly, you can type the color name or number into the tag preceding the text, as shown in Figure 9-18. Most colors have names, but typing the number is a more reliable method, even though some of the numbers are very similar and a typo can result in the application of a very different color than the one you wanted.

TIP Don't go crazy trying to match printed colors to Web colors. First of all, no one is going to hold your brochure or business card up to the monitor and exclaim, "Ah-HA! That's not the same shade of red!" Second, every person's monitor displays color a little differently. You can go to great lengths to find the closest Web-safe match to a printed color, only to have it look great on your monitor and lousy on someone else's. I had a client who thought the deep red shade I put in her site was purple. I had to go with brighter and brighter shades of red until she liked what she was seeing.

FIGURE 9-17

Select the text and then choose a color from the palette.

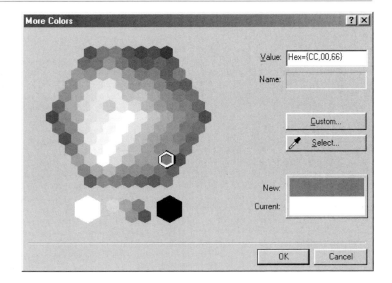

FIGURE 9-18

The color name or number goes in quotes within the HTML tag for the text you want to color.

```html
<html>
<head>
<title>Untitled Document</title>
<meta http-equiv="Content-Type" content="text/html; charset=iso-8859-1">
</head>
<body bgcolor="#FFFFFF">
<p align="left"><font color="#000099"><b><font face="Arial, Helvetica, sans-serif" size="3">
Changing</font><font face="Arial, Helvetica, sans-serif" size="3" color="#339999"></font><font
face="Arial, Helvetica, sans-serif">
  your lifestyle to exclude food, clothing, and other products that were derived
  from animals may seem like a big sacrifice, but it isn't, considering the sacrifice
  animals are forced to make in order for many of the things we eat, wear, and
  use to clean our homes, polish our furniture, and make ourselves look attractive
  to be manufactured. <br>
  There are plenty of delicious (and healthy!) meat substitutes, fabrics and fibers
  that rival wool, leather, suede, and fur, and products that aren't tested on
  animals, and with a small amount of time and thought, you can slowly add them
  to your life. You don't have to go &quot;whole hog&quot; immediately -- small
  steps in the right direction are very important, and they're much better than
```

Whatever colors you choose, and however you're applying them to your text, think about the tone you're setting and how well the color works with the rest of your site. There are calming colors, colors that imply action or tension, colors that are dignified, colors that are fun. Reactions to colors are fairly universal, so you can generally rely on your own perceptions in choosing colors. Very few people will argue that navy blue is dignified and moss green is soothing, or that bright pink is festive and fire-engine red is not a good choice if you want a "laid-back" feeling for your site. Use your best judgment, and always ask others' opinions if you're unsure—and do so *before* your site goes online.

ON THE VIRTUAL CLASSROOM CD-ROM Watch as your instructor demonstrates the techniques used in choosing the right fonts and formatting them for maximum legibility.

Adding Graphic Content

Which would you rather look at—a written description of someone's vacation to Europe or pictures they took while they were there? I thought that's what you'd say. Even the poorly composed, Aunt Mary-by-the-Eiffel-Tower pictures are going to be more entertaining and interesting than Aunt Mary's written treatise on French monuments. When it comes to the Web, the same holds true. People will respond more quickly to pictures than to text, will find the site's pages more compelling, and will spend more time visiting your pages if those pages include images.

That's not to say, of course, that text should be avoided. There are some things you can't explain with pictures, and some information that can only be conveyed with text. A site that includes articles from medical journals will have to include those articles, though they may be peppered with images of whatever's being discussed. Web pages that convey a lot of information, that share educational or instructional material, or that publish creative works of literature are going to be heavily text oriented. Even these text-based sites, however, will benefit from some eye candy in the form of images—line art and photographs artfully placed.

USING GRAPHICS EFFECTIVELY

Artfully placed, huh? Yes, that's what I said. If humans have a stronger, more immediate response to images than to text, you can use images to move your site's visitors over the surface of your pages. We've all seen a particularly moving photograph in a magazine or newspaper, and that image alone compelled us to read the accompanying article. Your site's images can be placed in such a way as to make sure the visitor reads as much of your site's text as possible. Think of the images as lures, drawing the visitor from shiny object to shiny object, with he or she hopefully stopping to read text (and maybe follow a link or fill out a form) in between, as shown in Figure 10-1.

FIGURE 10-1

Place a graphic image wherever you want the visitor's eye to fall and linger.

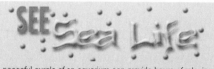

The peaceful gurgle of an aquarium can provide hours of relaxing fun for adults and children, and is a great way for children to learn the responsiblities of caring for other beings. Aquariums, both salt and fresh water, require a lot of care and attention. Don't let the creatures you invite into your tank become the victims of lost interest, ignorance, or a setup that's not healthy for one or more of the species, such as not using the right water temperature, not conditioning the water properly, or using the wrong (or too much) food. These are lives in your hands, and saying "They're only fish!" will only serve to show your children that some lifeforms are more valuable than others, which is surely not your intent.

Turtles are a good choice for a child who is careful, quiet, and will remember to keep the turtle's environment clean and provide fresh food. If your children share a noisy, often messy room, a turtle might not be the best choice. Pets aren't toys and they need attention!

Life for dolphins, seals, and other social animals is very unpleasant in captivity. Don't take your kids to see trained dolphins and whales, because you're contributing to a business that victimizes the animal performers with punative training techniques (isolation, starvation) and their life in captivity cuts their life span by as much as two thirds. If you want to SEE SEA LIFE, do it with a well-maintained fish tank in your own home.

WHEN AND WHERE TO USE GRAPHICS

When to use graphics on the Web? Often. Where to use them? Any place where they enhance the page design and provide information or draw attention to information nearby. The placement of your graphics can help you create the delicate balancing act that is good composition, as shown in Figure 10-2. Placing images on the page in such a way as to achieve a visual balance between them and with the page text helps set the speed of the page.

When I say *speed*, I refer to the visual speed at which the viewer's eye is compelled to move across the page. A fast page doesn't encourage lingering. A fast page never includes images that require or inspire dwelling on them. Photographs aren't fast, unless they're very spare, with very little detail. Detail invites the visitor to pause, to investigate. Line art—shapes, lines, graphical text—is fast, because there's no need and little impulse to pause and ponder it. If you want people's eyes to whip over the page and not linger in any one place—a reasonable goal for a page with nothing but graphical links to other pages, for example—don't use detailed photographs. Figure 10-3 shows a fast page, with images placed so that

> **TIP** Centering paragraph text makes it harder to read and should be avoided— that is, unless it's a series of individual sentences stacked in a centered pyramid arrangement (starting at the pinnacle and widening, or starting wide and narrowing to a point). This sort of stacking and centering is an interesting visual effect, and it slows the reader down. If there are links within the centered sentences, slowing the visitor down may result in more clicks on those links.

FIGURE 10-2

Big logo at the top? Put an image at the bottom to balance the visual weight.

Your local animal shelter and protective agencies can help you by providing names and numbers to call when you see animal abuse. Don't be afraid to report even a suspected abuse--it's better to be wrong than allow the abuse to continue without anyone's intervention.

Strict penalties for animal neglect/abuse are what's needed, along with vigorous enforcement of laws. Call or write you congressional representatives and demand that animal protection become a legislative priority.

FIGURE 10-3

Don't slow 'em down with details or images that require more than a few seconds for the eye to take it all in.

Educational Materials

Click the link to the left to for a list of educational videos to show students and seasoned activits as well. All videos are just $9.95 each, and run for just 30 minutes -- just long enough to get the message across without losing your audience.

Need handouts for your meetings, protests, and to include with mailings to members and prospective members? Order a pack of 10, 20, or 50. They're printed on light-weight paper so your mailing costs are kept to a minimum.

Home Page

the visitor's eye starts at the top of the page and does a quick zigzag down the page. Think of the path your viewer's eyes will travel as you place your graphics and text, and decide if that path should be traversed quickly or slowly. In this case, quick is better—the goal is to get people to click the buttons and move on.

A slow page does include photos and detailed, colored images, with a lot going on in them. These can range from detailed images of people and places that the likely visitor will be interested in to the emotional, one-picture-tells-a-story images such as those in *Life* magazine—the latter being images that will draw in anyone, not just someone who has already expressed an interest in an esoteric topic. Detailed images make people stop and look, even if it's for only a few seconds. This slows down the speed of the page, and that can be a good thing if you want people to linger and read or stop and consider something, such as the message of the picture itself. If the picture is a link to something, making people pause to look at it may be the only way to get them to click the link, so you don't want them to whip past on their visual way to another image. Figure 10-4 is an example of a page that invites lingering, by the nature of the image and the fact that the image is very detailed.

There are a lot of other ways to achieve balance on a page. Look at the page and figure out which item

> **TIP** You'll find more discussion of the ways to balance page content and achieve effective composition in Chapter 8, "Web Site Layout." There is also a discussion and demonstration of balancing techniques on the CD-ROM that accompanies this book. For more information on techniques for positioning graphics, see Chapter 12, "Structuring Web Pages with Tables, Frames, and Layers."

FIGURE 10-4

A lot of detailed, multifaceted images will slow down the page.

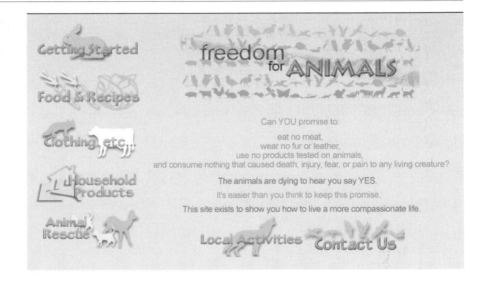

draws your eye immediately. Is that the only important thing on the page? Then you have balance already. If it's not the most important thing, you don't have balance yet. You can get it by drawing attention toward opposite corners, sides, or ends of the page (depending on where the current focus is) with graphics, horizontal rules, colored fills in table cells and layers, or enlarged text. Figure 10-5 shows how a variety of eye-catching elements—buttons, colored borders, interesting graphics—helps distribute attention on the page, moving the viewer's eye around

FIGURE 10-5

Like rearranging the furniture in a room to control traffic, conversation areas, and the appearance of space, you can rearrange all of your page elements to achieve the same results.

and making sure everything on the page gets noticed. The visitor won't mind scrolling down the page to see more.

AVOIDING THE VISUAL CIRCUS

Now, all this talk of adding images here, there, and seemingly everywhere might give the impression that you should load your page with images. That would be a mistake, for three reasons:

▶ Images take longer to load, so a graphic-heavy page will take longer to display, even if each of the individual images is small and quick-loading unto itself.

▶ Too many images overwhelm the viewer, and the message or impact of any individual image is lost by the sheer volume of surrounding images.

▶ A good rule of thumb for fitting content onto a page is to make sure 90 percent of the page content can be seen without scrolling when the page is viewed in an 800 x 600 pixel display. With a lot of graphics, you'd be hard pressed to achieve that goal without cramming the pictures together, which makes for a disorganized, scrapbook feel to your pages—rarely the impression you are trying to make.

If you're not sure whether your page has too many images on it, it probably has too many. If you have the slightest sense that you may have gone overboard (as in

---

FIGURE 10-6

A page that has photos and clip art all over it can begin to look like some sort of crazy quilt.

Figure 10-6), it's very likely that you have. Images should be like decorations—enhancements, icing, a little window-dressing. While a page can be made up entirely of images, you don't want all of the images to be pictures. Some of them should be graphical text, so there's something to read rather than just look at, offering a change in activity for the viewer's mind.

PLANNING YOUR USE OF IMAGES

What constitutes an "image"? Images can be buttons, photographs, clip art, horizontal rules, a page background graphic, graphical text in ornate fonts. Technically, anything that's not text you typed right onto the page or that you inserted to structure the page (tables, layers, frames) is a graphic. Graphic text, unless it looks like it was typed onto the page, will count as a graphic when you're tallying your graphic content to see if you have too much going on.

What if you need to use all of the stuff—images, background art, ornate fonts—but it's just too much for one page? Break the single page and its overwhelming amount of content into two or more pages. There are usually conceptual or topic changes that can warrant your placing some of the content on another page. Turn one of your graphics into a link to that second page, and one of the graphics on the new second page into a link that takes people back to the first page. Graphics that do something have much greater value on a page than ones that just sit there.

> **SEE ALSO** Read about how to turn graphics into links in Chapter 14, "Creating Hyperlinks to Connect Pages and Sites."

CHOOSING THE RIGHT IMAGES

What are the "right images"? That's such a subjective thing. The right images are the ones that fit the theme, the tone, and the feel of your Web page. If your page pertains to a high-tech service such as network administration or Internet hosting, you should have images that are sleek, strong, and modern (see Figure 10-7), like the technology with which you're involved.

On the other hand, if your page pertains to something earthy or more people-oriented, you want images that remind people of the feeling your product or service should invoke (see Figure 10-8). A furniture store, for example, should have warm, cozy images, such as soft couches in front of fireplaces, families at a

FIGURE 10-7

High-tech businesses such as software, pharmaceutical, and financial companies need images with a sleek, modern look.

kitchen table, or babies sleeping in cribs. That is, unless you sell modern furniture, and then you may want images that are a bit colder and less cozy and personal. See? It's never cut-and-dried, and most of the time you're going to have to rely on your own perceptions. Do your images feel right to you? What adjectives do they make you think of? If they're adjectives you'd like people to think of in conjunction with your organization, product, or service, you're on the right track.

FIGURE 10-8

Selling something that families use or that's of a personal or spiritual nature? Warm, homey images can be just what you need.

It sounds, perhaps, like I'm saying there are no "right" images. There are, but I can't tell you specifically which ones they are. What I can tell you is that you don't want to waste your visitors' download time and your valuable Web space on images that don't convey the message you want. You may not be sure about your choices or trust your own judgment—a common feeling, especially if you're designing your own Web site rather than designing for someone else. You may be too close to the topic to be objective. What to do? Ask impartial people to give you their opinion. Show them your images (on their own or in the context of the Web page) and ask what the images make them feel or think of.

Don't think that every page you design is going to be a struggle, or that every time you sit down to choose an image you're going to end up in some sort of turmoil over your selection. Most of the time, the right image is an obvious choice. It's just a good idea to have a clear idea of what your images should accomplish, and have a few good methods for making choices when the options aren't so obvious.

CREATING A CONSISTENT THEME WITH IMAGE PLACEMENT

As I said, image placement is important because it can help you achieve balance on the page and draw visitors' eyes to important page content. Placement is also important across all the pages in your site, so that people know where to look for things as they move from page to page.

For example, if your home page has navigation buttons down the left side of the page, don't move them to the top of the page on your subpages. If you have a "Back to Home Page" button in the upper-right corner of one subpage, don't put it somewhere else on your other subpages. People need to have a sense of where things are and will be as they navigate your site. Not being considerate of that will either make you look inconsiderate or give the impression that you're not paying attention to details. If one of your selling points (you hope) is your organization skills and detail-orientation, a site that looks haphazardly designed won't do much to get those points across.

If you're thinking that your page should be informal and friendly, and that details like consistency don't matter as much for your design needs, think again. What's more comfortable than reliability? Hotels that try to be "just like home" succeed in doing so if they lay out their rooms like a real bedroom. They create a sense of things being right where they should be—alarm clock on the night stand, lamp or light switch you can reach from the bed, a remote that isn't too complicated so you can work the TV. You feel at home because you don't have to think too much. Your pages and their features should allow people to concentrate on the page content rather than figuring out how to navigate your site.

Consistent placement doesn't just apply to functional page items, like graphical buttons for navigating from page to page. Consistency is important in terms of positioning photographs, drawings, and maps. You want to place them close to any text content to which they pertain, and it's a good idea to place them in the same spot on all of your pages. As shown in Figure 10-9, each page might have a key image on it—perhaps the name of the page, a heading, or a photograph that expressed the topic of the page. On each page, place that key image in the same spot so that people know where to look for it. If a visitor doesn't have to reorient himself or herself for each new page, much more attention will be paid to your pages' content.

SIZING AND FORMATTING GRAPHICS

Graphic images on Web pages should be small in terms of file size so that they load quickly. Keep a maximum of 35KB in mind, and make sure most of your images are much smaller, generally less than 20KB. This means that if your file is large in terms of its dimensions, it can't have a lot of pixel detail (high resolution) or its file size will be prohibitively large. You can have images that fill large areas

FIGURE 10-9

Each Web page should have a theme, and one consistently located image to express or represent it.

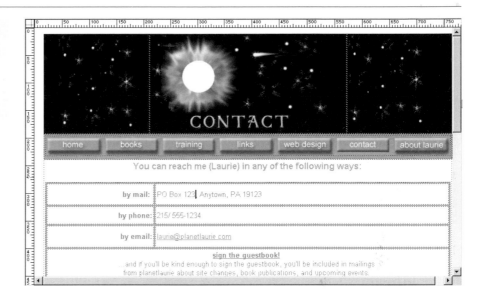

of your page, but be prepared to scale back their pixels per inch (also known as their dots per inch, or dpi) so you don't end up with a file that's more than 35KB. As shown in Figure 10-10, if an image takes up a lot of real estate on your page, don't expect it to be a sharp, detailed photograph with dazzling clarity. If you strive for that level of quality, people will get tired of waiting for the page to load and will go on to someone else's site.

FIGURE 10-10

Be prepared to sacrifice a sharp photographic image for a large one when you're working on the Web.

Smaller images can be sharp and clear, because they'll be smaller in file size anyway. This works out well, because smaller images need more clarity to be readable or for people to discern what's in the picture. A tiny group photo, for example, needs to be clear enough for visitors to recognize faces, and an image that includes graphical text needs to be sharp enough for all the letters in the text to be legible. Figure 10-11 shows a graphic with text in it that's not clear enough to read—in the interest of reducing file size, the designer sacrificed file usefulness.

When it comes to achieving the right file size and resolution, Web design tools, even WYSIWYG applications, aren't your best bet. Changing image width and height settings through HTML tags isn't advisable, either. While you can resize a graphic in Dreamweaver, FrontPage, or GoLive (or through the HTML code if you're designing in TextPad or some other text editor), you may not be very happy with the results. As bitmap images are resized, especially if you're enlarging them, the computer tries to guess at the colors to insert for the added pixels (for the added dimensions of the image). This results in those choppy edges you sometimes see on Web graphics, known as artifacts—the small spots and blocks that distort images that have been stretched, as these two illustrations show.

FIGURE 10-11

Smaller images need to be as clear and sharp as possible so that people can appreciate them.

KEEPING THINGS IN PROPORTION Another reason to resist the temptation to quickly resize an image by dragging its handles in a WYSIWYG workspace? It's very difficult to maintain horizontal and vertical proportions. Do you know your particular application's controls for maintaining *aspect ratio*? Sometimes it depends on which handle you use to resize, other times there's a key you need to press while resizing. If you don't know how to impose these controls, don't even try resizing an image in the Web design application. Manual resizing will usually result in stretching, squashing, and generally distorting the image, rather than keeping its original proportions.

CHOOSING THE RIGHT TOOL FOR GRAPHIC MANIPULATION

If you need to resize an image, use an application intended for that purpose. That means using something like Adobe Photoshop, Macromedia Fireworks, CorelDRAW, or Adobe Illustrator. Adobe Photoshop and Macromedia Fireworks are your best bets, and most Web designers swear by Photoshop—it's been around forever, and it's a very rich and powerful tool.

"Rich and powerful" can be daunting concepts. Don't be afraid. Graphics programs aren't difficult, they're just detailed. They need a lot of tools and features so that you have a lot of functionality at your disposal. Taking Photoshop as an example: it offers tools for retouching photographs, designing images from scratch, and adjusting image size in terms of both dimension and pixel depth. You can do everything from removing a coffee-ring on an old photograph, to adding a patch of green grass to obscure an unwanted mud puddle, to removing unwanted lines, as shown here in these before and after shots

TIP If the price tag on Adobe Photoshop and Macromedia Fireworks scares you, try the "lite" version, Photoshop LE. It gives you a reasonable set of retouching tools (and completely adequate tools for resizing an image) for much less than the full-fledged version. Macromedia Fireworks can be purchased as part of a package with Dreamweaver, and you realize substantial savings. You can also download a free 30-day trial version of Fireworks, so you know if you like it before you buy it.

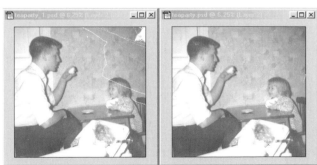

of the same old photo. Using a program like Photoshop or Fireworks, you can clean up an image, making it as crisp as possible for the size it will be, all while making it ready for use on the Web.

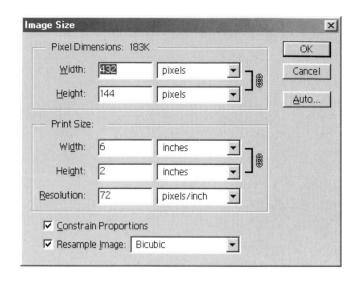

After making the image as clean and clear as possible (adjusting brightness, contrast, and sharpness as well as painting and smudging out spots and stains), you can reduce the pixel depth, thus reducing the file size, as shown here in Adobe Photoshop's Image Size dialog box.

Once you've cleaned up and resized your image, you're ready to save it in a format that's Web-friendly. As discussed in Chapter 6, "Gathering Your Web Content," the only acceptable file formats for Web graphics are .GIF, .JPG, and .PNG, the first two being the most popular and reliably displayed in all browsers. In Photoshop, the process of saving a .PSD (Photoshop's native format) file as a .GIF or .JPG file is achieved through the File | Save For Web command. You'll work in the window shown in Figure 10-12, where you choose the format and quality you want, and preview the results.

In Fireworks, you use an Export command to take the native .PNG format and turn the file into a .GIF or .JPG, as shown in Figure 10-13. There's an Export Wizard, for people new to the process, which coaches you through the steps involved in creating Web-safe images.

> **TIP** When you reduce image quality (reducing resolution), you'll lose some of the detail you had, but you shouldn't lose much. Remember, too, that viewing images on a computer monitor isn't the same as viewing them in person or in print. A lot of detail is lost just through displaying pictures onscreen.

WORKING WITH LOGOS AND WATERMARKS

Your organization's logo is an important image in your printed marketing materials (business cards, brochures, ads, and flyers) and on your Web site. Any time you can use your logo, you make it more recognizable, giving each successive use even more impact. If your organization has vehicles, signs, billboards—heck, even those promotional pens and desk calendars—with your name on them, each time

FIGURE 10-12

Pick .GIF or .JPG, and watch the size and estimated download time as you tinker with quality settings.

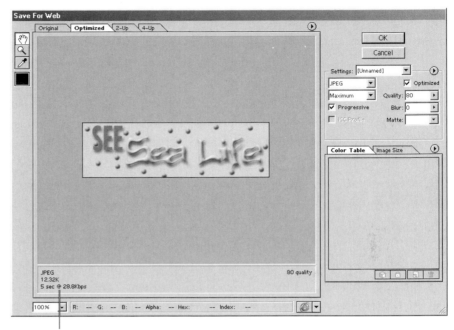

Estimated file size and
time to download

FIGURE 10-13

Use Fireworks' Export Wizard to take the process of saving a file for the Web step-by-step.

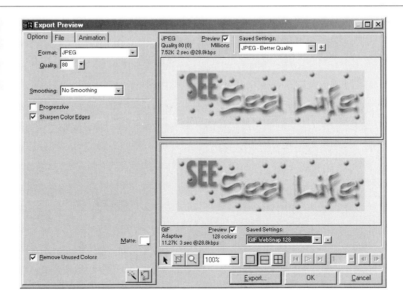

and place you use your logo and organization name, you're making the public more aware of you. Making sure your logo is prominently displayed in or used as an integral part of your Web pages is essential to the visual and conceptual connection between your other marketing efforts and your Web presence. As with repeated use of your logo, repeated and varied marketing efforts help each other.

So how do you use your logo creatively on your Web site? Is it passé to slap it in the upper-left corner, just like it is on your letterhead? Perhaps. Should it be a major focal point or more subtly used? It depends on your design, the tone of your marketing and advertising, and whether or not your logo is in fact a symbol. If your logo is just your company name, as shown in Figure 10-14, you can simply place it on the home page as an identifier and repeat it on your site's subpages for consistency's sake and so people know that they're still at your site.

If, on the other hand, your logo is or contains a symbol—think of the instantly recognizable logo for a certain German car manufacturer, or the checkerboard symbol that a famous pet food company uses—you want to integrate that into your site's design, using it both as an identifier along with your organization name and as a graphic unto itself. Just such a logo is shown in Figure 10-15. If your logo isn't as ubiquitous as you'd like it to be, you can start by making it a prominent and consistent image on your Web site.

FIGURE 10-14

Not all logos are graphical—some are simply the organization's name—and don't have to be used as a graphical element on the page.

The selected image can be made smaller in Photoshop or Fireworks and used on subpages in the site.

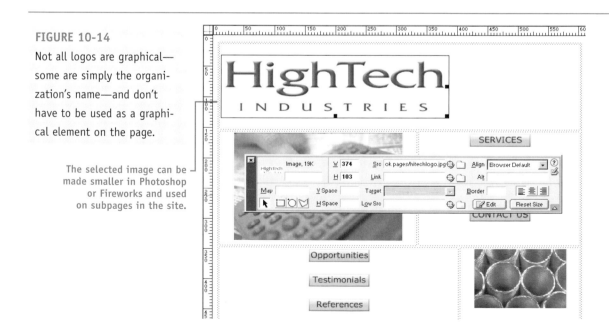

FIGURE 10-15

Creative use of an organization's symbol is part of an effective page design.

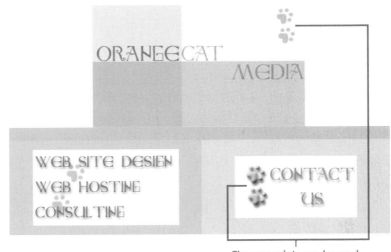

The paw prints can be used throughout the site as a reminder of the company name.

One subtle yet effective way to utilize your organization's logo/name/symbol is to turn it into a watermark. A watermark is an image that appears behind the text and other graphic content on a page, as shown here. Typically, a watermark image is semitransparent, with reduced brightness so that it doesn't compete visually with what's on top of it, but it remains recognizable.

USING GRAPHIC BACKGROUNDS

When you add your logo or any other graphic image behind your Web page content, you're adding it as a page background. A Web page has two levels: the background and the page content. You can use any graphic file as a background image. Depending on its size and the controls your Web design software gives you, the image may be tiled (repeated over the surface of the page) or centered (appearing only once). Whatever graphic background you choose, make sure it's not so bright or busy that it renders any text on top of it illegible. If graphics will be used on top of a graphic background, make sure the background doesn't overwhelm the images. Figure 10-16 shows a background that's just too dynamic to

FIGURE 10-16

Background images that will have content on top of them should be much more subtle than this one.

literally function as a background, and Figure 10-17 shows a background that's a perfect choice.

CREATING A GRAPHIC BACKGROUND

Like resizing and formatting graphics, turning an image into a suitable background is the job of a real graphics application. You want to use a program like Photoshop or Fireworks to take an image, whether it's original computer-generated artwork or a scanned image, and adjust the color levels and size so that the graphic has the visual effect you're looking for. As shown here, Photoshop provides tools for reducing image opacity—one technique for fading an image out to the point that it will fade effectively into the background.

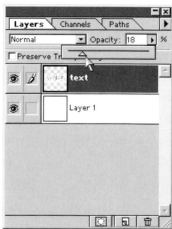

If you're creating a background image from scratch, reduce the opacity of the colors you apply, and consider gradient fills (colored fills that go from dark to light or bright to faded) for an interesting effect. Avoid using too much detail, because if the image fades into the background as it should, that detail will be lost on the viewer. Figure 10-18 shows an interesting background effect. Site-relevant text is repeated in different fonts and sizes, all in

FIGURE 10-17

A background that supports your page content doesn't overwhelm it. This one enhances the page.

FIGURE 10-18

Anything can become a background graphic—a photograph, a simple piece of line art, even text.

faded colors, overlapping to create an interesting graphic that can't literally be read, but that repeats words that are important to the site's message. It's not quite subliminal seduction, but it makes a point.

APPLYING THE BACKGROUND TO PAGES AND STRUCTURAL ELEMENTS

Once you have a background graphic ready for use, you can apply it to your page or frame. If you're using layers on your page, you can apply your graphic to one layer, and place another layer with no fill on top of it, thus turning the bottom layer into a background for the top layer. Your options are virtually unlimited. You can even create a background for a table by placing the background in the page or frame that contains the table, as tables are transparent by default. The use of tables, layers, and frames to provide structure for your Web pages is discussed in detail in Chapter 12.

> **TIP** Is your page background great for most of the page, but creating too much competition for your table? Give the table cells their own background color, which will block out the background. This can be an effective technique for improving the legibility of table text without having to get rid of an otherwise useful page background.

To apply a background graphic through a WYSIWYG application such as Dreamweaver or FrontPage, you can modify the page properties and specify the image to be used for the background. It's that simple. The image will tile in the page, repeating as many times as needed to fill the page dimensions. As shown in Figure 10-19, an image that's 100 pixels square will tile eight times across and six times down a page viewed at 800 x 600 pixel resolution. Not all images are effective when tiled, though this one is. The image used as the background is inserted at full opacity on the page so you can see how the image was tiled for the effect displayed in the background.

> **TIP** There's a lot to be said for a solid color background. You don't have to worry about an image competing with page content, how an image will tile, or the download speed of the image. On the other hand, an image can provide a more interesting texture for the page, which can come in handy if the page content is sparse or dull by nature.

If you don't like the tiled look, you can either resize the image to fill the screen (which will make it take

FIGURE 10-19

If you know your image won't fill the page on its own, think about how it will look when it appears over and over again.

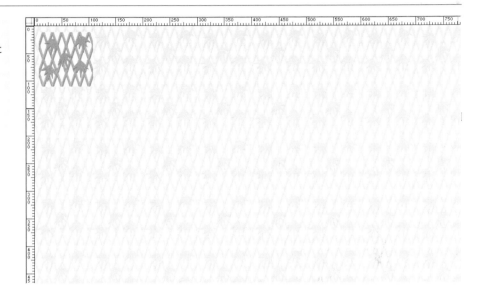

a long time to load, because it will be a much bigger file), or you can, through some Web design applications, change the way the image is applied to the page background. In Dreamweaver, you can specify how or if the image will tile, and if it won't tile, where on the page the single image will fall—top, bottom, left, right, or center.

 ON THE VIRTUAL CLASSROOM CD-ROM Sites without pictures can be pretty dull—learn to choose the right images and place them effectively through this video demonstration.

Working with Color on the Web

If you've ever designed for print media—such as

brochures, posters, or packaging—you know how expensive it

is to print things in more than two colors. When it comes to the

Web, however, you can use as many colors as you want, as often

as you want, and the use of color is absolutely free. The only

limitation is that you have to stick to a palette of 256 colors

that are considered "Web safe." Now, either you think 256 is

more colors than you'd ever need or you're upset to find out

there are so few from which to choose—in either case, however,

it pays to understand the Web's color requirements and be pre-

pared to work within the palette.

WHAT ARE WEB COLORS?

Web colors are the colors that Web browsers (such as Internet Explorer and Netscape) can display reliably on any computer. Of course, the browsers are limiting themselves to work with the lowest common denominator in terms of computer hardware. An older monitor with a low-end video card can only display 256 colors, so that became the "standard" for browser software (there are 216 colors that all browsers display, and 40 more that are displayed differently by different browsers, for a total of 256 web-safe colors). Even though there are monitors that can display millions of colors, browser software engineers don't want to leave anyone out, so they aim low. Figure 11-1 shows the Windows Display Properties dialog box, through which the monitor's color display settings can be adjusted.

That last paragraph probably didn't do much to charm those of you who feel that a palette of 256 colors is just too limiting. But think about it—256 colors is plenty of colors to use when it comes to changing the color of text, choosing a page background, or filling table cells, layers, or frames with color. Most Web design

FIGURE 11-1
As a Web designer, you must take the limitations of your visitors' monitors into account.

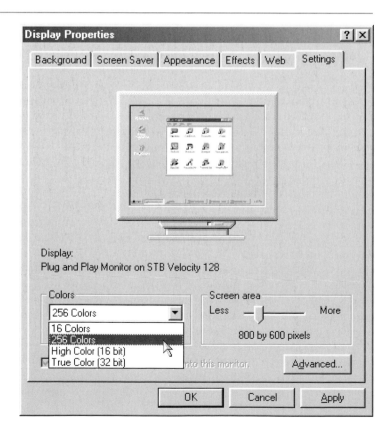

applications allow you to select a color from anything onscreen, so if your site contains a color photo, you'll be able to select a color from within it, and the software will determine the closest Web-safe color to it. As shown in Figure 11-2, the Dreamweaver color well tool allows you to select a color from any object onscreen. When a color from the artwork already on the page is chosen, a Web-safe equivalent is displayed in the Dreamweaver Properties Inspector. This makes it easy, for example, to match your page background to a shade found within one of the images on the page.

Notice the number next to the color. That's the hexadecimal value of the color selected. Colors are represented by numbers so they can be referred to in the HTML code that makes the page. You can use color names such as "red" or "light blue" in your HTML code, but imagine trying to name all 256 colors and to make sure everyone knew the names. You'd end up with color names like the ones you see on cosmetics or paints—"muted sage" isn't something an HTML programmer wants to remember if all he or she wants is a dirty-looking green. It's a lot easier to look at a palette of Web-safe colors, click on the one you want, and have the software insert the color and enter the color number into the underlying HTML code.

When selecting colors for Web page elements, you can enter the color number if you know it, or find out the color number by selecting the color by eye in a dialog box such as the one seen in Figure 11-3. Adobe Photoshop, which is used to create

FIGURE 11-2

Use Dreamweaver's eyedropper to sip up color from one place for use in another.

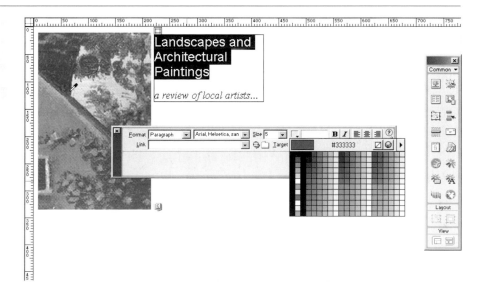

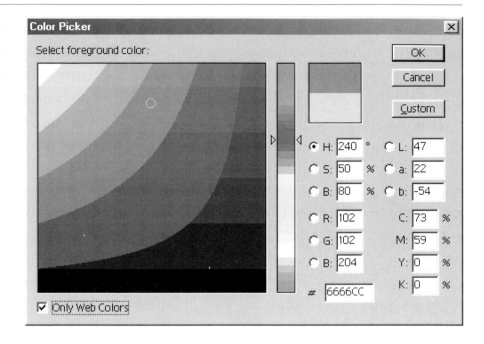

FIGURE 11-3

Click on a color in the palette and note its hexa-decimal value.

artwork and retouch images for both print and Web work, offers two main palettes—one that's Web safe, and one that's not.

WORKING WITH PROCESS AND PRINT COLORS

A lot of Web sites, especially those belonging to businesses, need to match their Web site design to existing marketing materials—letterhead, logos, business cards, and so on. This can affect the overall design in terms of using the organization's logo and recognizable graphic elements, but most often it affects the range of colors the Web designer can use.

If the organization for which you're designing a site has selected a color scheme for its marketing materials, you'll need to match that scheme in the colors you apply to the pages and their elements.

TIP **Different monitors do display the same colors differently—what appears as a dark red on one person's monitor may look like purple on someone else's monitor. In addition, people visiting your site may have adjusted the brightness for their display, so that what's bright white to you is a light gray to them. With all of these influences on how color is perceived by individual visitors to your site, you can see why attempting to find a perfect match for a print color or the color something is "in real life"—like the color of a rose, for example—is pointless. Find the closest match, and leave it at that.**

Because the existing materials are probably on paper, you may run into colors that don't have an exact Web-safe match. What to do? You have lots of options, and worrying isn't one of them. It's easy to find a near match using the color values of each shade you want to use. You'll need to find the color names or numbers (yes, even print colors have numbers), and then view the values for those colors. Color values are viewed through a dialog box that shows the amount of each color used to make up a particular color, based on a color model.

UNDERSTANDING COLOR MODELS

When it comes to Web color, the RGB (red, green, blue) model is used. This means that all colors are seen as containing some level of red, green, and/or blue. For example, what you might call "pink" is really R=255, G=102, B=153, with a hexadecimal number FF6699. As shown in Figure 11-4, you can use programs such as Adobe Photoshop to view the RGB or CMYK levels of different colors, make note of them, and then find a Web-safe equivalent.

If you're worried that the non-Web color you want to use is a few digits off on the R, G, and/or B level when you find the closest Web-safe color, don't. First of all, every person's monitor shows color a little differently, and no one expects to hold a brochure up to a Web page onscreen and see an exact match.

FIGURE 11-4

Pick a color and jot down the color levels. Then go to a Web-safe palette, and find the closest match by entering those levels.

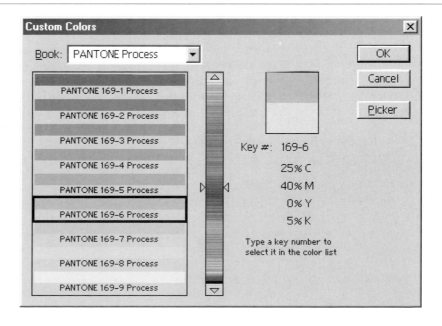

RGB, CMYK, PANTONE, AND PROCESS COLORS For print work, the RGB and CMYK models are both popular. The CMYK model interprets all colors as containing a level of cyan, magenta, yellow, and black. The Adobe Photoshop color picker shows both RGB and CMYK levels for each color, plus HSB (hue, saturation, and brightness) levels. Other printed artwork may contain Pantone or process colors from a commercial palette of numbered/named colors that professional printers use. Just like matching any other color, you can determine the RGB levels of a Pantone color and then find the Web-safe equivalent or the closest match. Any application (Photoshop, Illustrator, CorelDRAW) that's used to create artwork for print will offer a process or Pantone palette, and display the RGB levels for each one.

Choosing the Right Colors

Whether you're matching print colors or just trying to find the right colors for the page at hand, it's important to choose colors that evoke the appropriate feeling for the page and that are easy on the eyes. What does "easy on the eyes" mean? Imagine staring for any length of time at bright red, screaming yellow, or that shade of green you only see in highlighter pens. Your eyes start to feel strained; they may even water a little bit. This is not a good thing when it comes to colors for use on a Web page, because you want people to linger—to read the whole article, visit all of your links, browse your online catalog until they find what they need. If your color scheme is hard to look at for more than a nanosecond, you won't find too many people hanging around or revisiting your site.

This doesn't mean you're stuck using soothing earth tones for everything, or that all text should be black on a white field. Absolutely not! You can use bright or intense colors as accents. If you love navy and fuchsia together, use navy text on a white background, and have a pink border or graphic element nearby.

Aside from color preference, you have to think of what feeling or response your site should evoke. If you're designing a Web page for a stockbroker, you probably want to stick to a conservative color scheme, using colors you'd find in that same stockbroker's closet—gray, black, brown, navy, dark green—even if you don't personally love these colors for your own wardrobe or decor. These colors are serious, no-nonsense colors. On the other hand, if you're designing a Web page for a day-

THE WAY COLORS MAKE US FEEL You know why the British painted their phone boxes red? So people wouldn't hang around making long, personal phone calls. Red makes people tense and invites action. It can make some people angry, and for just about anyone, red inspires motion. Light pinks and greens, on the other hand, are soothing colors that allow people to take a deep breath and relax. You'll find light shades of pink and green in hospitals and prisons, places where people tend to be under stress of some kind. The color may not make the stay more pleasant, but it doesn't add to the tension, either. Earth tones (beiges, creams, mossy greens) are also calming, and are rather neutral in feeling as well as tone. The person in a beige environment is unchanged by the colors around them, having little or no reaction to the color at all.

care center, you can go a little wild, using bright colors that appeal to children and make people think "fun." Pinks, yellows, oranges, bright blues and greens, rainbow colors—anything that inspires a feeling of playfulness would be appropriate.

When it comes to page backgrounds, a clean, white background would be great for a child-oriented Web site; black would not. Remember, the rules for choosing colors for a Web site are no different than the rules you'd apply when selecting paint for an office versus a daycare center or picking the colors for an invitation or announcement. When it comes to a background color, though, as opposed to accent colors, you want to pick a color on which text can be easily read. Even if bright yellow is an appropriate choice for a site based on the desired tone or feeling, it's really hard on the eyes to look at a large, bright yellow space for more than a few seconds.

If you're feeling as though there are just too many variables and too many things to consider as you choose your site colors, think of it this way: you probably have the same reactions to colors as the majority of other people in the world. Pick the colors *you* think "work" for the page in question. Unless other people look at the page and say, "Yuck! What were you *thinking*?" you've probably made good selections. Getting other people's opinions is a good idea, too, just in case you're too close to the subject or you think your own personal color preferences are getting in the way of choosing what's right for the site.

WORKING WITH THE COLOR WHEEL

When choosing colors for your site, it helps to choose a central color and then stick with colors that are either related to that color or that are compatible with it. By "central" color I mean the color that's used for major accents or for the background (if it's a color on which text can be read). If, for example, the organization's logo includes dark blue text, you might want to use that as your central color, applying it to borders, heading text, and horizontal rules.

So what do you do once you've picked your central color? How do you know which colors go with that color? Most people feel fairly confident about their ability to match up colors when they get dressed, so this shouldn't be that difficult.

> **TIP** **Want to see a color wheel online? Type** "color wheel" **(with the quotes) into a search site's keyword text box. From graphic design firms to paint manufacturers, there are plenty of places where you can view the color wheel online. For example, try http://painting.about.com/ hobbies/painting/library/weekly/ aa110398.htm.**

FIGURE 11-5

Yes, this image is in black and white, but the colors are labeled to assist you!

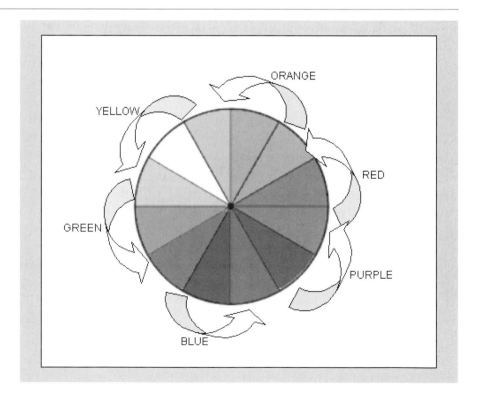

There are some people, however, who either don't feel confident about their choices or are told that their choices are bad—people who wear brown socks with a black suit, for example. If you fall into either of these categories, don't despair! The color wheel is there to help you, as shown in Figure 11-5.

IDENTIFYING PRIMARY AND SECONDARY COLORS

The color wheel is made up of primary, secondary, and tertiary colors. A primary color is a color that cannot be made by mixing other colors. The primary colors are red, blue, and yellow. The secondary colors are those that are made by mixing two primary colors, such as yellow and blue to make green, or red and blue to make purple. The secondary colors are green, purple, and orange (the product of red and yellow). Tertiary colors are made by mixing secondary colors, and they're the colors you get in the 64-color box of crayons, such as burnt sienna and other complex shades.

> **TIP** Here's a little color tip—white is the presence of all color, and black is the absence of it. You'd think that by mixing all the colors in the wheel you'd make black, but you wouldn't—you'd get a dark brown. If you truly mixed all the colors (and not on paper, but on some sort of light-reflecting palette), you'd get white. Trust me.

UNDERSTANDING COMPLEMENTARY COLORS

If something is *complementary*, it goes well with something else. Complementary colors are those that go with other colors. How do you know which ones go with which other ones? Again, we turn to the color wheel. Colors directly next to each other on the wheel are related colors, and they go together well. If your central color is red, shades of red, from a deep crimson to a pale tomato red, will work together, as will shades of blue if your central color is navy.

The color directly across from another color on the wheel is its opposite and is also complementary. Yellow/blue and purple/green are good pairs of complementary colors. You may find that your wardrobe options increase after getting used to the color wheel, as you discover color pairings you never thought of before!

APPLYING COLOR TO YOUR WEB PAGE

So now you know how to pick the colors for your site, or at least have a better sense of what role color plays. It's not just a matter of picking colors you like, but of picking colors that work. The process of literally applying those colors to your Web page is simple, especially if you're using a WYSIWYG application such as FrontPage or Dreamweaver. You can apply color to anything on the page, from the text to the background of individual cells, frames, and layers. You can apply color to the page as a whole, and you can insert horizontal rules and apply color to them, as well.

USING COLOR AS A BACKGROUND

Most pages you'll find on the Web have a white background. There may be a lot of color used on the page, but the page itself is white. Why? Because white works with any color scheme, and text is very legible on a white field. Black backgrounds are also popular, because colors look very bright against a black field—think about white or yellow chalk on a blackboard.

You can, of course, apply any color you want to your page background, but there are some things to keep in mind as you make your selection:

► **Eye strain** Test your background by staring at it for 30 seconds. If your eyes feel strained or if when you look away things in the room are a funny color, choose something else. Here's a trick to see what I mean: stare at a bright pink background for 30 seconds and then look around you—everything will look a little greenish.

► **Legibility** Have a lot of text on your page? Pick pale colors (or white, of course) rather than bright or deep colors. While you may love purple, it's very hard to read on purple, and what color would the text be? White? Yellow? People's eyes get tired looking at bright text on a dark background. You want reading your text to be effortless.

► **Visual competition** Will your page have graphics on it? Will the color of the background complement or compete? If you'll be using photographs or complex drawings with bright colors in them, a more muted background (of course, in a shade that works with the predominant color in your graphics) is a good idea. If you'll be displaying artwork or photographs that you want people to really look at, use a white background, like the walls in an art gallery—nothing should compete with the image colors.

After considering these points, and weighing in with your own personal preferences, you can apply your background in any of several different ways, depending on the Web design tool you're using:

▶ If you're working in a WYSIWYG environment such as Dreamweaver, you can choose Modify | Page Properties to display a dialog box through which a background color can be chosen. The resulting Page Properties dialog box (see Figure 11-6) allows you to apply a solid color background or a background image. If you're using FrontPage, choose Format | Background.

▶ If you're working in a text editor and typing your own HTML code, the background color is established through the bgcolor attribute, part of the `<body>` tag, as shown in Figure 11-7. Type the color's hexadecimal number in quotes.

> TIP If your page contains frames, each frame is really a page unto itself. Therefore, the background of each frame can be established individually, using the same procedure as you used for applying a page background color. Click inside the frame to be colored, and choose Modify | Page Properties (in Dreamweaver) or Format | Background (in FrontPage). You can apply a different color to each frame in your frameset, repeating the command for each frame as you click inside it.

FIGURE 11-6

Page Properties include the color of the page background. The default is white.

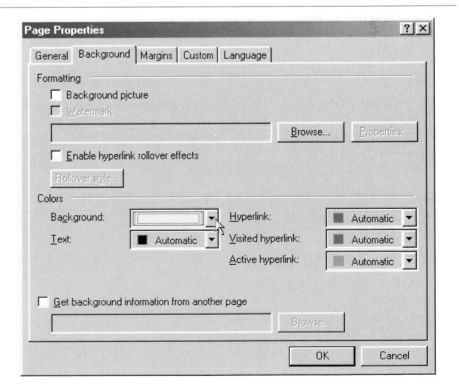

FIGURE 11-7

The background color is set within the `<body>` tag, at the beginning of your HTML document.

```
<html>
<head>
<title>Untitled Document</title>
<meta http-equiv="Content-Type" content="text/html; charset=iso-8859-1">
</head>

<body bgcolor="#CC9999" text="#000000">
<img src="/oil3.jpg" width="208" height="324">
<div id="Layer1" style="position:absolute; width:200px; height:115px; z-
index:1; left: 222px; top: 15px">
  <p><font size="5" face="Arial, Helvetica, sans-serif" color="#333333">
Landscapes
    and Architectural Paintings</font></p>
  <p><i><font size="4">a review of local artists...</font></i></p>
</div>
</body>
</html>
```

APPLYING COLOR TO PAGE ELEMENTS

Colored fills can be applied to table cells and layers (see Figure 11-8), creating blocks of color on the page. Your choices here are nearly as important as your selection of a page background color. If the cell or layer will contain text, the choice is even more important, because legibility comes into play.

The technique for applying color to page elements varies with the design tool and with the element to which you're applying color:

FIGURE 11-8

Apply accent colors by adding background color to cells and layers.

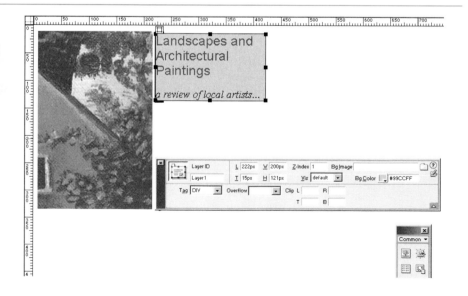

▶ To apply color to a table cell through FrontPage, right-click the cell and choose Cell Properties from the shortcut menu. In the Cell Properties dialog box (see Figure 11-9), pick a color from the Background Color palette.

▶ In Dreamweaver, click inside a cell and use the Properties Inspector to apply a Bg Color. Click the color well, and use the eyedropper to select a color from the palette or from any onscreen element by clicking it (see Figure 11-10).

▶ In HTML, go to the `<td>` tag for the cell in question and add the bgcolor attribute, followed by a pound sign, and the hexadecimal color number in quotes (see Figure 11-11).

When it comes to layers, Dreamweaver offers a more flexible set of tools than FrontPage does. Once you've inserted a layer through Dreamweaver, you can click the layer's tab and use the Bg Color color well in the Properties Inspector to choose a color (see Figure 11-12).

If you're working in HTML, the layer's `<div>` tag should include a background-color attribute, followed by the color number with a # sign in front of it, as shown in Figure 11-13.

FIGURE 11-9

View and edit cell properties in FrontPage.

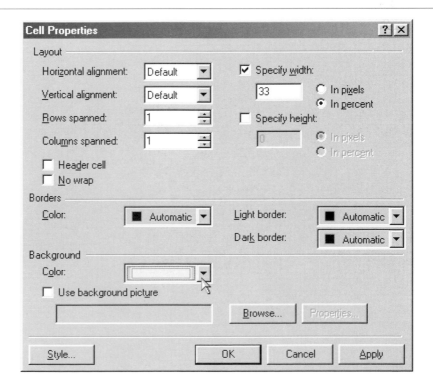

FIGURE 11-10

Select one of 256 Web-safe colors from the color well.

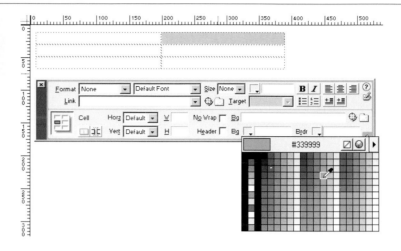

FIGURE 11-11

Don't forget to put quotes around the six-digit hexadecimal number for the color you want to apply.

```
<tr>
  <td> </td>
  <td bgcolor="#33CC99"> </td>
</tr>
<tr>
  <td> </td>
  <td> </td>
</tr>
</table>
```

FIGURE 11-12

Dreamweaver's Properties Inspector offers color tools for whichever page element is selected.

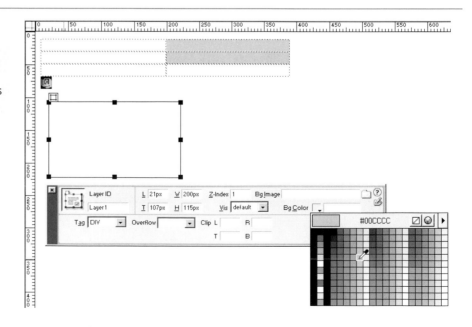

FIGURE 11-13

To color a layer through HTML, look for the layer's `<div>` tag.

```
</tr>
<tr>
  <td> </td>
  <td> </td>
</tr>
</table>
<div id="Layer1" style="position:absolute; width:200px; height:115px; z-index:1;
left: 21px; top: 107px; background-color: #00FF33; layer-background-color:
#00FF33; border: 1px none #000000"></div>
<p> </p>
</body>
</html>
```

Applying color to any other element—such as horizontal rules and table or frame borders—employs very much the same process you use to apply color to other things. In FrontPage, select the element to be colored, and use the Format menu or appropriate toolbar button to apply a color. If you're in Dreamweaver, use the Properties Inspector while the element is selected. In HTML, a color attribute can be added to virtually any element's tag.

Using Colored Text

The color of text can make or break your site, depending on the importance of the text itself. If the only text on your page is single words or short phrases acting as text links to other pages, the text can be marginally legible and you can get away with it. As long as someone can make out the words without squinting or pressing his nose to the monitor, you're okay. If, on the other hand, your page contains a lot of text in paragraphs, you'll want to make sure the text is entirely, indisputably legible. While choosing a clear, simple font (Arial, Helvetica, or Times New Roman) in a size large enough to read without a struggle (at least 12 points or the pixel equivalent) is a big part of this legibility, the color you choose is even more important. Big, clear letters will still be impossible to read if your text color is too light on a light or white background or too dark on a dark or black background. Figure 11-14 shows several errors in text color.

Beyond the pairings of light text on a dark background or dark text on a light background, color combinations are also important to keep in mind. You don't want red text on a blue background, or vice versa, because the text will appear to jump if a visitor moves her head while reading the text. Yellow text on white is obviously a bad choice, as is red text on a green field or green text on a red field. Why the problem with green and red? Because 15 percent of the male population (and about 7 percent of the female) is color-blind and won't be able to tell green from red.

FIGURE 11-14

Can you read this? Don't commit these text color sins on your Web pages!

— Unlike what's been done here, when the background is light or white, use dark-colored text.

This layer has a dark background, and the text color is too dark to be read against it.

Just like choosing colors for your background and other page elements, let common sense and your own experiences with color be your guide. If you can read the text without squinting or rubbing your eyes after a while, your color choices probably work. Keep your audience in mind, however. If you don't need glasses and can read the small print on a sign 50 feet away, don't apply those standards to your site visitors. Many people need glasses and may or may not be wearing them at the time they visit your site. When making choices for text color (and any other text attributes that affect legibility), play to the lowest common denominator: someone who can't see very well, with a short attention span. If you can make your text legible and keep their interest, you've got it made.

ON THE VIRTUAL CLASSROOM CD-ROM **The Web makes it cheap and easy to use color, unlike printed materials where using color can be prohibitively expensive. Learn about colors—types, models, and concepts—as well as how to choose colors, and see how the use of colors alone and in combination can increase a site's effectiveness.**

12

Structuring Web Pages with Tables, Frames, and Layers

Without tables, most of the pages you see on the Web would look very different. Tables are probably the most often-used structural device in Web pages, and for good reason—they're easy to create and control, and both old and new browsers can "see" them and display them properly. Running a close second to tables in terms of use on the Web are frames, which have their share of positive and negative attributes. Due to limitations imposed by older browsers, layers are the third most-common structural device you'll see on the Web, but they too have a significant number of benefits. This chapter will show you how these devices are used, which situations require one over another, and how to work with them in both WYSIWYG and HTML development environments.

UNDERSTANDING STRUCTURAL OPTIONS

A Web page is like a word processing document in terms of how text and images are positioned. You type headings, paragraphs, and lists, and the text flows from line to line within the page margins. When you press ENTER or SHIFT-ENTER, a break is inserted that forces the text to flow according to your terms. As shown in the following illustration, the text on a Web page is rather limited in terms of what you can do with it—you can change the font, size, color, and alignment. Other than that, your only manipulative powers are in terms of how much space you create between lines or paragraphs of text by pressing ENTER to move text down, and allowing word wrap to work unrestrained.

Heading Text

This is paragraph text, flowing from the left side of the page to the right, running along until it hits the right side of the page at which point it flows back to the left side on a new line. This word wrap will keep text going and going until you press Enter to indicate the beginning of a new paragraph. You can also press Shift + Enter to create a line break but not break the paragraph into two pieces.

More Heading Text

Your manipulative powers with regard to graphics are just as limited. As most Web pages also contain graphics—photographs, line art, logos, shapes—the need to position them in and among lines and paragraphs of text becomes important. Again, if you simply insert graphics on a page, they'll stack like lines of text, just as they do in a word processing document. Figure 12-1 shows the same page as shown in the previous illustration, but this time, a graphic has been added between paragraphs. The text doesn't flow around the image nor does it sit beside it. This presents problems if text pertains to an image, as in the case of an online catalog where a product description must accompany an image of the product. While you can place text above or below a picture to which the text pertains, you'll waste a lot of space on the page by stacking images and text without using space left to right.

FIGURE 12-1

Text and graphics sort of
ignore each other, at most
forcing one onto the next
line to make room.

Heading Text

This is paragraph text, flowing from the left side of the page to the right, running along until it hits the right side of the page at which point it flows back to the left side on a new line. This word wrap will keep text going and going until you press Enter to indicate the beginning of a new paragraph. You can also press Shift + Enter to create a line break but not break the paragraph into two pieces.

More Heading Text

So how do all the pages you see on the Web that don't look boring and horrible manage it? With structural devices such as tables, frames, and layers. The use of these devices makes it possible to have a picture next to text rather than just above or below it. Tables and layers provide the most free-form effects in terms of size and placement, and frames offer considerable control in terms of viewing page content. Your pages can contain one, two, or all three of these devices, and you may even nest one inside the other—layers can contain tables, tables can contain layers, and frames can contain both tables and layers. You can nest tables inside of tables, and frames inside of frames, and you can stack layers so that one appears to be inside of another.

The options for using tables, frames, and layers are virtually unlimited, which is part of their power. Without them, you can't move things around on the page, place items on top of or alongside other items, or apply background colors to anything other than the entire page. Layers and tables (and individual table cells) can have background colors, and because each frame is a page unto itself, each frame can have a background color or image. By placing these elements in your Web page, you gain the ability to turn your imagined layouts into reality.

With all the creative possibilities presented by tables, layers, and frames, there are some limitations:

▶ Tables are rather rigid and must follow a grid structure of some sort, and cannot be dragged at will on the page surface—table position is limited by size and content. All browsers (in versions anyone is likely to have at this point in time, anyway) can see them and display them properly, and you don't need to learn any new skills to place text or graphics inside a table's cells. Tables can be invisible to the site visitor, or they can have colored fills and borders applied to them so that they become a graphical element as well as a structural element.

▶ Frames are also rather rigid. While they can be sized without regard for what they contain (unlike tables, which can only be as small as their largest element), they cannot be moved at will. You can resize frames to achieve the illusion of moving them, but they aren't free-floating entities on your page, they're part of the page itself. Frames also have another significant limitation—search engines can't index them based on their content. If you need people to be able to find your site based on the first 100 words on the home page, frames aren't for you.

▶ Layers are a tool for creating free-form page layouts. You can place, move, and resize layers at will, unbound by any grid structure. They are, however, invisible to browsers prior to version 4.0 (of either Internet Explorer or Netscape). You may think this is not a big deal, but there are a surprising number of people out there with old browsers and no immediate plans to upgrade. As a designer, therefore, you must work around this problem by using layers only when you know the browser version your visitors will have or when the layer content isn't essential to the effectiveness of the page. You can also design content for the visitor who can't see layers.

Now, with these basic pros and cons in mind, think about how you might use tables, frames, and layers in your Web pages. They can simply help you place text and graphics in more creative and compelling arrangements, or they can become a significant part of the design.

WORKING WITH TABLES

Tables are simply blocks of cells. The blocks can be uniform, as shown here, creating a grid to house text and graphics in a tidy structure where columns are of equal width and rows are of equal height. They can also be less uniform, 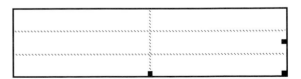 arranged as shown in Figure 12-2. The structure you choose to create is dictated by your needs for positioning text and graphics on the page, and for creating blocks of color and space.

FIGURE 12-2

Drawn on the page rather than created through typing HTML code, these cells are anything but regimented.

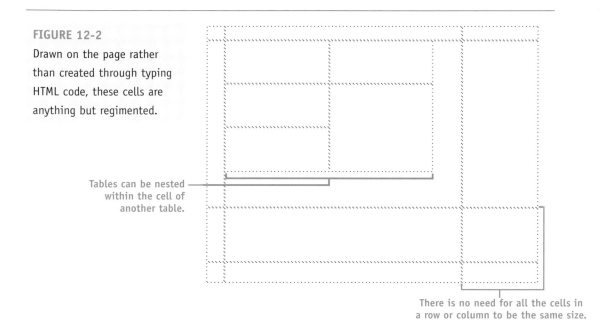

Tables can be nested within the cell of another table.

There is no need for all the cells in a row or column to be the same size.

CREATING TABLES

The method you use for creating a table can often affect the appearance of the table, and your need for a particular type of table can dictate your choice of tools for creating it. If you don't have a WYSIWYG application such as Dreamweaver or FrontPage at your disposal, and you're not a devoted HTML programmer, you may opt for a simpler table structure. Creating a more elaborate or free-form table is easier in a WYSIWYG program, because you can draw the cells onscreen as you're picturing them in your mind. This can be done in straight HTML, but it's much more difficult to translate a layout you have in your head to a very complex series of table tags and settings. Figure 12-3 shows the HTML code required for just a portion of the table seen in Figure 12-2.

USING WYSIWYG TOOLS

Table-creation tools vary within and between WYSIWYG applications. For example, in Dreamweaver, you can draw tables freehand (using your mouse or other pointing device), or you can insert tables, answering a series of dialog box questions about the intended dimensions of the table. The former technique, as you can imagine, results in a more free-form table, and the latter in a simpler, more uniform table. Dreamweaver also offers two views to work in, one that facilitates drawing and resizing table cells, and another that caters to the needs of the

FIGURE 12-3

The more complex your table, the less you'll enjoy hand-coding it with HTML, and the more you'll like using a WYSIWYG tool for the job.

```html
<table width="369" border="0" cellpadding="0" cellspacing="0">
  <tr>
    <td width="20" height="16"></td>
    <td width="265"></td>
    <td width="84"></td>
  </tr>
  <tr>
    <td height="184"></td>
    <td valign="top">
      <table width="88%" border="0" cellspacing="0" cellpadding="5" height="145">
        <tr>
          <td> </td>
          <td> </td>
        </tr>
        <tr>
          <td> </td>
          <td rowspan="2"> </td>
        </tr>
        <tr>
          <td> </td>
        </tr>
      </table>
    </td>
    <td valign="top"> </td>
  </tr>
```

designer who is stocking an existing table with content. As shown in Figure 12-4, in Dreamweaver's Layout view, your mouse turns to a crosshair, and you can draw tables within tables, cells within cells, and create as complex a tabular layout as you want.

Dreamweaver's Insert | Table command (and the Insert Table button) is a close match for FrontPage's table-creation tools. FrontPage's table tools are very much like the table tools in Word, and result in fairly simple grids. You can, of course, nest cells and tables within other table cells and resize each cell as desired for a less uniform layout, and you can also use the Draw Table command to draw freehand cells singly or in groups. Figure 12-5 shows the Insert Table dialog box in FrontPage.

Adobe GoLive provides a table-creation environment with a grid to help you position your cells and tables. As shown in Figure 12-6, apply a layout grid from the palette, and then drag a table onto the grid. Using the Table Inspector, change the table's dimensions, border, and other settings.

CREATING TABLES WITH HTML CODE

The HTML code required to create a table includes table tags: `<table>` to open the table, marking its beginning, and `</table>` to close the table, marking where the table ends. Between these tags are `<tr>` tags for each row (including a closing

FIGURE 12-4

Draw layout tables and cells in Dreamweaver's Layout view.

Each new cell results in a grid of supporting cells around it.

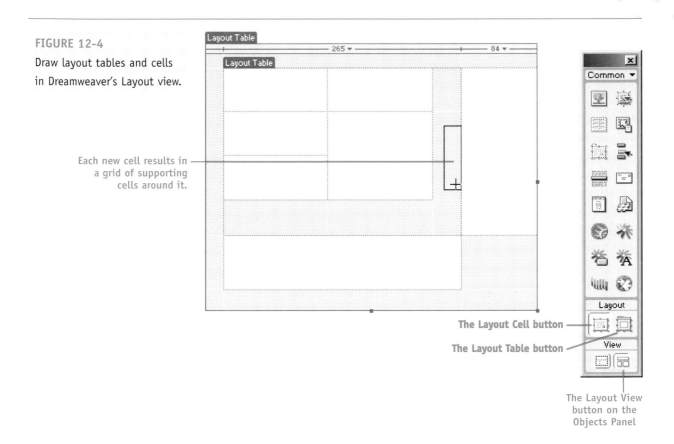

The Layout Cell button

The Layout Table button

The Layout View button on the Objects Panel

FIGURE 12-5

You have to plan ahead when building a table, knowing the number of columns and rows you want, and how much space to add inside and between them.

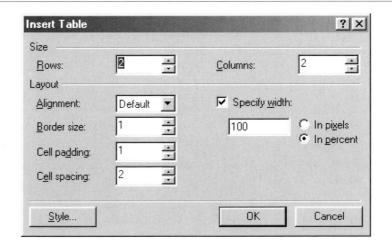

FIGURE 12-6

Create tables using the grid and palette.

The grid makes positioning tables easier.

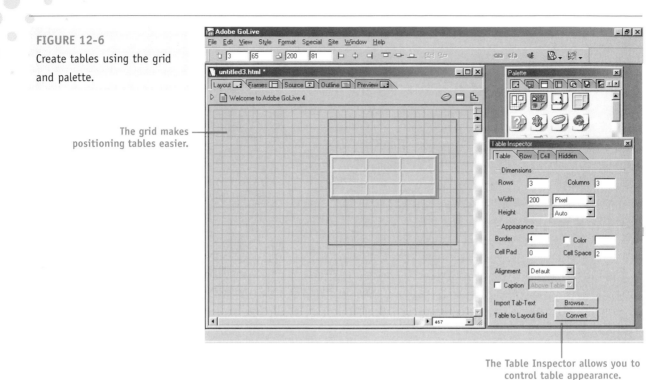

The Table Inspector allows you to control table appearance.

</tr> tag for each row, too) and <td> </td> tags for each cell in each row. The attributes for each row and cell can include width and height settings and background colors. The main table tags include attributes for the overall size of the table, a color for the table's background, and settings for the distance between cells and between the walls of the cells and their contents. Figure 12-7 shows the code

FIGURE 12-7

If you're not an HTML expert, creating tables and editing the code for them is a great way to learn more.

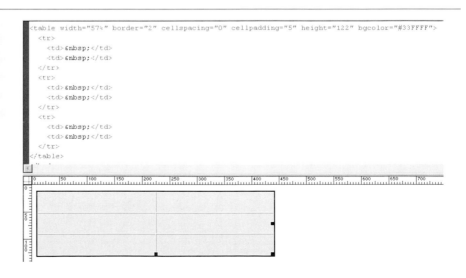

```
<table width="57%" border="2" cellspacing="0" cellpadding="5" height="122" bgcolor="#33FFFF">
  <tr>
    <td> </td>
    <td> </td>
  </tr>
  <tr>
    <td> </td>
    <td> </td>
  </tr>
  <tr>
    <td> </td>
    <td> </td>
  </tr>
</table>
```

required for a three-row table, with two cells per row, plus the table that is created by the code. The table has a light blue background, a two-pixel border, and there is no space between cells, but a five-pixel space between the walls of the cells and the text or images inside them. If you're building a table in HTML, remember that you'll be working within the table, row, and cell tags when you insert your text and graphics.

WORKING WITH TABLE CONTENT

Adding content to a table cell is just like adding it to a blank Web page document. Simply click to place your cursor in the cell, and begin typing or issue the command to insert a graphic image. Once the content is in the cell, you can resize the cell to accommodate it (perhaps widening a cell so text wraps more legibly or so an image isn't cramped within its walls). You can adjust the way the content is positioned by changing the cell's horizontal and vertical alignment settings.

ALIGNING TABLE TEXT AND GRAPHICS

To change the alignment of cell content, you can use various onscreen tools if you're working in a WYSIWYG environment, or you can add alignment attributes to the cell tags in HTML. As I generally recommend using a WYSIWYG tool for building and manipulating tables (it's faster and easier, I find), our examples will come from Dreamweaver, FrontPage, and GoLive.

The placement of content in a table cell can be adjusted both horizontally and vertically. You can center an image horizontally, and also place it in the middle of the cell in terms of its vertical position. This places the image in the cell's true center. Text can be aligned to the left (best for paragraph text) and set to start at the cell's top, so that the entire cell can be filled with text. As shown here, the Dreamweaver Properties Inspector displays alignment tools for both horizontal and vertical alignment as long as your cursor is in a table cell.

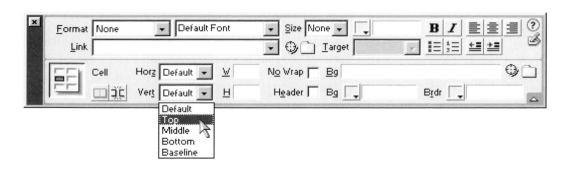

ADJUSTING TABLE FORMATS

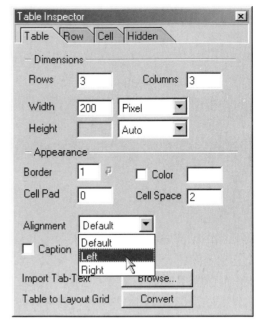

At the time you create a table, you can set the table borders, cell padding (space between cell walls and cell content) and spacing (the distance between cells), and color attributes for the entire table, using the Insert Table dialog box and other onscreen tools. You can also change them after the table's been created, using onscreen palettes. As shown here, Adobe GoLive displays table settings whenever a table is active, and you can adjust borders, colors, spacing, and padding settings quite easily. You might find that it's easier to adjust table and cell formats after you've started adding content to the table cells—it can be helpful to see what the content requires.

Of course, when it comes to color, you'll want to match the colors of your table cells and borders with colors already on the page—images, page backgrounds, and text. When you choose the colors for cell and table backgrounds, make sure your text is still legible on top of it. Nothing's worse than a bright or dark table background that renders table text impossible to read.

When choosing the spacing between cells and the padding within them, again, think of your content. If you want to make sure that text in two adjoining cells don't run together visually, increase the padding (5 or 6 pixels is a reasonable amount of padding) and if that's not enough, add a few pixels of space between cells, too. Figure 12-8 shows cell padding set to 6 pixels in the table on top, and no padding for the table below it. Notice that the text in the bottom table seems to run into the table walls, making it difficult to read.

Cell spacing can also be used to create an interesting table border. Apply a background color to the entire table, and then apply a different background

> **TIP** Are there any circumstances where no cell padding is best? If your table exists solely for structure and will have no border, and if there are no graphics or other text right next to a cell containing the unpadded text, cell padding set to 0 will work. The problems arise when there are other table elements running into the outside of the cell—if the cell's text runs right to the edge, it also runs into these adjoining elements.

FIGURE 12-8

Give your text and graphics some room by setting cell padding of at least 3 pixels, preferably 5 or 6.

This table has cell padding set so that there is distance between cell content and the cell walls.

Even when cells are side by side, there's some breathing room

The text in this cell wraps right up to the cell walls on the left.

The text in this cell wraps right up to the cell walls, too. There is no space between the wall and the text.

color to the table's cells. The cell spacing will allow the table's background color to show through, and the cell's background color will block the table background except for the border created by the spacing. As shown here in a table with a three-pixel "border," a dark background for the entire table creates the illusion of a border when the cells are given a lighter fill.

Applying color to a table or cell is done through dialog boxes, toolbars, or onscreen palettes, depending on the software you're using. Figure 12-9 shows the FrontPage tools for filling individual cells with color. You can make each cell in a table a different color or apply a uniform color to

TIP Older versions of Netscape (prior to 6.0) ignore the colored background in tables. Designer's lives will be much improved when everyone is using new browser software!

FIGURE 12-9
In the Cell Properties box, pick a background color for the selected cell.

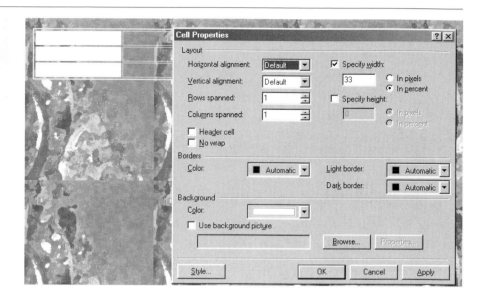

a block of cells. By default, tables are transparent, and the background color of the page shows through.

RESIZING TABLE COLUMNS AND ROWS

The size of a table is dictated by the size of its cells. The size of a table's cells is dictated by the content of the cells and by your resizing actions, made through the design software you're using or by editing HTML code. The size of individual cells is limited by the cell's content—you can't make a cell smaller than its content, be it text or graphics inside the cell. When a cell has text in it, you can resize it and make the text rewrap to fit the new cell dimensions, but you can't make the cell so small that any of the text is obscured. If your cell contains a graphic, the size of the graphic (plus any cell padding you have set for the table) is the smallest the cell can be. If, for example, you have an image that's 100 pixels wide by 200 pixels tall, if the cell padding is set to 3 pixels, the cell containing the image can only be reduced to 103 x 203, and no smaller.

Cells can, of course, be made larger than their contents, but only within the constraints of anything that holds the table itself. For example, if the table is within another table, the nested table can't be any larger than the cell of the table that contains the nested table (see Figure 12-10). Say *that* five times fast! Further, if a table is within a layer, the table cannot be made larger than the size of the layer.

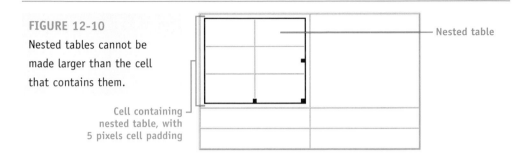

FIGURE 12-10

Nested tables cannot be made larger than the cell that contains them.

Nested table

Cell containing nested table, with 5 pixels cell padding

Page size doesn't restrict tables—if you set your table to 100% width, that means it will resize to the page size depending on the display properties of the visitor. Someone viewing the page on a monitor set to 800 x 600 resolution will see the same amount of content left to right as someone viewing the same page on a monitor set to 1024 x 768. If, however, the table width is set to a specific number of pixels, such as 900, the visitor using an 800 x 600 monitor will have to scroll left and right to see the entire width of the page, as 100 pixels of the page will be beyond the horizontal display area of the monitor.

TIP If your entire page is made up of one or more tables, center them on the page. Why? If someone is viewing the page on a monitor set to a higher resolution than the one for which you designed the page (most designers aim at the 800 x 600 resolution, despite probably not viewing pages at that resolution themselves), they'll see the page centered, not off to the left with a huge vertical strip of whitespace on the right. The centered table will look like it was made for their display settings, especially if you set your main table to be 100% of the page.

MERGING AND SPLITTING CELLS

One way around all the limitations on cell size is to merge and split cells. Merging cells means that you take two or more contiguous cells and turn them into one cell, as shown in Figure 12-11. Splitting cells does just the opposite—you take one cell and split it into two or more cells. As shown here in a table that's had some splitting done, the additional cells create more small containers for fields in a form.

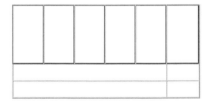

The process of merging and splitting cells is easiest to perform in a WYSIWYG application such as Dreamweaver, FrontPage, or GoLive. As shown in the next illustration, the Merge and Split buttons on the Dreamweaver Properties Inspector become available as soon as either two or more cells are selected for merging or a single cell is selected to be split. As soon as you've selected the cells to be merged

FIGURE 12-11

FIGURE 12-11

Need to create a large, unseg-
mented block within a table?
Merge two or more cells.

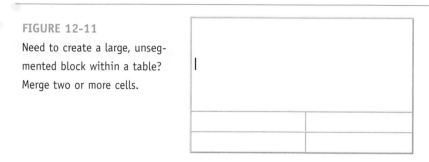

or split, click the appropriate button. Using the Properties Inspector (or the merge/split tools in any WYSIWYG application) is much easier than changing table structure directly through HTML.

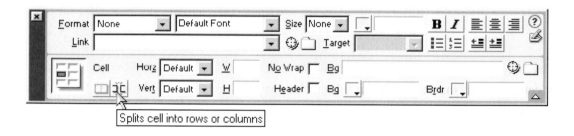

Splits cell into rows or columns

If you choose to split the cell, the application will want to know how many cells to split it into. Continuing in Dreamweaver for continuity's sake, this illustration shows the Split Cell dialog box, in which you specify how many new cells you want to create with the split, and whether you want to break the selected cell into rows (horizontally arranged cells) or columns (vertically arranged cells).

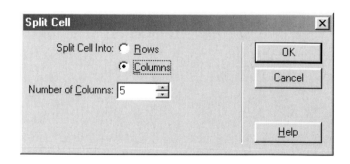

If you're still not sure when and why you'd split or merge cells, consider these design dilemmas:

▶ You have a multiple-row table with two cells per row. You need to pair product images on the left with text on the right (the text describes the products
pictured). This is fine until you get a product with two images. If you want to
have two images in a cell next to a single cell with text describing the product,

FIGURE 12-12

Simplify the layout process by turning two or more cells into one.

Visit the Dolphins!
Come diving with our trained team of experts.
Our focus is on reef ecology and wildlife, examining the wonders of this native ecosystem, and the precarious balance that is in danger of being lost forever. Of course we can't guarantee any dolphin visits, but we certainly don't keep them in a pen for the public's viewing pleasure.

as shown in Figure 12-12, you need to merge the two cells on the right, creating a large block for the text describing the two images on the left.

▶ You have a table that contains one row with three cells in it. Each cell contains a long text article, and the overall effect is that of a newsletter or a page from a newspaper. On one of the long "columns," however, you want to nest another table to contain the results of a survey form. You need to split one of the long cells into two cells, and confine the article to one of the cells. In the new, empty cell, you can insert a table, in which the data is displayed, as shown in Figure 12-13.

FIGURE 12-13

Break one cell into two to gain control over the content of a table.

Nested table in cell created by split

Survey data in nested table

The Animal-Free Times

Compassionate Consumers: The Animal-Free Grocery Cart

Ridding your diet of animal products can seem like an insurmountable goal. Even if you stop eating meat (which millions of people have already done to reduce the risk of cancer, heart attack, and stroke), what about eggs, milk, cheese? These foods may not seem like they come at the expense of an animal, but they do. Chickens lead horrible lives, packed thousands to a barn, unable to even flap their wings. Some of them are packed so tight their feet don't touch the floor. Chicks are de-beaked (with a hot, electrified wire) so that when the horribly tight quarters drive them to violence, they can't peck their fellow chickens. These conditions are not the exception, they're the sad, terrible rule.

One of the things that keeps people from switching to a vegetarian or vegan diet is not knowing what foods are available, what you can eat instead of meat, dairy, and eggs. Here are just some of the things a typical vegan eats:

Vegetables (yeah, big shock there), fruit, pasta, rice, nuts, and beans. Sound boring? It isn't. It's healthy, and you can serve all of these foods in delicious ways. To add more protein, try seitan, a wheat product that tastes like beef. Sauté it in a wok or frying pan with teriyaki sauce or any other marinade you like. Add sautéed onions, mushrooms (portobellos are very meaty-tasting and textured), green onion, and fresh garlic. Serve it over pasta or rice. Filling, good for you, and not a single animal suffered or died to feed you. That feels even better.

Click here for more recipes.

SURVEY: 50 random shoppers were asked:

Why would or do you not eat meat?:

It's healthier not to	45%
Concerns about animal welfare	40%
Don't know	15%

Of the carnivores responding, 35% said they've reduced the amount of meat and/or animal products in their diets.

Lunches are easy. Avocado and tomato on toast with soy mayonnaise. Add soy cheese or a soy-based "turkey" or

New cell

WORKING WITH NESTED TABLES

As shown in Figure 12-13, a nested table is simply a table placed inside the cell of another table. The nested table cannot be made larger than the cell that houses it, but it can be treated in every other way as you would any other table. It can have borders and background colors, and you can adjust the alignment both horizontally and vertically within the cells (for the cell content). You can also adjust the alignment of the nested table within the cell that holds it, just as you would adjust the alignment of a table in relation to the entire page.

Sometimes nesting a table is easier than splitting cells because you have more control over the resulting cell structure and can set up new rules for the nested table. For example, if your main table has cell spacing set to 2 pixels and cell padding set to 3 pixels, if you split cells within that table, the new cells inherit those settings. If you nest a table within the main table, however, the nested table can have entirely different cell padding and spacing settings, as well as different colors, border width, and alignment.

STRUCTURING A PAGE WITH FRAMES

Unlike a table, frames aren't part of a page—they become the page, or rather turn a single page into several pages called a *frameset*. When you break a page into frames, each one becomes a page itself, and the group of frames, even if it's just two, is the set of frames or frameset. Frames have some interesting benefits and some serious drawbacks. Depending on what you think frames will do for you, you may feel the drawbacks are no big deal.

Frames are great because you can set up one part of the page to be scrollable, to house, say, a long article or series of images and related text. In another frame on the same page, you can have a graphic and navigation bar that never moves. One frame can be scrolled at will, but the other frame's content remains onscreen throughout the entire time that the page is displayed (see Figure 12-14). Without a frame, as soon as the visitor scrolled down to read the rest of the text, the top of the page (where, presumably, the organization logo or advertising images appear, along with a set of navigation buttons) would disappear. Because frames are really a group of pages all displayed on one page, you have the ability to treat each one differently.

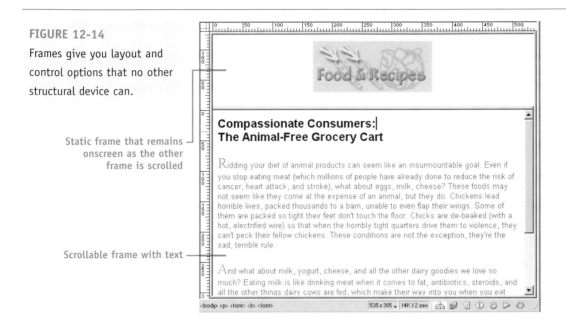

Each frame in the frameset can have a different background color or image, as shown in Figure 12-15. This makes it possible to create a Web page that is broken into visually distinct blocks, each containing different information, each with a visual look and feel all its own.

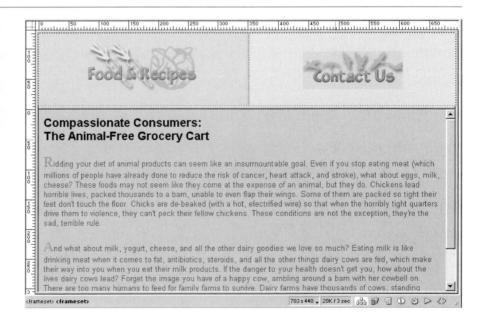

You can set up links within a frame that lead to pages within the site or to external sites, and control where the linked pages appear: in the very frame that contained the link to them, in a new window, or in a separate window on top of the frames window, resulting in two browser windows being open at the same time.

Okay, here's the downside. Frames pages can't be searched by search engines the way a single page can. A single page has meta tags, a list of keywords in the HTML code that assist search engines in displaying a given page in the list of results for a user's search criteria. For example, if you run a soup kitchen and you're looking for volunteers to serve and donors to give you money and supplies, your keywords might be "soup kitchen," "homeless," "donors," "volunteers," "charity," and "donations," as shown here. If someone types any of those words into a search bar at a site such as Lycos, AltaVista, or Google, your site should be in the results because of the matching keywords. Also, if you list those words in the actual text on your home page, this increases the chances of your site being in the search results. If your page is made up of frames, however, this can't happen because there isn't one single page with meta tags to be indexed.

```
<html>
<head>
<title>City Cares Soup Kitchen</title>
<meta http-equiv="Content-Type" content="text/html; charset=iso-8859-1">
<meta name="Keywords" CONTENT="soup kitchen, homeless, donors, volunteers, charity,
donations">
```

SETTING UP A FRAMESET

Creating a frameset happens automatically when you insert frames on a page in any WYSIWYG application. When you go to save the page, you're prompted to save the frameset and then to save each of the frames within it, giving each a distinctive name. The frameset can be updated (resaved to include changes) each time you add or delete frames, move and resize frames, or in any way change the configuration of frames on the page.

The individual frames are pages themselves, and they, too, must be saved. When working with the individual frames, you can use all of the page-oriented tools in the application, such as the Dreamweaver Page Properties dialog box, as shown in Figure 12-16.

FIGURE 12-16

Click inside a frame and then choose to view the Page Properties.

Page Properties ☒

Title: The Animal-Free Grocery Cart

Background Image: [   ] Browse...

Background: ☐ #99CC99

Text: ■ #000000   Visited Links: ☐ [   ]

Links: ☐ [   ]   Active Links: ☐ [   ]

Left Margin: [   ]   Margin Width: [   ]

Top Margin: [   ]   Margin Height: [   ]

Document Encoding: Western (Latin1) ▼   Reload

Tracing Image: [   ] Browse...

Image Transparency: ───────────────┘ 100%
                    Transparent   Opaque

Document Folder:

Site Folder: C:\Sites\freedomforanimals\

OK   Apply   Cancel   Help

INSERTING FRAMES

Inserting frames in a WYSIWYG environment is very simple. As shown here in Dreamweaver's Frames Objects Panel, you can choose to insert a set of preset frames, or you can use the Frames Pages templates available through FrontPage (see Figure 12-17). FrontPage offers a series of several different frames configurations and creates an instant frameset for you. Once the page is created, you can manipulate the frames as desired, using the Frames menu.

Dreamweaver also allows you to create your own frames by dragging frame borders from the perimeter of the page. This lets you create a completely original frameset, not following any preset configuration. Choose View | Visual Aids | Frame Borders, and thick borders appear along the left and top sides of the workspace. Drag the borders onto the page with your mouse, and continue dragging in new borders until the desired frameset is created. Figure 12-18 shows some frames in place and a new frame in progress.

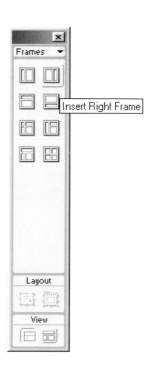

FIGURE 12-17

Build a frames page from one of FrontPage's templates.

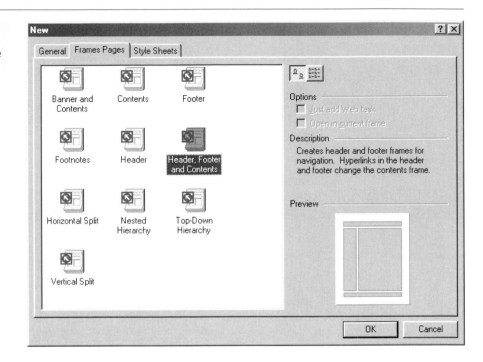

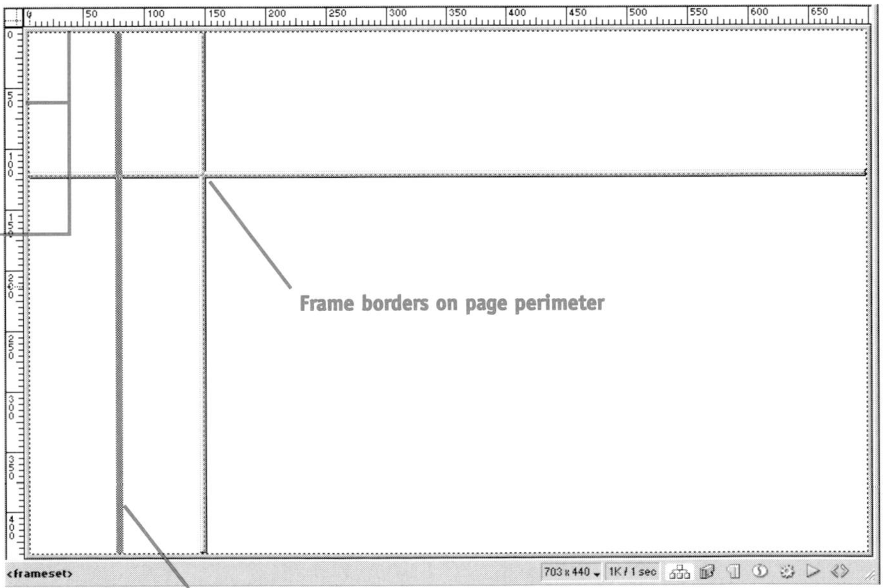

FIGURE 12-18

Create a customized frameset by dragging frame borders in Dreamweaver.

Frames already created

Frame borders on page perimeter

New frame's walls being dragged into position

Adobe GoLive's frame-building tools are a cross between Dreamweaver's more free-form procedure and FrontPage's canned set of frames. As shown in Figure 12-19, you can click the Frames tab to indicate that you're building a frames page, and then use the Frames palette to choose a frameset configuration and drag the one you want onto the page. Once the frames are in place, they can be adjusted in terms of height and width, and frames can be nested inside other frames.

MOVING AND RESIZING FRAMES

Frames can't really be moved the way a layer can be dragged around on the page (see the Layers sections later in this chapter), but you can change their placement on the page by resizing them. Resizing a frame is simply a matter of dragging the frame borders with your mouse. As shown in Figure 12-20, you can make a frame taller or shorter, wider or narrower, depending on the border you drag and the direction in which you drag it.

It's generally a good idea to make sure your frames are big enough to show their entire content, except in the cases of frames that contain long articles or several paragraphs of text that can't possibly fit on one page. In these cases, it's okay to have the visitor scroll through the frame. If your frame contains images, however, it's best to make sure no one needs to scroll to see the whole picture. If there are

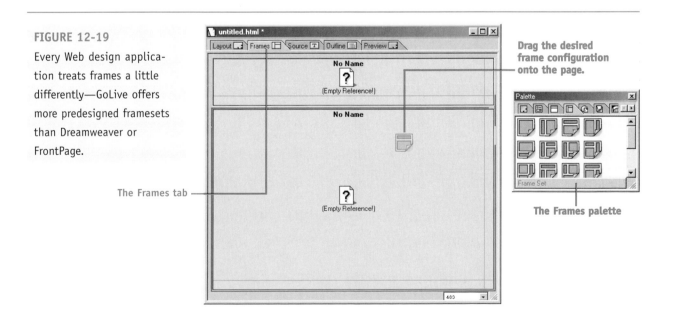

FIGURE 12-19
Every Web design application treats frames a little differently—GoLive offers more predesigned framesets than Dreamweaver or FrontPage.

The Frames tab

Drag the desired frame configuration onto the page.

The Frames palette

FIGURE 12-20

Resize a frame by dragging its side or corner handles.

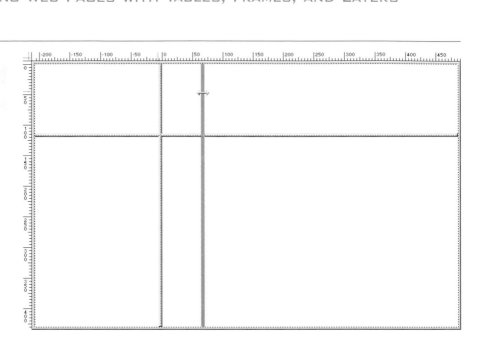

links in your frame, make sure they're visible at all times, or no one will follow them, not knowing they're there to be clicked!

MODIFYING FRAME OPTIONS

As stated previously, each frame is a page unto itself. This gives you some options for the appearance and function of frames that you don't have over tables or layers. For example, you can apply a background color or image to each frame in your page, making each frame stand out as an individual entity. You can also control the visitor's interaction with your frames, dictating whether the frames have a scroll bar on them and preventing the visitor's resizing the frames.

Frame controls are set through your software's tools for adjusting page and element settings. In Dreamweaver, you'll use the Properties Inspector to adjust such things as frame borders and size, and you'll use the Page Properties dialog box, shown in Figure 12-21, to apply page backgrounds and adjust the colors of text and links. Anything specific to the page can be adjusted for an individual frame. Because each frame is seen as a page on its own, you need only click inside a frame to make it the active frame, and then choose Modify | Page Properties to see current settings and make settings adjustments for the frame.

FIGURE 12-21

You can have a different background, and different text and link colors for each frame on your page.

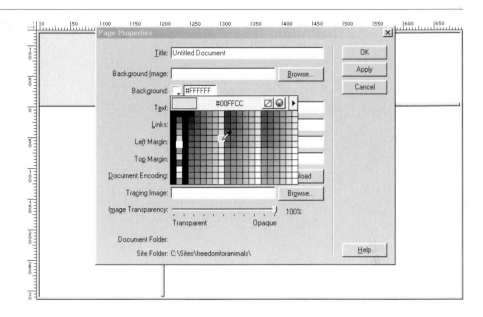

APPLYING BACKGROUND COLOR AND IMAGES

To change the background color or apply an image to a frame background, you need to select the frame in question and employ your software's tools for changing page properties. All the WYSIWYG applications—Dreamweaver, FrontPage, GoLive—offer a Page Properties dialog box through which anything pertaining to the entire page can be adjusted. Browsers see each frame in the frameset as a distinct page, and so each frame's settings must be adjusted individually. You can stick with the defaults, however—white background, black text, browser-dictated link colors, and so on.

While you can stick with the defaults and leave no dynamic sign that your page is made up of separate frames, you can set up a frame with a different background image than the other frames on the same page to make it stand out (see Figure 12-22). When you set your frames up to have no borders, a different background image or color can be the only immediate indication that a frame is in use.

Does it pay to hide the fact that your page is made up of frames? It depends on your reasons for using them in the first place. Frame borders (the primary indicator of frames' existence) can be a negative design element, because they make a page look boxy and structured—a no-no if you want a page that looks rather

FIGURE 12-22

Make a frame stand out by applying a distinct image to its background.

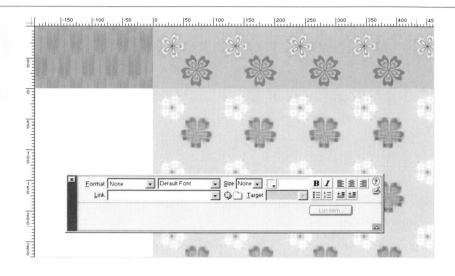

fluid and free-form. The color of borders can also be a problem. Some browsers only display them in gray, others honor your color choices. If gray clashes with your color scheme, frame borders may be something you want to get rid of.

If you're using frames so that you can keep one part of the frame static while another part is scrolled, the scroll bar on the section that's meant to be explored will suffice to let visitors know that one area of the page can be treated differently than the other. If all the frames on your page are large enough to show their entire contents (no scrolling or resizing by the visitor required), you have to ask yourself why you're using frames to begin with.

The only other reason to use frames (if not to allow for scrolling on one area of the page) is to be able to have linked pages (in your site or on another site) appear within a frame. By so doing, you keep your site's information visible (your logo, your phone number, and so on) while visitors visit other pages.

ADJUSTING FRAME BORDER SETTINGS

If you don't want your frame to have borders, or if you want to change the thickness or color of the borders you have, you'll want to add or edit the appropriate attribute to your frame tags, as shown next, or use your software's frame properties tools to adjust the size and color of frame borders.

> **TIP** When using a WYSIWYG application to design your page, note that a frame border width of 0 will result in no visible border.

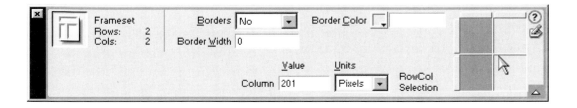

PREVENTING VISITOR MEDDLING

By default, site visitors can resize your frames. I know, isn't that awful? Some interloper, messing with your page layout. The nerve! Don't worry, though, because you don't have to let them meddle with your frame sizes. You can designate one or more (or all) of your frames as "noresize," which means the visitor won't be able to drag your frame borders and resize the frames. You can apply this setting through HTML code (add the word "noresize" to the `<frame>` tag), as shown here:

```
<frameset rows="116,314" cols="201,486" frameborder="NO" border="0"
framespacing="0">
  <frame src="/UntitledFrame-7.htm">
  <frame src="/UntitledFrame-8.htm" frameborder="NO" noresize>
  <frame src="/UntitledFrame-9.htm" frameborder="NO">
  <frame src="/Untitled-5.htm" frameborder="NO">
</frameset>
```

If you're using Dreamweaver, FrontPage, or GoLive (or any other WYSIWYG application) to develop your pages, you can issue a "no resize" command for an active frame, and the aforementioned attribute will be added to the HTML for you. In Dreamweaver, if you click inside a frame, the Properties Inspector shows frame options, one of which is a No Resize check box. As shown here, if you click to place a check in the box, the frame can no longer be resized.

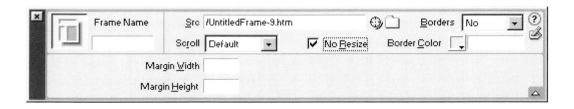

SETTING SCROLL OPTIONS

If left to its own devices, a frame will display a scroll bar if the content you place inside it (text and/or graphics) exceeds the size of the frame. If the content fits entirely within the frame's confines, no scroll bar will appear. This default is usually fine, but sometimes you want to exert more control. Perhaps you want a scroll bar to appear all the time, even if the frame content doesn't require it, or maybe you don't want a scroll bar at all, no matter what. Some reasons to control scrolling:

▶ A given frame's content changes from month to month (or week to week, whatever your update schedule is). In cases where someone else is doing the content update, you want to be sure the frame is scrollable should the new month's content be longer than last month's. Imagine a newsletter or online bulletin board with postings that a variety of people update to the site. You don't want to remove scrolling for one week (when it's not needed) and have someone forget to turn scrolling back on when content requires it.

▶ You want to hide something low on the page. Some people like a counter on their site to show off their traffic. Some people don't like to show off, or perhaps traffic is light, and the number on the counter isn't terribly impressive. A neat trick is to tuck the counter way down on the home page, many blank lines below the last of the legitimate page content. Visitors don't scroll down because there's no reason to (their browser window will have a scroll bar regardless of the frames' scroll settings) as far as they can see. If your frames have their own scroll bars, however, visitors will think there's something there to scroll down to and may discover your "hidden" counter. By turning off scrolling (for frames where you always size the frame to match the content), you prevent visitors nosing around where they're not wanted.

To control scrolling, you can add one of the following attributes to the `<frame>` tag:

▶ `scroll="YES"` This will result in a scroll bar at all times, no matter how big the frame is in relation to its content.

▶ `scroll="NO"` No matter what, the frame won't display a scroll bar.

▶ `scroll="AUTO"` This setting means that if content exceeds the frame's dimensions, a scroll bar will appear.

If you don't insert any scroll attribute, the frame will operate as though the AUTO option is in place—a scroll bar will appear whenever needed. This illustration shows the scroll attribute in a `<frame>` tag:

```
<frameset rows="116,314" cols="201,486" frameborder="NO" border="0"
framespacing="0">
  <frame src="/UntitledFrame-7.htm">
  <frame src="/UntitledFrame-8.htm" frameborder="NO" noresize>
  <frame src="/UntitledFrame-9.htm" frameborder="NO" noresize scrolling="YES">
  <frame src="/Untitled-5.htm" frameborder="NO">
</frameset>
```

As in the case with resizing, WYSIWYG applications make it easy to turn scrolling on or off, or leave the scrolling set to AUTO. In Adobe GoLive, a Frame Inspector (which appears when you click in a frame) has a Scrolling drop-down list, from which you can choose No, Yes, or Auto, as shown in this illustration.

CONTROLLING LINK EFFECTS

One of the best reasons to use frames is to control what happens to your page (the page the visitor is on) when a link is clicked. If the link leads to a page in someone else's site, frames allow you to keep your important information onscreen while the other site's page is viewed. As shown in Figure 12-23, you can keep your organization's logo, key navigation buttons, and other pertinent information onscreen while the visitor checks out another Web page within the large center frame. Controlling where linked pages appear is known as controlling the *target*.

By default, when someone clicks a link on your page, the window changes to display the linked page. Your target alternatives are:

▶ **_blank** When a link to another page is clicked, the new page is displayed in a new window on top of the current window. When the visitor is finished, they can close the new window, returning to yours because yours is back on top.

FIGURE 12-23

Put another person's site in its place—within your site!

▶ **_parent** If the frame containing the link is nested inside another frame, the parent frame (the frame containing the nested frame) houses the linked page. If the frame isn't nested, the linked page opens in place of your frames page.

▶ **_self** This is the default, so if you like what it does, there's no need to specify this. The _self attribute tells the browser to load the linked page within the frame that contained the link. This is the one that allows your other frames to remain onscreen even if a link within another frame is clicked.

▶ **_top** The linked page opens in an additional window on top of your frames page. When the visitor is finished with the linked page, he or she can close that window and will be returned to your page which has returned to the top of the "stack" of open windows.

▶ **mainFrame** If you want the linked page to open in the main frame (the one containing all the other frames on your page), pick this option.

▶ **leftFrame, topFrame, rightFrame, bottomFrame** These options appear singly or in combination, depending on your frames' configuration. For example, if your link is in the frame on the right side of the page and there is a frame to the left and above, rightFrame and topFrame will appear in the list of target options.

If you want to add the target choice to your HTML code manually, you add it to the `<a href>` tag that indicates a hyperlink in your page. As shown next, the attribute is target="*option*", where *option* represents the target you want to set for the link in question.

```
<div align="left"><a href="www.yahoo.com" target="_top"><img src="/yahoo.jpg"
width="800" height="600" border="0"></a>
</div>
```

WORKING WITH LAYERS

Layers are the free spirits of Web page layout. You can place a layer anywhere on the page, even on top of other page elements. Layers can overlap each other, and they can be animated so that when a page is loaded (or some other event occurs, such as a mouse click), the layers move around on the page.

Inserting a layer through WYSIWYG software is almost criminally easy, making it all the more tragic that older browsers don't recognize layers at all. If your audience consists of a lot of people with older computers and/or software, you might not be able to use layers, or you may have to design a less creative page for non-layer users, squirreling the nonlayer content under the layers that the rest of us can see.

Layers can contain anything you want—text, graphics, tables, even other layers. Unlike frames, layers are not viewed as pages, so you can't apply a background graphic. You can apply a colored fill, however, or insert a graphic and size it to fill the layer so that it looks like a background graphic.

Why use layers if they aren't older (pre-4.0) browser friendly? Because of the layout freedom they give you. You can place anything anywhere, unbound by the grid structure of a table or the location limitations of frames. You can create a layout that mimics a photograph or schematic, with page elements placed freely on the page wherever content appears in the picture or blue-print. This makes it possible, for example, to set up a page layout that looks just like the floor plan

TIP Dreamweaver allows you to place a *tracing image* on the page—a graphic that you can size to fit in part of the page or fill the page entirely. The graphic doesn't show when the page is previewed through a browser or viewed online. You can use the tracing image to help you position layers and their content, and leave it in place (to assist in future editing), or remove it after the page layout is set up. To apply a tracing image, choose Modify | Page Properties and insert the path and filename of the graphic you wish to use. Once in place, use the View | Tracing Image submenu to size and position the image.

for an office or a convention. You can place layers where each office or booth will be placed, and the layer can contain information pertaining to the object in the picture/schematic in the same spot.

INSERTING LAYERS

As I said, inserting layers is very simple. You can draw them with your mouse (as though you were drawing a rectangle in a graphics application) or insert a default-sized layer on the page at the cursor. Specifically, use any of the following application-specific methods to add a layer through your WYSIWYG application:

▶ In Adobe GoLive, click to place your cursor on the page where the layer should appear. In the palette (see Figure 12-24), click and drag the Floating Box icon onto your page and release the mouse. A layer appears, awaiting content.

▶ In Dreamweaver, choose Insert | Layer. A layer appears wherever your cursor is at the time you gave the command.

▶ Also in Dreamweaver, use the Objects Panel and click the Draw Layer button (as shown in Figure 12-25). After clicking the button, move your mouse onto the page (it appears as a crosshair), and drag to draw a layer the height and width you need.

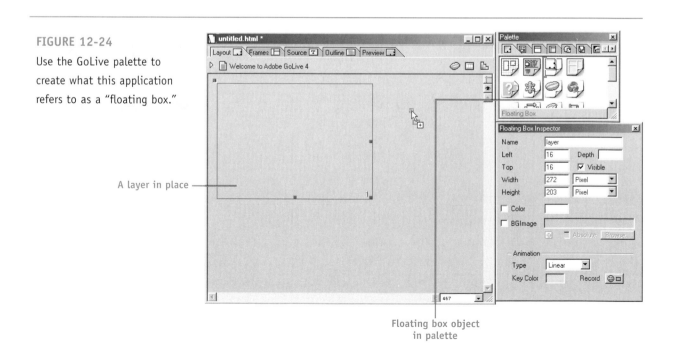

FIGURE 12-24

Use the GoLive palette to create what this application refers to as a "floating box."

A layer in place

Floating box object
in palette

FIGURE 12-25

Draw a layer with your mouse, making it any size you want, anywhere you want.

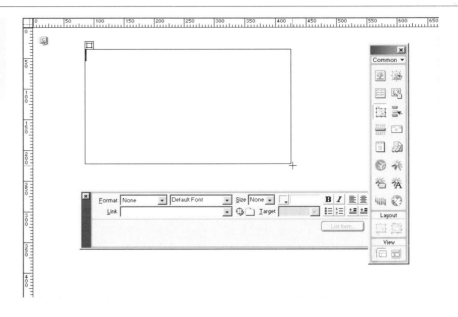

▶ FrontPage deals with layers a little differently. You can draw individual table cells on the page, and the cells can be filled with color, text, and graphics. You can't move them, and they can't overlap. Essentially, they aren't layers. Why is this? Because FrontPage is part of the Office suite, and for the sake of cohesiveness, the table insertion and formatting tools that exist in Word and PowerPoint are repeated in FrontPage so that the skills you use in one application are more easily applied in another. Figure 12-26 shows a single cell being drawn in FrontPage.

> **TIP** It's much easier to use a WYSIWYG application to create and manipulate layers than to do it through manually created HTML code. If you like the control that working in HTML gives you, create the layer in the WYSIWYG tool and then switch to the Code view of your page to make changes to the `<layer>` tag and attributes.

FORMATTING LAYERS

Layers can have a solid color fill, and you can control their stacking order, which is important if your layers overlap. Your WYSIWYG application will present the right tools for altering your layers' format whenever a layer is selected. As shown here, Dreamweaver displays layer-related tools in the Properties Inspector, including the

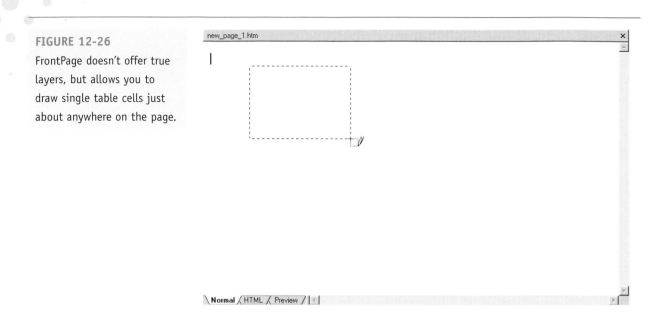

FIGURE 12-26
FrontPage doesn't offer true layers, but allows you to draw single table cells just about anywhere on the page.

Bg Color color well, and a Z-index option. The Z-index of a layer is its order in a stack, and the higher the number, the higher in the stack that layer will appear if layers overlap.

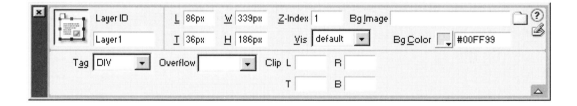

The same design rules apply to layer color and content as you'd use in designing a table or frame. Use colors that don't clash and that allow graphics and text to stand on their own and be noticed. If you're stacking layers, remember that layers are see-through by default. You can use this to your advantage, allowing a transparent layer to overlap a layer that has a colored fill—the result is a partially filled layer on top, as shown in Figure 12-27.

MOVING AND RESIZING LAYERS

Moving and resizing a layer is so simple it almost doesn't require any coverage here. In Dreamweaver, which is the most layer-friendly of the WYSIWYG applications, simply click the layer's tab and drag the layer (your mouse will appear as a four-

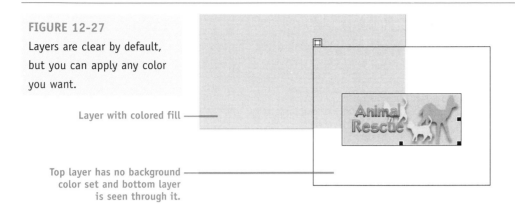

FIGURE 12-27

Layers are clear by default, but you can apply any color you want.

Layer with colored fill

Top layer has no background color set and bottom layer is seen through it.

LAYERS: LEEWAY AND LIMITATIONS How do you want to handle layer content that doesn't fit within the layer? You can use the Overflow option in the Dreamweaver Properties Inspector. GoLive doesn't allow layers to be smaller than the content you place inside them—if the layer contains three paragraphs of text, it can be resized to a different width and height, but you'll be limited in terms of reducing the layer size. Dreamweaver, on the other hand, allows you to designate a scroll bar for layers that will have more content than can be seen in the layer's current size, and to apply margins that hide portions of the layer content. Click inside a layer and observe the Clip settings for L (left), R (right), T (top), and B (bottom). Enter pixel depths for one or more of these sides of the layer, and that portion of the content will be hidden along the selected edge.

headed arrow) to any desired spot on the page. If you want to make it larger or smaller, drag the handles—a corner handle to keep current proportions for width and height, or a side handle to change the height or width alone. Figure 12-28 shows a layer being resized in Dreamweaver.

TIP GoLive won't let you drag layers around on the page—you have to enter new pixel locations for the left side and top of the layer. Use the Floating Box Inspector's Left and Top boxes to enter the coordinates for your selected layer.

ANIMATING LAYERS

Again, we turn to Dreamweaver to demonstrate this feature, because Dreamweaver generates the JavaScript required to move a layer from point A to point B on the page, and to associate the movement with an event such as a mouse click or the

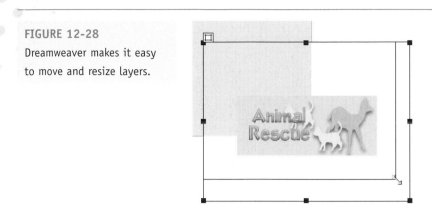

FIGURE 12-28
Dreamweaver makes it easy
to move and resize layers.

loading of the page. Animation of layers can be a nice addition to a page that's not terribly exciting from a visual standpoint or can enhance an already exciting page. Drawbacks? The animation may take some time to happen for visitors on a slow dial-up connection, and if they don't have a current JavaScript plug-in, they'll have to download one. Simple animations are the best choices, such as moving a layer from the left side of the screen to the right, or having a layer move from page top to page bottom, the motion implying some action related to the layer's content. Don't animate layers just for the sake of doing so.

To animate a layer in Dreamweaver, create a layer, and position and size it as you want it to appear prior to the animation occurring. Next, choose Modify | Timeline | Record Path Of Layer. The next and final step is to drag the layer around on the page, following the path that the layer should follow on its own when the animation occurs. A series of dots will appear in your path, as though you're leaving a trail of breadcrumbs, as shown here. The Timelines palette appears onscreen as well (see Figure 12-29), and shows the frames created (think movie frames, not Web page frames) to move the layer from its starting position to the last location in its path.

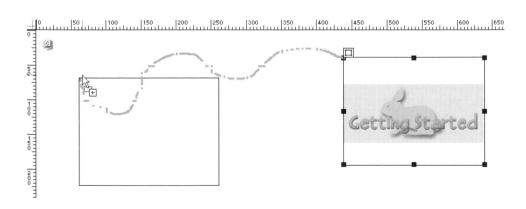

FIGURE 12-29

The Timelines palette shows you the process of moving the layer, gives you animation speed options, and indicates how often the animation will occur.

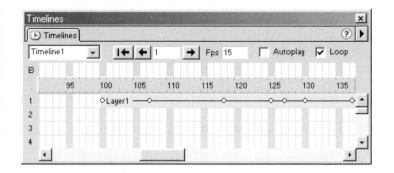

You can change the number of frames in the timeline, and even alter the path the layer takes. Just click on a frame within the Timelines palette, view the position of the layer (it will move to the spot where it would be in that frame), and either delete the frame or move the layer to a new location.

To check your animation, preview the page in a browser (press F12 to see the page displayed in the browser designated as your default). From within the Timelines palette, you can set the animation to loop (play over and over) or to play once by leaving the Loop option off.

TIP If you want your animation to happen faster or slower, adjust the fps (frames per second) setting. The default is 15, which is a good rate for most computers. If you make it too fast (more than 20–25 fps), the animation might look choppy or halting on older computers.

13

Using Multimedia on the Web

As the computer-using public, both at home and at the office, becomes more sophisticated in their use and knowledge of the computer, they start to expect more from their Web experience. While not all sites lend themselves to the use of multimedia, those that do can be "expected" to include some sound and animation if only to keep things entertaining. This chapter will help you decide if your site will benefit from multimedia, and if you feel it will, what to use and how it all works.

JUST WHAT IS MULTIMEDIA, ANYWAY?

Literally, the term *multimedia* means more than one type of media, and *media* refers to forms of expression or methods of communication. If your Web site consists solely of static text and images, that's one form of media, much like a magazine or newspaper. If you have sound and/or movies playing or playable from your site, you have more than one form of media going on, and are thus considered to have multimedia.

Should you use multimedia? The often annoying answer, "Well, that depends," is all-too appropriate here. Some sites really benefit from some sound or movies happening. Sites that pertain to entertainment are certainly good candidates. Does your site sell the services of a disc jockey or singing telegram service? Sound would probably be a good idea. Does your site serve as the repository for all information pertaining to a particular celebrity or famous movie? Songs and movie clips relevant to your topic will be enjoyed by those people who visit your site. Does your site strive to inform, to educate, to inspire? Pertinent videos, playing automatically at your site or playable by interested visitors, can help make a point that text and still images sometimes can't.

On the other hand, if you're a stockbroker, dermatologist, or landscaper (just some random examples), the need for sound and movies is limited, if not nonexistent. If people should see you or your organization as conservative and no-nonsense, skip the distraction of sound and video when it doesn't inform visitors of something important. If your site has movies, they should be of the documentary variety, something that informs in a way text can't. You'll want to use the same criteria in choosing media for your site that you would in choosing colors. If bright, exciting colors aren't appropriate, music probably isn't, either. While it might be amusing for a dentist's site to have "dentist's office music" playing, it could make site visitors (potential patients) think you're not responsible and serious. If, on the other hand, you're a dentist specializing in the treatment of children's teeth, some fun music might give the desired impression that a visit to you will be a stress-free, kid-friendly experience. See how "it depends" is really the only answer to the questions about using or not using multimedia?

Beyond the appropriateness of multimedia, you have some technical considerations to keep in mind—things that might prevent your visitors from appreciating your multimedia goings-on. If your site's effectiveness hinges on someone hearing a song or watching an animation or movie, it's important to consider whether all of your visitors' computers can play the sounds and movies, and whether their Internet connections are adequate to download the multimedia files quickly. A slow download and poor sound or visual quality will torpedo your site's effectiveness every time.

UNDERSTANDING PLUG-INS

When a visitor to your site does whatever it is that triggers your sound or movie to play, the success or failure of the sound or movie is determined by a *plug-in*. A plug-in is an extension, a software addition, that allows the visitor's computer to run the multimedia file you've added to your site. If your site includes a Flash or Shockwave movie, visitors must have that plug-in in order to play the movie. Many sound file formats also require special plug-ins—simple WAV files don't, because Windows has the requisite tools to play WAV files on its own.

You can supply the plug-in through your site or provide links for the visitor to follow to download the plug-in. You can add a plug-in check to your site's HTML code, which will alert visitors if they don't have the plug-in, and automatically take them to a site where the plug-in can be downloaded. If you don't add this sort of alert and URL to the plug-in source, the visitor will simply see a prompt that the sound or movie cannot be played. The onus is then on the visitor to go seek out the plug-in (assuming he or she knows to do so), download it, and then come back to your site. You don't need to be a psychic to guess how many visitors will do so—very few or none of them. If you make the plug-in acquisition process easy by providing a link to where the plug-in can be found, people will generally comply and go through with the download, assuming that they (1) are interested in seeing the movie or hearing the sound your site offers, and/or (2) realize that having the plug-in will help them at other sites using the same kinds of multimedia files, so acquiring it to facilitate visiting your site has future benefit.

There are four ways to handle the whole plug-in situation:

▶ Avoid it entirely by not using anything other than simple WAV sound files, because anyone with Windows can play WAV files with no special software.

▶ Avoid it by offering a "Skip the movie" or "Don't play the music" link that takes visitors to a multimedia-free version of your page.

▶ Insert a plug-in check into your page's HTML code (using JavaScript) that determines if the visitor has the plug-in, and if not, takes them to a URL you specify where the plug-in can be downloaded.

▶ Offer a link within your site to the plug-in file (stored on your Web server) so the visitor can download it from within your site and then play the sound or movie.

The first two options require no further explanation—you're avoiding a potential problem by not including any page content that a visitor won't be able to see or hear. The latter two require you to add some extra elements to the pages in your site that contain multimedia.

The plug-in check is done through JavaScript, and a WYSIWYG design application such as Dreamweaver will create the code for you and add it to your page. All you have to do is click on the object on your page (in the Dreamweaver workspace) and open the Behaviors panel. As shown here in the list of Behaviors (click the plus sign to see the list), Check Plugin is one of the options. If you choose it, a dialog box appears (see Figure 13-1), through which you can choose the plug-in to check for, and which Web site the visitor should be sent to get it if the plug-in isn't found on his or her computer.

This Check Plugin process adds JavaScript to your page's HTML code, as shown in Figures 13-2 and 13-3. Unless you know JavaScript, you probably want to let Dreamweaver do this little bit of work for you.

The last option for handling plug-ins is to provide a link to the plug-in at your site. This requires your having the plug-in files stored on your Web server, and a link to the files from the page containing your multimedia objects. You want to call visitors' attention to the link in some way so they'll click it—no sense being subtle about it. You've probably gone to sites that have some text or even a graphic that states, "If you don't see the movie playing, click here to download the necessary software."

FIGURE 13-1

Customize the Check Plugin process.

```
Check Plugin                                              [X]

        Plugin:  (•) Select:  [Flash            ▼]          [  OK  ]

                 ( ) Enter:   [                 ]          [ Cancel ]

                                                          [  Help  ]
    If Found, Go To URL: [                ]  [Browse...] (optional)

    Otherwise, Go To URL: [http:/www/macromedia.c]  [Browse...]

                  [ ] Always go to first URL if detection is not
                      possible
```

FIGURE 13-2

The JavaScript appears in two places in your HTML code—at the beginning and around the selected multimedia object.

```
<script language="JavaScript">
<!--
function MM_checkPlugin(plgIn, theURL, altURL, autoGo) { //v4.0
  var ok=false; document.MM_returnValue = false;
  with (navigator) if (appName.indexOf('Microsoft')==-1 || (plugins && plugins.length)) {
    ok=(plugins && plugins[plgIn]);
  } else if (appVersion.indexOf('3.1')==-1) { //not Netscape or Win3.1
    if (plgIn.indexOf("Flash")!=-1 && window.MM_flash!=null) ok=window.MM_flash;
    else if (plgIn.indexOf("Director")!=-1 && window.MM_dir!=null) ok=window.MM_dir;
    else ok=autoGo; }
  if (!ok) theURL=altURL; if (theURL) window.location=theURL;
}
//-->
</script>
```

FIGURE 13-3

See the URL you set for downloading the needed plug-in.

```
<script name="Used by MM_checkPlugin" language="javascript">
<!--
with (navigator) if (appName.indexOf('Microsoft')!=-1 && appVersion.
indexOf('Mac')==-1) document.write(' '+
'<scr'+'ipt language="VBScript">\nOn error resume next\n'+
'MM_dir = IsObject(CreateObject("SWCtl.SWCtl.1"))\n'+
'MM_flash = NOT
IsNull(CreateObject("ShockwaveFlash.ShockwaveFlash"))\n</scr'+'ipt>');
//-->
</script>
```

Don't take all of this to mean that using multimedia is a big problem, a path fraught with difficulty that is best avoided. Not true at all. Every day that goes by, more and more users are downloading plug-ins to fortify their older computers with the "juice" to experience multimedia, and more people are buying new computers that come with the plug-ins already on them for virtually any kind of multimedia file. This means that fewer of your site's visitors will need to worry about downloading a special plug-in to experience your movie or sound. Eventually, the number of people who don't have plug-ins for any kind of movie or sound file will be so small that it won't be useful to continue designing around them.

WORKING WITH SOUND

Sound files can be set to play as soon as someone visits your page or when a particular link is clicked. Most people who use sound set it to play as soon as the page loads, so that the visitor takes a passive role in the multimedia experience—no motivation on the visitor's part is assumed, and none needs to be cultivated.

The process of playing a sound on a Web page requires that JavaScript be added to the page's HTML code. As I said about the Check Plugin feature, if you don't know how to write JavaScript, you will want to use a WYSIWYG tool such as Dreamweaver to choose the sound and set it to play at a desired time (associated with a specific event). Dreamweaver will create the JavaScript for you and insert it where needed in the HTML code. All you have to do is pick the sound file and choose what will trigger its playing, loading the page being the most popular and effective way to go.

The process of adding a sound to your page with Dreamweaver is simple: Just display the Behaviors panel and click the plus sign to display a list of potential behaviors. Choose Play Sound, and the Play Sound dialog box appears, as shown in the following illustration. You can type the path and file name of the sound file that should play, or you can browse to find the file if you're not sure of its name and location.

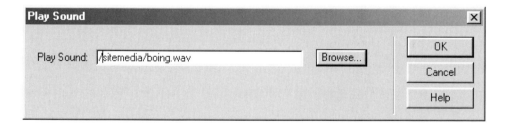

As soon as you pick a sound and click OK to add it to your page, the JavaScript is created. By default, the sound is set to play onLoad, meaning when the page is loaded in the visitor's browser window. If the file is a simple .wav file, the visitor will hear it as soon as the page and the sound file itself are downloaded. For this reason, you want to use small sound files so that the download time isn't so long that the visitor gets bored and moves on before the sound ever plays.

There are other sound file formats, some requiring plug-ins (which many people already will have, just from visiting other sites with the same sound file types in use) and others that are more obscure and require additional software beyond a simple plug-in. Listed below are some popular sound file format choices (in addition to WAV):

▶ MIDI (.mid) files are supported by nearly all browsers and don't require a plug-in. The files tend to be small, so download time is reduced. The sound quality is quite good. The downside to this file type is significant: MIDI files are created with a computer, using special hardware and software. Unlike WAV files, which can be created with a microphone and software that comes with Windows, you can't play a song into your microphone or read a script and save a MIDI-format file.

▶ Even if you're never played one, you've probably heard about MP3 files because their availability online has been in the news for the last year or so. MP3 files are very small, and the sound quality is good. To create them, you need special software, and to play them, you also need special software and a plug-in, such as RealPlayer or the Windows Media Player. Most people have these plug-ins, so this isn't a huge stumbling-block.

▶ RAM, RPM (RealAudio) files create very small files, which is great for Web use. You can stream the files so that the music starts before all the page images are finished loading, which is very convenient. While the sound quality isn't great, it's fine for a page "soundtrack"—mood music while your page is onscreen—so RAM files are quite popular. To record and play them, you need to download and install RealPlayer (go to http://www.realplayer.com/ to get the software).

If your Web page will be offering sound files for download, you can create a link (text or a graphic) on the page that points to the sound file, stored on the Web server. When visitors click the link, a prompt will ask them if they want to open the file or save it to their own local drive. Of course, you only want to add something like this if you're offering music or other sound files on your site for visitors to download, not to get them to open and play the sound so they can hear it while viewing your pages. Also, be careful not to provide links that people can use to download copyrighted material—music, speeches, news clips, and so on—unless you're the person singing, playing, or speaking. You could end up in trouble with the copyright holder, and justifiably so!

USING ANIMATION

Not to be confused with movie files, animations are quick, usually *looping* (repeating) visual effects, similar to the e-mail and "under construction" graphics you've seen at Web sites—an envelope spinning around a globe or a mailbox opening and producing a letter for e-mail animations, and the road sign stick figure hammering the ground in an animation symbolizing the fact that the site is still being built. Animations can add some visual interest to a page, drawing attention to a link that might otherwise go unnoticed, or add some fun, a little frivolity to a page that may be a bit more serious or dull than the designer intended. Figure 13-4 shows an animated image on a Web page. Yes, I know it isn't moving here on the page, but when the animation occurs, the phone's receiver lifts and then the words "Give Us a Call" appear, the animation occurring in three stages. When visitors click the link, they're taken to a page of customer service and other contact phone numbers.

USING ANIMATED GIF FILES

Animated images are a type of GIF file, and like static GIFs, look best when used with images that contain solid colors and lines rather than photographs or drawings with subtle shading and a lot of color gradients. You can turn a photograph into an animation, but the image won't be as clean and clear as it would have been as a static JPG file.

How does a GIF file become an animated GIF? By storing the image as a series of frames (think movies, not Web page frames) and making all of the frames part of the image. For example, you can have an animated GIF that looks like a traffic light—red, green, and yellow circles, flashing in succession. All three circles are part of the graphic, but the graphic contains three layers—one where the red circle is

FIGURE 13-4
Most animations are simply an on/off arrangement between two versions of an image—here, the phone is either on the hook or off, at which point the text appears.

visible (and the green and yellow are not), one where the green circle is visible (and the red and yellow are not), and one where the yellow circle is visible (and the red and green are not)—and each frame of the animation has a different layer visible. When the animated GIF file is saved, the information about which layers are visible and when they appear is stored as part of the file so that when the file is displayed through a browser, the animation takes place.

> **SEE ALSO** Refresh your memory about graphic file formats by reviewing Chapter 10, "Adding Graphic Content."

BUILDING ANIMATIONS

You can create animated GIF files through Adobe ImageReady or Macromedia Fireworks. Both of these applications allow you to build an image as a series of layers and to specify which layers are on and which layers are off in each frame of the animation. The software also allows you to move layer content so that it appears as though the image (or a section thereof) is actually moving on the Web page. Figure 13-5 shows the aforementioned traffic light image being built in

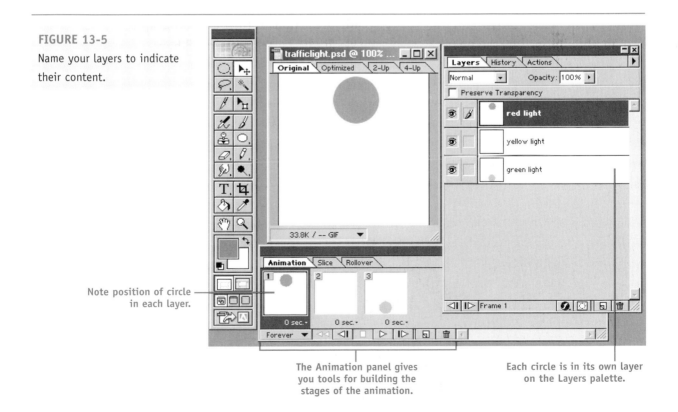

FIGURE 13-5
Name your layers to indicate their content.

Note position of circle in each layer.

The Animation panel gives you tools for building the stages of the animation.

Each circle is in its own layer on the Layers palette.

Adobe ImageReady. Note that there is one layer for each of the circles so that the "lights" can be animated to turn on and off in a specified order.

If your animation needs to show a more complex motion or effect, you can ask the software to create the intervening frames. For example, as shown in Figure 13-6, you can create an animation that shows a sunrise—the animation starts at night with a full moon, the sun rises, replacing the moon, and the sky brightens from black to blue. You would be responsible for creating the frame that shows night (consisting of a moon layer, a night sky layer, and a ground layer) and the frame that shows day (consisting of a sun layer, a day sky layer, and a ground layer). The frames between these "before and after" frames were created by ImageReady through the Tween command (that is, creating frames be*tween* the existing frames), found in the menu accessed through the triangle on the far right end of the Animation panel. When you choose to create the "tween" frames, you can specify how many, and whether they appear before or after the active frame, as shown in Figure 13-7.

FIGURE 13-6

Six layers (three for day, three for night) turn into an animation that shows night becoming day.

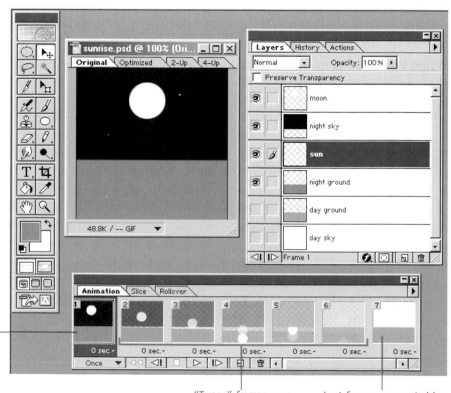

First frame was created by turning the first three layers on and the last three off.

"Tween" frames were created by the software.

Last frame was created by turning the last three layers on and the first three off.

FIGURE 13-7

Choose Tween from the Animation menu and tell ImageReady how many frames to create.

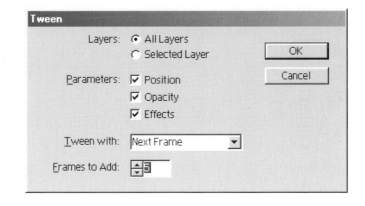

ADDING AN ANIMATION TO YOUR PAGE

The good news is that despite all the steps involved in creating an animated GIF, there are no extra steps involved in adding one to your page—you insert it just as you would a static GIF or any other image. Simply click on the page, in the layer, in the table cell, or in the frame where the image should go, and use your WYSIWIG application's command for inserting a graphic. If you're working in HTML code, simply insert an `<img src>` tag and identify the path and filename of the GIF you want to add.

When you view your page through a WYSIWYG application, it won't move—you have to preview the page through a browser to see the animation happen. If you don't like something about the animation, such as the speed at which the animation occurs or the fact that it loops (happens over and over) or doesn't loop (happens only once), you can return to ImageReady or Fireworks—whichever application you used to create the GIF—and adjust the timing and loop settings. As shown here, you can use the ImageReady Animation panel to adjust the loop setting, choosing between Once, Forever, or some number of repetitions.

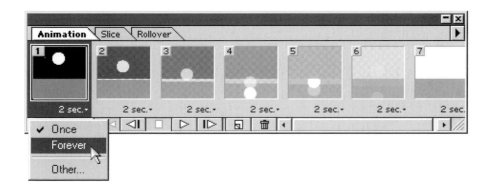

TURNING TWO IMAGES INTO A SINGLE ROLLOVER GRAPHIC

Another type of animation effect you can add to your Web pages is a *rollover*. A rollover is a set of two images that swap when someone rolls over an image with his or her mouse. You can create rollovers directly through the WYSIWYG applications by specifying the image that should appear when the visitor's mouse is not on the image, and then choosing the image that should appear when the mouse is on the image. Rollovers are most often used with images that serve as a link to another Web page or a file, but they can be used to add motion to the page that responds to a visitor simply moving the mouse around. Figure 13-8 shows the first image (the one that appears when no one is mousing over it) on the left, and the second image (the one that appears when the visitor points to the first image with the mouse) on the right.

Using Dreamweaver as an example, the process of creating a rollover is quite simple. It requires that both images exist before you go to set up the effect, but other than that, no preparation is needed. After choosing Insert | Interactive Image | Rollover Image, the Insert Rollover Image dialog box appears, as shown in Figure 13-9.

> **TIP** If you're setting up a rollover that will serve as a link, be sure that the first image is the one that tells the visitor to click the image, using text that's part of the image or using a picture that indicates that the image is a link.

As with an animation, you can't see the rollover effect until you preview the page in a browser. To test it, open the page in Internet Explorer or Netscape, and point to the image. It should change from the first image to the second, and when you move your mouse away, it should revert to the first image again.

FIGURE 13-8

The first and second images can be virtually identical—except for a change in drop shadow or the color of the image.

FIGURE 13-9

Choose your two images and, if they should link to another page, enter the URL.

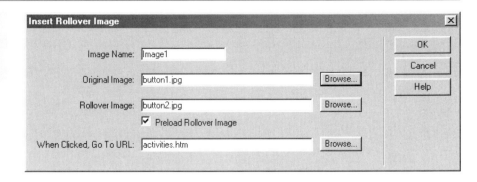

WORKING WITH MOVIES

Movies, created in applications like Macromedia Flash, are only integral to your Web page design if they're viewed as part of the page as soon as it loads. If the movie is activated by a link on the page, and run in a separate window that appears after the link to the movie file is clicked, only the link is part of the page design. You can design a Web page in Macromedia Flash, creating a page that's a movie unto itself, but that's a whole different ballgame. Flash pages take a long time to load for visitors using a dial-up connection to the Internet. While the concepts of good composition and color that I've discussed in this book can and should be applied to them, all other bets are off, because the use of structural devices and methods for inserting and formatting text and graphics are all different, adhering to the commands and features found in the Flash application.

For the purposes of this book, and for the vast majority of Web pages, Flash and other format movies are elements that provide (from a design perspective) a moving graphic on part of the page or are activated when visitors click a link to indicate that they want to see the movie. The only design element involved is the link that activates the download of the movie file. In either case, the visitor will also need a plug-in for the movie, and as discussed earlier in this chapter, you can add a plug-in check to your HTML code so the user is taken to the right place to download the necessary plug-in.

As shown next, you can offer visitors the choice to watch the movie through a text or graphic link. It's

> **TIP** How do you know how long it will take to download the movie? You can benchmark it yourself, by loading the movie (if it's a movie people will download) or loading the page that contains the movie. Try dialing in at 28.8 Kbps, and 56.6 Kbps, and note the number of seconds it takes before the movie is running onscreen.

a good idea to provide visitors with some idea as to the content of the movie and let them know how long it might take to download so they can make an educated decision about viewing it. And don't underestimate the download time because you think people won't wait—people appreciate the truth, and if they really want to watch the movie, they'll be willing to wait for it.

ADDING FLASH AND SHOCKWAVE MOVIES

If the movie will be running on the page from the time the page loads, you can insert it similarly to the way you insert a graphic—the procedure for the insertion varies between applications. In Dreamweaver, you can use the Objects panel and click the Insert Flash or Insert Shockwave (another Macromedia movie format) button. Either button opens the Select File dialog box, from which you select the movie file that you want to add to the page. The dimensions of the movie canvas will determine the amount of space that the movie takes up on the page.

Like an animated GIF, the movie won't play in your WYSIWYG workspace—you'll have to preview the page to see the movie play. One exception is Dreamweaver, which offers a Play button in the Properties Inspector, available when the movie placeholder (shown here) is selected.

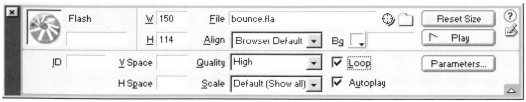

CONTROLLING MOVIE ACTIVATION AND TIMING

Most of the movie's settings—frames per second, the size of the movie canvas, and the order of the movie's frames—are controlled through Flash or whatever application was used to create the movie. Your WYSIWYG application offers some control, such as the looping, automatic play, and quality settings seen in the Dreamweaver Properties Inspector in the previous illustration.

OFFERING MOVIE FILES FOR DOWNLOAD

If you want visitors to click a link and download your movie for viewing in a separate window now (or later, at their leisure), create a text or graphic link that points to the movie file. Like the tools for downloading sound files discussed earlier in this chapter, the link, when clicked, will open a dialog box that allows visitors to download the file. They can choose to open it immediately or save it to their local drive.

STOP! LOOK! LISTEN! (OR NOT) Movies can be a wonderful addition to your page. They're eye-catching, they make a more "high-tech" impression than a static page (assuming the movie quality is good), and they make the page more interesting. On the other hand, with most people connecting to the Web via modem, the time it takes to load a page that contains a movie can be prohibitive. Visitors are likely to get bored and move on, or if they actually wait for the page to load, they're annoyed and this can adversely affect their reaction to your page and their willingness to buy what you're selling or read what you have to say. When it comes to using movies, keep the files small (this is done through the movie-production software, such as Macromedia Flash or Adobe LiveMotion). Consider offering a link on the page that allows visitors to skip the movie if they don't want to wait for it. Visitors who've been to your site before may not want to watch the movie again, and new visitors who are on 28.8 modems might be unwilling to wait several minutes just to see your page.

14

Creating Hyperlinks to Connect Pages and Sites

Without hyperlinks, what would the Web be? Not much.

Links are what give Web sites depth. The ability to hop from

page to page or site to site is what makes us sit for hours

in front of a computer screen, combing through "dot-coms"

until the wee hours. Links on Web pages are the ultimate "See

Also..." that we've all used in an encyclopedia or dictionary.

One term or concept invites exploration of another. The Web is

very much like an encyclopedia, packed with information and

ideas, most of it related in one way or another, if only by virtue of the fact that someone might be interested in seeing or reading about it. In this chapter, you'll learn to turn text and graphics into hyperlinks, to control how the linked content appears, and to connect your site visitors to files for download. You'll also learn to create links that open e-mail message windows, pre-addressed to the recipient of your choice.

UNDERSTANDING THE ROLE OF LINKS

Links make connections, between pages in a site and to pages in other sites. They also connect site visitors to files that can be downloaded or played (sounds and movies), and to e-mail so that visitors can make contact with a site's owner or contributor.

Your links can be set up as you build your pages, or you can go back to your finished pages (finished in terms of the design and content) and turn text and graphics into links. Links can be made from text—single characters, whole words, phrases, or sentences—and graphics. When it comes to graphic links, you can turn the entire image into a single link or map out sections of the image into *hotspots*, geometric shapes drawn on top of an image that are assigned to individual links. If you've ever gone to a Web site that asked you to click on a section of a map to indicate where you were or the region in which you were interested, you've used hotspots—sections of the map cordoned off so that a single graphic can be linked to several different files or pages.

SITE NAVIGATIONAL LINKS

One of the most important roles of links in your sites is to help visitors move around in the site itself, going from page to page and back again. While these navigational links are set up like any other link, their purpose is essential to the effectiveness of your site's pages. Navigational links should be easy to spot and should be in the same place on virtually all the pages in your site. Why? As discussed in the chapters of this book pertaining to composition and how repetition and consistency play a major role in good design, you don't want visitors scanning each page wondering where the button that takes them back to the home page is. You don't want to distract them from the information your site is sharing by making it hard to find their way around.

When you set up links to pages within your site, it's helpful to use your WYSI-WYG software's site creation and maintenance tools. Site management is one of the most important and labor-saving features any WYSIWYG application offers. One of the areas where it will save you serious time is in setting up links and keeping them intact as you rename and move pages, add new links, and update your page content. As shown in Figures 14-1 and 14-2, both FrontPage and Dreamweaver offer site management views of your linked pages.

Site maintenance is very simple if you let the software do most of the work. Aside from establishing which page will be your home page (typically the first page you design, although you can work around it and design subpages first), all you have to do is set up the links between your pages and the hierarchy of your site, and its pages will build itself by virtue of those links. The way you insert navigational links varies by application. FrontPage offers direct menu commands for inserting navigational buttons. The buttons automatically match the site's theme—the background, fonts, and colors you chose for your site from FrontPage's list of Themes—and the text on the buttons is drawn from the names you gave your site's pages. Dreamweaver, on the other hand, tracks any links to pages within the site and sets up page relationships accordingly. Dreamweaver also has a menu command for creating a navigation bar,

FIGURE 14-1

Dreamweaver's site window shows you a list of files on the right, and the "family tree" created by your linked site pages on the left.

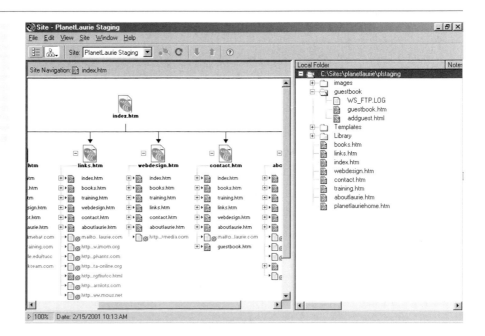

FIGURE 14-2

FrontPage offers a Navigation view of your site, which shows the hierarchical relationship between pages.

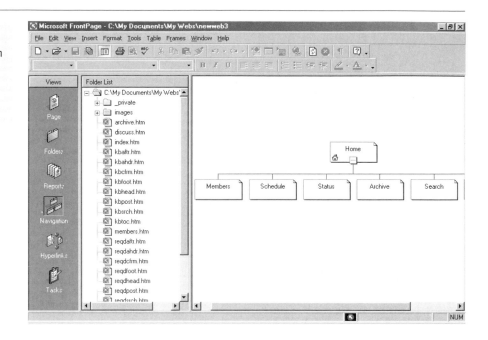

but assumes that designers will be creating or using their own images to serve as the buttons in that bar—there are no predesigned themes in Dreamweaver.

LINKS TO OTHER SITES

When you create a link to a page outside of your site—say, to the site of an organization to which you belong or to a supplier of products your site visitors may use—all you need to know is the correct URL (Web address) of the site to which you're linking. One of the steps in preparing to design a Web site is to gather the Web addresses to which your site will link, and to contact those sites' owners to make sure that it's okay to (1) link to them and (2) get any graphics—logos, photographs, and so on—that will serve as the links. If you're linking to a well-known organization or to an organization with a recognizable logo, it's a good idea to use that image as the link to that organization's site. As shown in Figure 14-3, if you're linking to Amazon.com because you want

TIP If the site to which your site links is owned by a peer—someone on the same level as you are in your industry, field, or area of interest—you may be able to get him or her to create a link back to your site. By contacting the site's owner and letting him or her know you'll be sending visitors from your site to theirs, you may be able to convince the owner of the merits of adding a link to your site. If your sites aren't direct competitors, and if visitors will benefit from something your site offers, they should be amenable to such an arrangement.

FIGURE 14-3

Take advantage of well-known logos and ubiquitous images by using them as the graphic links from your site to theirs.

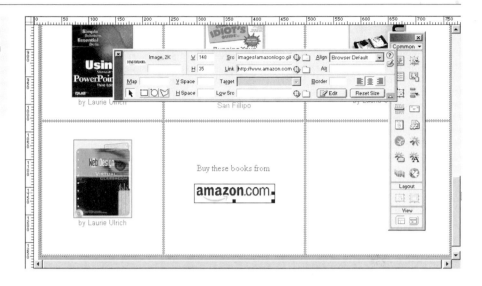

your visitors to buy a particular book, use the Amazon logo as the link to their site. Many sites that sell also have programs through which you can be paid a commission for sales made to people who followed a link from your site. It's worth getting in touch with these organizations before setting up your links to them, if only to find out if such a program exists.

OFFERING DOWNLOADABLE FILES VIA LINKS

If you want people to download or open a file from your site, you can make a link to that file (document, worksheet, sound file, or movie) and when visitors click that link, they'll be prompted to open the file or save it to their local drive. If they're smart, they'll opt to save it, thus protecting themselves from viruses that your document could contain (just as you shouldn't open files from others' Web sites without scanning them with virus software first). It's also the best choice if the file is large; visitors will only spend time saving the file, not loading it and running it at that time. Figure 14-4 shows the dialog box and options offered to a visitor who has clicked a file link.

If the file you're offering requires a plug-in in order to be played (I told you all about plug-ins for sound and movie files in Chapter 13, "Using Multimedia on the Web"), the visitor will be prompted to download it if the plug-in isn't found on his or her computer. If the file is a simple document of some kind—such as a

FIGURE 14-4

The default action for any file
is Save This File To Disk.

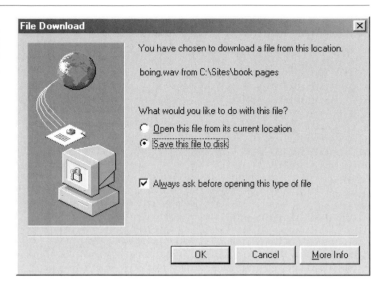

letter, report, or spreadsheet—the visitor can download it and open it in an appropriate application such as Microsoft Word or Excel.

The link to such a file doesn't look different than any other link. You can turn text into a link to a file, or you can use a graphic. The only difference between a file link and a link to a Web page is in the information you provide about where the link should take the visitor. Figure 14-5 shows the HTML code that supports a file link.

CONVERTING TEXT TO A LINK

Enough about the types of links and how they work—you need to know how to create a link in the first place. Starting with text links, which are quite common, you'll find them appearing on a panel down the left or across the top or bottom of a page, or within a paragraph. Generally, two things will indicate text that's set up

FIGURE 14-5

The path to and name of

the file appear within the

`<a href>` tag.

```
<body bgcolor="#FFFFFF" text="#000000">
<a href="/boing.wav">Click Here to Download</a>
</body>
</html>
```

as a link—your cursor will turn into a pointing hand when you point to the link text, and the text itself is underlined. Figure 14-6 shows text links on a page.

The key to setting up text as a link is to select the text and then indicate where that selected text should take the visitor once the link is clicked. If you're using WYSIWYG software to design your pages and set up your links, select the text, and then use the relevant dialog box or palette to indicate where the selected text link points. In the case of FrontPage, you'll click the Insert Hyperlink button on the toolbar, and then use the Edit Hyperlink dialog box (shown in Figure 14-7) to set up the link.

If you're working with Dreamweaver, you can use the Properties Inspector to set up the link for selected text. Either type the link into the Link box, or click the Browse For File button in the Properties Inspector to find the file through the Select File dialog box. Figure 14-8 shows both the Browse For File button and the resulting dialog box.

> **TIP** When you're setting up a link that points to a page outside of your site, be sure to type the http://www. before the Web address. Otherwise, when the page is viewed online, the visitor's browser will search for the page within your site's pages rather than going out to the Web to find the page. If the page is within your site, just put the filename (including the .htm extension) in the Link box, and skip the http://www.

FIGURE 14-6

Underlined text links stand out in paragraph text.

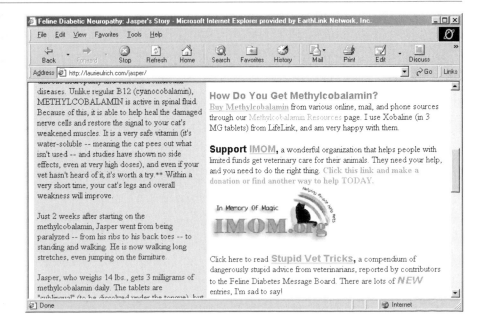

FIGURE 14-7

Enter the Web address or file-name to which your text links.

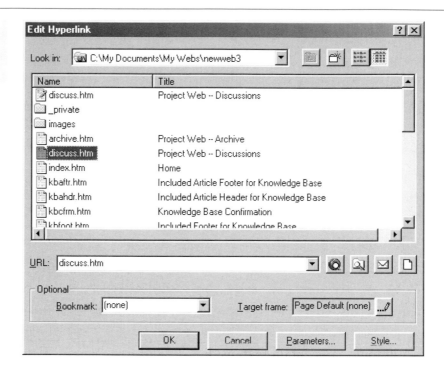

FIGURE 14-8

If you don't know the exact filename or location, browse for it.

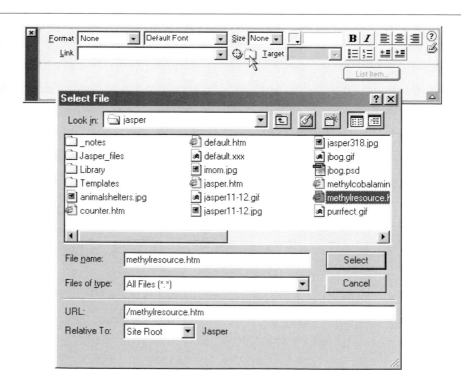

IT'S ALL RELATIVE When you're setting up links to pages within your site, be careful about slashes. If you place a slash (or allow the software to put one in for you) in front of the page filename, you're setting the link up so that the browser software will go to the root directory to find the page. If you remove the slash, the browser will look in the folder containing the active page to find the page to which the link takes you. This is known as a relative link—the page will be sought relative to the location of the active page. If the slash remains, you're creating an absolute link—telling the browser that no matter where the active page is, go back to the root (represented by the slash) to find the page to which the link points.

CREATING GRAPHIC LINKS

Graphics make good links because pictures are often more interesting than text, and simply because people gravitate toward pictures more immediately than to words. A graphic can contain text, as discussed in Chapter 10, "Adding Graphic Content," and often, if you want to use elaborate fonts or combine text and pictures, you have to use graphic text, as discussed in Chapter 9, "Adding Text Content." So whether your graphics contain text or simply communicate their purpose as links through the content of the image, you can literally make a picture worth a thousand words by using it to connect to another Web page, site, or file.

To turn a graphic into a link, select the graphic onscreen (assuming you're working in a WYSIWYG environment) and observe that the graphic has handles around it, indicating that it's selected. Next, use the software's tools for setting up a link—the Create Hyperlink dialog box in FrontPage, or the Properties Inspector in Dreamweaver. If you're using GoLive, click the New Link button on the toolbar, and then use the Image Inspector's Link tab to set up the link itself. Figure 14-9 shows a selected image on the page and the Image Inspector with a link in progress.

Whatever you're doing in whichever WYSIWYG application you're using, remember that HTML code is being created as you select text and graphics and set up links. Figure 14-10 shows the HTML code created by turning a graphic into a link to Amazon.com. The `<a href>` tag indicates the destination of the link, and the

FIGURE 14-9

All WYSIWYG applications work similarly when it comes to setting up links.

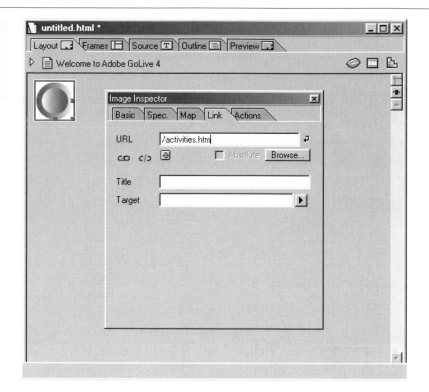

img src= attribute indicates the filename and location of the image that's serving as the link.

WORKING WITH MOUSE-OVER EFFECTS

Graphic links can also be set up as interactive images such as rollovers (also known as *mouse-overs*). The key here is to have two images—one that appears when the page loads, and one that is swapped when the visitor points to the original image. In Chapter 13, you learned to create a rollover image by choosing two different images, one for each state that the graphic can be in: no one's pointing to

FIGURE 14-10

Selecting a graphic and setting up the URL to which it points creates the code your browser will use in making the link work as expected.

```
<body bgcolor="#FFFFFF" text="#000000">
<a href="http://www.amazon.com"><img src="images/amazonlogo.gif"
width="148" height="35" border="0"></a>
</body>
</html>
```

it (Image 1), and someone's pointing to it (Image 2). Normally, the only difference between the first and second image is a change in color or the addition or deletion of a drop shadow, giving the impression that the image was physically clicked, like an actual button.

What's useful about rollovers? They draw attention to the link. In a lot of cases, visitors might not know that a given graphic is a link to another page or site. Perhaps the image itself isn't doing a good job of indicating that it's a link—there's no text on it, or the image doesn't relate to the page to which it links—so people don't think to click it. If the visitor doesn't notice his or her mouse pointer turn to a pointing hand, the fact that the image is a link can remain a mystery. If, however, when the visitor mouses over the image, the image changes to something else (or changes color, or seems to sink into the page as though pushed in), the image will have caught the visitor's attention, and the link will be clicked. As shown

here, an image can do two things to make sure people click it: (1) the graphic includes the word "click," and (2) when the rollover effect occurs, the image changes from the way it looks on the left to the way it looks on the right (it looks like someone pushed a button and depressed the image).

SETTING UP HOTSPOTS

As stated earlier in this chapter, hotspots are sections of an image that are mapped out and set up as links to other pages, sites, or files. Rather than turning an entire image into one link to one place, hotspots allow you to take a single image and turn it into several links. Figure 14-11 shows a graphic that includes text, and each of the questions can become a different link.

Hotspots are much easier to set up in a WYSIWYG environment than through HTML code. The resulting HTML code, shown in Figure 14-12, isn't necessarily hard to type or figure out, but the process of drawing the hotspots using drawing tools through an application such as Dreamweaver is much simpler. It also gives you more visual control over the process of establishing hotspot areas and sizes.

Using Dreamweaver for demonstration purposes, the process of creating hotspots couldn't be much easier. To set up hotspots on an image, select the image, and

FIGURE 14-11

A graphic with text and/or a variety of images within it can become a group of hotspot links, each taking the visitor to a different page.

then use any one of the three hotspot drawing tools—the rectangle, circle, or polygon shapes—to draw hotspots on the surface of the image. When you've created a closed shape (as shown here), type the Web address to which the active hotspot will link, or use the Browse To File button to select an address or file to which the hotspot will point.

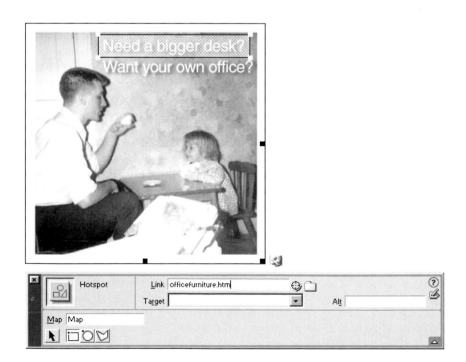

FIGURE 14-12

From the usemap= attribute through the `<area shape>` tags, hotspots create a lot of HTML code.

```
<body bgcolor="#FFFFFF" text="#000000">
<img src="/mewdad.jpg" width="300" height="299" usemap="#Map"
border="0">
<map name="Map">
   <area shape="rect" coords="91,15,285,41" href="ofcfurn.htm">
   <area shape="rect" coords="93,41,287,70"
href="biggerspace.htm">
</map>
</body>
</html>
```

The only thing to be careful of when drawing hotspots is that the image itself makes it clear where one hotspot ends and another begins. A map is a good example of an image that leaves little mystery as to the shapes and logical purpose of the hotspots. Using a map of the United States, each state can be a hotspot, or sections of the country—the northeast, New England, the South—can be mapped out as hotspots. Visitors will know where to click to activate a specific link and know what to expect when the link is clicked (their knowledge will also be based on the topic of and other information provided by the page).

CONTROLLING THE LINK'S RESULT

Whether your link is text, a graphic, or a section of a graphic mapped out as a hotspot, you have some additional options for how the link will work. When your link points to a Web address, you can choose to have the linked page appear in the same window as the page containing the link to that page, in a new window, or in a new window on top of the current window. If your link is within a frame, you can open the linked page within that frame, or within the parent window if your frames are nested (one frame within another frameset). These choices are offered through the Target settings in any WYSIWYG tool's link setup dialog box or Inspector, or by setting a target= attribute in HTML. Figure 14-13 shows the list of target choices as shown in Adobe GoLive, and Figure 14-14 shows the resulting HTML code.

Your target options depend on the location of your link and the makeup of the page containing it. If you're using frames, you have more options than if your link is sitting on a single frameless page:

▶ **_top** The _top target option loads the linked page in place of the active page. To get back to the original page, the visitor will have to use his or her browser's

FIGURE 14-13

Want your linked page to appear in a new window? Choose _blank as the target.

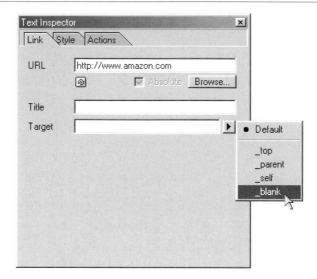

FIGURE 14-14

Don't forget the underscore in front of the target attribute value, as in target="_top".

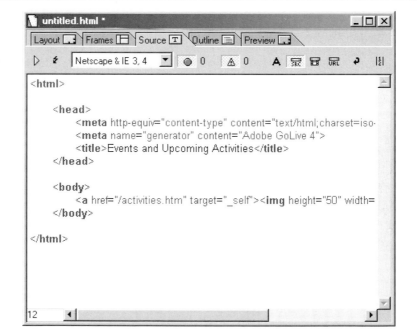

Back button, or if the linked page has navigational buttons pointing back to the previous page, the visitor can use them.

▶ **_parent** The _parent target option is the same as _top if your page has no frames or if the frames on the page are not nested. If the link is in a nested frame, this option will open the link pages inside the parent frame.

▶ **_self** The _self target opens the linked page in the same window as the active page. This is the default target, so if this is the effect you want, don't set a target at all.

▶ **_blank** The _blank target option causes the linked page to open in a new, untitled browser window on top of the window containing the page that contains the link.

When choosing a target, think about how visitors will react. If you choose to have the linked page open in a new browser window, visitors will have to know to close that window when they're finished. The Back button won't work to take them back to the original window that contained the link. If you choose to have the linked page take over the window and replace your page, you can be sending a visitor off to someone else's site, never to return to yours. If you're working with frames, your options are increased, because you can keep your content onscreen in some of the frames, and have the linked page appear in a separate frame on the page.

> **SEE ALSO** Chapter 12, "Structuring Web Pages with Tables, Frames, and Layers," shows you how to build, format, and use frames. The chapter also provides a discussion of the target options for links as they apply specifically to links within frames.

MAKING CONTACT WITH E-MAIL LINKS

One of the most convenient links you can create is an e-mail link. It's convenient for you as the page designer (and perhaps owner) because you can make sure if someone e-mails you from the Web page, the e-mail is addressed to you and addressed properly. If you're the visitor, the e-mail link is convenient because it eliminates the margin for error in terms of opening an e-mail message window and addressing it to the intended recipient.

To set up an e-mail link, first select the text or graphic that will serve as the link. Where you'd normally type a Web address or filename, type **mailto:** followed by the exact e-mail address to which the messages should be sent, such as **laurie@planetlaurie.com** if you want to set up a

> **TIP** If you want your visitor's messages to go to more than one person, type more than one address after the mailto: in the Link box. Separate the addresses with commas (with no spaces between commas and addresses) and the browser and e-mail software on the visitor's computer will do the rest.

link that sends a message to me. Of course, the visitor must click Send in the message window, but the message will be properly addressed (assuming you didn't make a mistake when typing the mailto: information) and should arrive in the appropriate person's e-mail Inbox.

As shown here, the Dreamweaver Properties Inspector allows you to set up mailto: information for an e-mail link. Figure 14-15 shows the resulting Outlook Express message window, the To box already filled in as per the mailto: link setup.

FIGURE 14-15

The recipient information is already in place—the visitor need only fill in a Subject and message, and click Send.

Web Maintenance
and Mastery

Your pages are beautiful, informative, and compelling.
All of your links work. Your graphic images display quickly and
cleanly, and you couldn't be happier with the way your site
turned out. Now what? Well, unless you want to be the only
one admiring your Web design handiwork, it's time to upload
your site to the Web, copying your locally stored Web pages
and graphics to the Web server so that people around the
world can stop by for a visit.

POSTING PAGES TO THE WEB

Although Dreamweaver, FrontPage, and GoLive (the three main WYSIWYG Web design tools I've used to demonstrate concepts throughout this book) all provide tools for uploading to the Web through their user interface, I recommend that you invest in some FTP (File Transfer Protocol) software to use in uploading your pages. Why? Because you don't want to be tied to the application-based FTP tools. What if you need to upload files and the design software isn't working? What if you're loading a stray page that's not part of an established site? The WYSIWYG applications base their FTP process on the uploading of site files, pages that are part of an established site, linked to other pages within that site. If you're designing an ad hoc page that's not technically part of a site, you won't be able to use the application-provided FTP tools, at least not without difficulty.

When I say "invest in" some FTP software, I don't necessarily mean money. There are some great FTP programs that are freeware, meaning you can download and use them at no cost. Some are shareware, meaning that you can download and test them for free, but must buy them (usually at a very low price) when the evaluation period is over. Some of the shareware programs stop working when the evaluation period is over, others keep working indefinitely. In any case, it's stealing if you keep using the shareware without paying for it.

Where do you find these great programs? The Web, of course! You can go to sites like www.hotfiles.com or www.tucows.com and do a search for "FTP software," or simply search through a site like www.google.com or www.yahoo.com and use the same search criteria. The benefit of going through a software distribution site like Tucows is that you can usually get product ratings supplied by people who've downloaded and used the software. Figure A-1 shows the www.tucows.com site and the FTP search criteria entered.

Once you've searched for and found a list of FTP products, pick one and click the link to download it. Normally, you'll be downloading a self-extracting zip file (a compressed file that consists of all the parts of the FTP program) or an installation/setup file that you double-click after the download is complete and the installation process begins automatically. Don't worry that you'll need any special skills to download this software—the installation process is automated. At most, you'll be asked to enter your name and company name and to choose a folder into which

FIGURE A-1
Search for FTP software through a site that offers product ratings and technical support.

the program files should be copied. The questions you're asked will be clear, and you'll see a prompt telling you when the software is installed and ready for use.

USING FTP SOFTWARE

FTP software works by connecting you to an FTP site. This is a repository for files—sort of an electronic file cabinet on the Internet—to which you can upload your Web page files and any graphics, movies, sounds, or other files appearing on or linked to your pages. Files uploaded to an FTP site are then on your Web server, making them visible to anyone who types your Web address through a browser such as Internet Explorer or Netscape.

To connect to an FTP site, you need three things:

▶ **The FTP server name/location** This is a designation such as ftp.*domain*.com, where *domain* is the same as the Web site domain. For example, when I upload files to the server where my planetlaurie.com site is stored, I go to an FTP site named ftp.planetlaurie.com. Remember, the FTP software is just a vehicle for uploading files to your Web server. The server is the actual location of the uploaded files, and the FTP site is the intermediary that accepts the files on behalf of the server.

▶ **A user ID** This is assigned by the person who administers the Web server. If you have your own Web server, you can create user IDs for anyone who needs access to the FTP site. Most user IDs are from four to eight characters long, with no punctuation or spaces.

▶ **A password** The password is associated with the user ID and only works for that ID. This makes it possible for different people to maintain different sites on the same server and/or to maintain different parts of the same site. Passwords should be at least six characters in length, and be something that no one other than the user would know. Security for Web servers is very important, especially if you're tracking visitor data, selling products directly through your Web site, or storing potentially sensitive information in a database that your site accesses.

Once you have these three things, you can set up an FTP location through the FTP software, in preparation for making the actual connection to that FTP site. As shown in Figure A-2, you'll fill out a simple form that contains all the information needed about the FTP site and your connection to it.

After you've set up an FTP location, you can connect to the FTP site. Of course, you must be online (connected to the Internet) before you can do this. Assuming you're online, in most cases you'll simply double-click an icon representing the FTP site you want to connect to, or you'll click once on the site by name and then click a Connect button. Figure A-3 shows a connection being made.

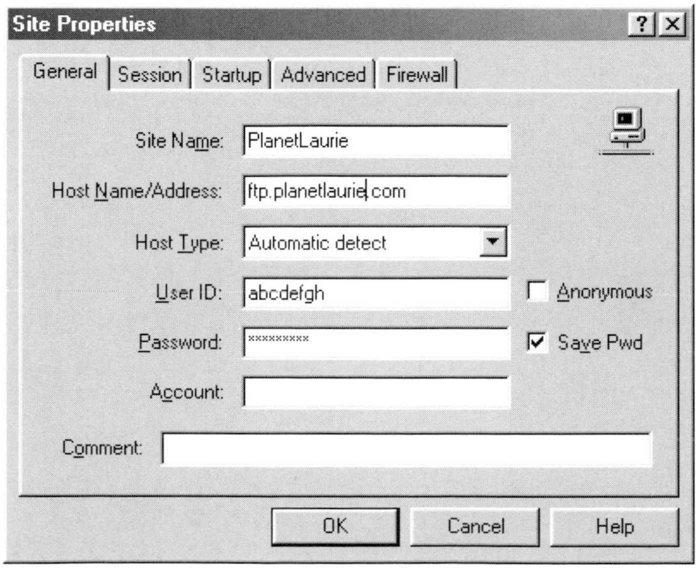

FIGURE A-2

Tell the FTP software all about your intended FTP connection.

FIGURE A-3

Select the site you want to reach and click to connect.

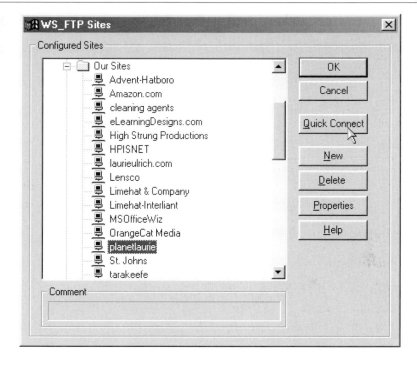

As the connection is being made, you'll see a progress report of sorts—the status of each part of the connection process is documented in the window. When a connection is completed, the word "Connected" or something similar (it varies by application) will appear, and you know you're connected to the FTP site.

Most FTP applications offer a two-sided window. One side displays the folders and files that are on the local hard drive, and the other side displays the folders and files on the FTP site. To use the window, click on files on your local drive and either drag them over to the FTP site side of the window, or click a Copy button to indicate that the selected local files need to be copied to the remote FTP location. Of course, you can also go the other way, copying files from the FTP site down to your local drive. Figure A-4 shows a group of selected Web page files ready for copying to the FTP site.

ORGANIZING YOUR FILES ON THE WEB SERVER

When you upload your files, it's important that you maintain the same folder hierarchy that you had on your local drive. This means that if you had page files in the site's root folder and graphics in an Images folder, you should make sure the page files are in the FTP site root folder and the graphics are in an Images folder on the

FIGURE A-4

Press and hold the CTRL key as you select multiple files to be uploaded.

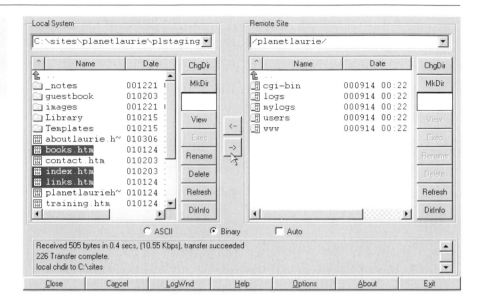

FTP site, too. Why is this important? Because as you created links between your site's pages and to graphic images (so the image would appear on the page when you view the page through a browser), the path to those files was added to the HTML code and saved as part of the HTML file that makes your page. If the files are not in the same relative places on the FTP site, the paths are invalidated, and the browser won't find linked pages and graphics where it's told to look for them.

The process of establishing identical folder hierarchies on both your local drive and FTP site is not complex or difficult. Your FTP software will offer tools for creating folders, so that if you have an Images folder locally, you can create one on the FTP site, too. If you have page files stored in folders by topic, you can create those folders, too. Figure A-5 shows the Windows Explorer view of a site's folders and files. This is the same structure that exists in the view of an FTP site shown in Figure A-6.

There may be extra files or folders on either the local drive or the Web server for a variety of reasons. The key is to make sure that if your page files are in the site root folder on the local drive, they're in the site root folder on the Web server. If you store your pictures in an Images folder on your local drive, be sure you copy them to an Images folder on the Web server. You may have to create the Images folder if it's not already there, although many Web hosting companies set up the servers to already have an Images folder because it's such a common element in their customers' setup.

FIGURE A-5

The site folders as stored on the local drive

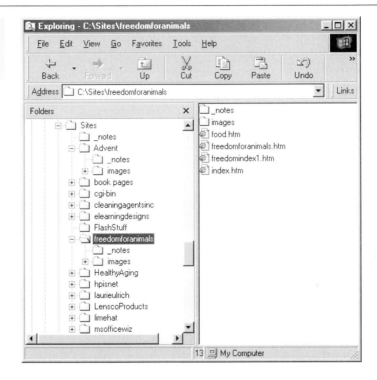

FIGURE A-6

The same structure is repeated on the FTP site.

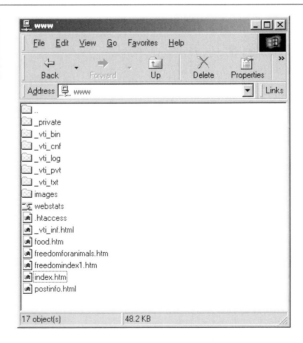

> **TESTING, TESTING, 1-2-3** When I'm designing for myself and for clients, I like to upload the site to a staging area first, a folder off the site's root folder, so the pages can be tested online without making them available to the public. This saves you the embarrassment of displaying to the whole world a page with spelling or factual errors, missing graphics, nonworking links, or other difficulties. You can name the staging folder anything you like, and that way, only psychic visitors will know to type "www.domain.com/testarea/testhome.htm" to get to your home page in the staging area. Once you've tested everything (or allowed the client to view the pages and give you the thumbs up), you can move the files to the domain's root folder so the pages are available to anyone who types the domain name into his or her browser window. Don't forget to rename your home page to index.htm before moving it to the root—otherwise, it won't appear when someone types the domain name.

TESTING YOUR PAGES

Once you've uploaded your files to the Web server via an FTP site, your pages are officially online. You can type the Web address for the site you've designed, and the index.htm (the name of the home page) file will display automatically. If you want to go to another page within the site, type the filename after the domain name, as in www.planetlaurie.com/links, to go to a page called links.htm within my planetlaurie Web site. If you simply type www.planetlaurie.com, you'll go to my home page.

As you were designing your Web pages, you no doubt previewed them in a browser during the design process for each page and after each page was completed. Assuming you didn't upload pages that had any display or functional problems (such as missing graphics or nonworking links), the pages should work properly once they're online. It's important, however, to test them anyway. The testing process gives you the peace of mind of knowing what your visitors will see, how long it will take them to see it (assuming that you're testing the site through a dial-up connection, which most of your visitors will have, rather than through a fast network connection), and whether you successfully uploaded everything you need.

CHECKING LINKS AND GRAPHICS

When you test your site pages, check every link. Even if it worked seamlessly when you tested it locally, test them all again. Go to every page in the site and make sure all the graphics appear where they're supposed to. If you have rollover images on your pages, make sure the images swap properly when you mouse over them. If you have a sound or movie on your page, make sure it plays. Leave no stone unturned. Figure A-7 shows the one thing any designer dreads—a broken graphic link, indicating that a graphic file can't be found by the browser.

> **TIP** When you reload a page after editing it, always click the Refresh or Reload button to make sure that the browser is going back to the server for the latest version of the page, rather than loading the version that's in your computer's memory.

If a link doesn't work, whether it points to a page within your site or to someone else's Web page, the test will result in your ending up either on the wrong page or in the display of the dreaded Error 404 – Page Not Found. Of course, you have no control over someone else's server. There will be times when your links to another person's page don't work because their Web server is down or their page is temporarily unavailable. When this is the case, an entirely different error appears, as shown in Figure A-8. Rarely will a visitor (or your Web design client)

FIGURE A-7

If you spot this when testing your pages, go back and check your page setup for the right image file and location.

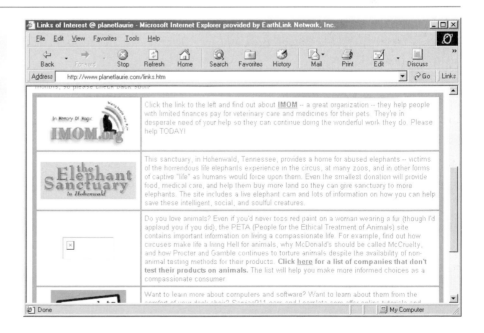

blame you for this error, because it clearly indicates that the problem is with the page to which you're attempting to link.

VIEWING THE PAGES IN MULTIPLE BROWSERS

When you do your site tests, check the appearance and functioning of your pages in both of the main browsers (Internet Explorer and Netscape). If possible, check the pages in multiple versions of both browsers, too. Why? Because there are significant differences between the ways the two browsers deal with page content, most of which have been discussed in this book. You want to know what display glitches your visitors will encounter, and perhaps go back and make some design changes to accommodate a browser's shortcomings.

> **TIP** If you designed the site for someone else, don't skimp on the testing. There's nothing worse than calling or e-mailing your clients to tell them the site is up and running, only to have them call you back to say that something doesn't work. It's bound to happen sometimes, and as nobody is perfect, problems will occur, but you'll want to have checked the pages thoroughly before letting clients know the pages are online.

FIGURE A-8
Most server problems are transient, and if visitors try the link later, they'll get to the desired page with no further difficulty.

ⓘ The page cannot be displayed

The page you are looking for is currently unavailable. The Web site might be experiencing technical difficulties, or you may need to adjust your browser settings.

Please try the following:

- Click the Refresh button, or try again later.
- If you typed the page address in the Address bar, make sure that it is spelled correctly.
- To check your connection settings, click the **Tools** menu, and then click **Internet Options**. On the **Connections** tab, click **Settings**. The settings should match those provided by your local area network (LAN) administrator or Internet service provider (ISP).
- If your Network Administrator has enabled it, Microsoft Windows can examine your network and automatically discover network connection settings.
  If you would like Windows to try and discover them, click Detect Network Settings

MAINTAINING A WEB SITE

If a Web site was painstakingly designed and serves an important role in the life of the person, business, or organization who owns and/or designed it, a site won't be forgotten and left idle. While many individuals who take advantage of the free Web space offered by ISPs may design a personal page and forget all about it, rarely is a Web site uploaded, tested, and then forgotten by the designer and/or owner of the site if they care about the site's appearance and functionality. Typically, business and nonprofit Web site content is changed once a month— new products are offered, newsletters need updating, calendars are edited to reflect current and future activities—and you'll need to upload new versions of your existing pages.

You'll also have new pages to add and old pages to get rid of. If you're working for clients, be prepared for them to request changes. These may be minor tweaks: "Can we move this graphic down an inch?" "Can this text be blue instead of pur-ple?" Or they could be major overhauls: "Can we have these graphics in a group over here and have them link to pages with full-size versions of each image?" "We have a new logo and we want it on every page, in the upper right instead of the lower left, and someone said we should have a Flash movie on our home page!" If your job as designer includes making these changes after the initial site is delivered, make sure your timeframe for responding to requested changes is spelled out ahead of time, and that the client knows that changes after the initial site is approved are billed separately.

MAKING CHANGES AND ADDITIONS

When you go to make changes, you'll use the FTP software again, copying files to the FTP site from your local drive. If the file is an updated version of one that's already on the Web server, a prompt, such as seen in Figure A-9, will appear to ask if you want to overwrite the file that's already there. Make sure you're copy-ing the correct version, and click Yes to overwrite the file.

If you're copying a new page, make sure that you also copy any graphic files or other elements (sounds, movies, files that people will download through the new page) to the appropriate folders on the Web server.

FIGURE A-9

Be careful when uploading new versions of existing files. Don't overwrite unless you're sure you're uploading the latest and greatest version.

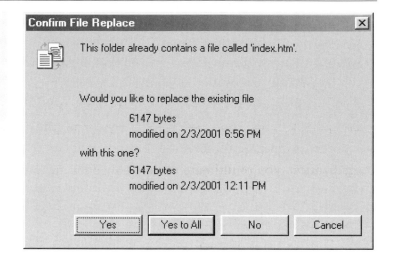

BACKUPS AND ARCHIVES It's a good idea to keep copies of your pages in a separate folder. Why? Because if you accidentally overwrite the wrong file, you'll want a place to go to get the file that was overwritten so you can upload it again and put things back to the way they should be. Further, it's a good idea to maintain some sort of page archives. If your site has a newsletter or calendar, keep copies of the various versions of the pages for reference. If you're working with a client, there could be a dispute over what was posted last month, and if you already uploaded this month's version, you'll want an archive version of the file to check. When you store archive versions, change the filenames to reflect the date. For example, if it's a calendar page that's posted to the Web server as calendar.htm, save the archive versions as calendar_feb.htm (for February's calendar) or calendar_feb01.htm if you want to save more than a year's worth of files for reference.

UNDERSTANDING THE WEBMASTER'S ROLE

The term *webmaster* really says it all. A true webmaster is the omniscient, omnipotent ruler of the Web site. Nothing is uploaded by anyone else or without his or her consent and approval after the fact. Changes are requested in writing and submitted to the webmaster, or they don't happen. All testing is done by the webmaster, unless he or she appoints someone else to do it. A schedule for periodic testing of links (in case a site to which your site links has moved or is shut down) is established and maintained by the webmaster.

All this power comes at a price, however. The buck stops with the webmaster in terms of blame, as well. If you're the webmaster and a visitor can't load a page or a graphic is missing, you'll get the irate phone call from the client or the irritated e-mail from the visitor (if you have a "Contact the Webmaster" link on the site). Even if you, as webmaster, delegate some of the maintenance and testing jobs to others in your organization, you're ultimately responsible for the proper functioning of the site.

Many designers offer to perform webmaster duties for their clients, especially if their clients are small organizations that don't have the staff or funds to appoint their own person to maintain their site. This dual role can be a good thing, because many designers feel a certain attachment to the sites they create, and staying on as webmaster helps assure them that no one is going to come in and monkey with their masterpiece. The dual role can be a bad thing, though, if the client is one that makes a lot of demands—change this, move that—on a daily or weekly basis. You can end up with so many webmaster tasks to perform that you can't make time for new design work. If you're building (or thinking about building) a Web design business, don't bite off more than you can chew in terms of the support you promise to existing clients and the number of new clients you're cultivating. You could end up with too many clients and too much to do for them, long before you have enough income to afford an assistant.

> **TIP** If your Web design business is growing beyond the point where you can wear all the hats—designer, webmaster to several sites, marketer, salesperson, customer service rep—consider bringing in an intern. Local universities and technical colleges are often eager to find such positions to help students learn about the real-world, day-to-day life of a Web designer, webmaster, or graphic artist.

HTML Basics

While it's not essential that you understand HTML in order to design Web pages, it can be a big help. Because the design software you'll be using—Dreamweaver, GoLive, FrontPage, and a variety of other applications—all convert your pages to HTML, it pays to at least be able to read that code and be able to recognize its parts and have a general understanding of what's going on. You'll also find that, at some point, you may be required to edit a Web page when you don't have your trusty design software by your side. Knowing enough HTML to edit text, change a graphic from one image to another, or redirect a hyperlink will save you a lot of time, and if you're designing pages for clients, make you look like a genius.

WHAT IS HTML?

HTML is a markup language (the letters HTML stand for Hypertext Markup Language) that consists of *tags*, *attributes*, and *values*. You enter the tags, attributes, and values by typing text into a word processor or text-editing program, and save the file as HTML. Virtually any text-editing program or word processor offers the HTML format (.htm) through its Save As dialog box (click the Save As Type drop-down list). You can use WordPad or Notepad, both of which are part of the Windows operating system and are found in the Accessories submenu. You can also use programs such as TextPad (from Helios Software Solutions), or you can use the code view features in Dreamweaver, GoLive, FrontPage, or any other WYSIWYG application.

THE "GRAMMAR" OF HTML

HTML consists of tags, which are directions. They say such things as "insert this here," "go there," or "do this." For example, every Web page begins with a tag that tells the Web browser, "This page contains HTML code, and you should do what it says." The tag that makes this statement is the `<html>` tag, and it's the first line in the code of any Web page. At the end of the page, a closing `</html>` tag is inserted, saying, "The HTML ends here." Note the leading slash `(/)` which is part of any closing tag.

In order for HTML code to work and be interpreted correctly by the Web browser software, it must be structured properly. This includes the order in which basic tags appear (the tags every page must have) and the order and content of lines of code within the page. For example, something as minor as a missing set of quotation marks or an unwanted slash can result in an image not appearing or a link not working. Figure B-1 shows the HTML code for a blank Web document—there is no text or graphics yet, just the skeleton of the HTML code that every page must have.

WORKING WITH TAGS AND ATTRIBUTES

Most tags need both an opening tag and a closing tag, but some don't. Some tags are accompanied by *attributes* and *values*, further instructions that tell the browser how a tag's instructions should be fulfilled. As an example, imagine a tag

FIGURE B-1

These basic codes tell the browser what kind of document this is and help define its basic parts.

```
<html>
<head>
<title>Untitled Document</title>
<meta http-equiv="Content-Type"
content="text/html; charset=iso-8859-1">
</head>

<body bgcolor="#FFFFFF" text="#000000">

</body>
</html>
```

that says, "Insert an image here." That tag must include information about the image, such as where the image file can be found, and if the image serves as a link to something else, the link information must be there, too. Figure B-2 shows the HTML tag and attributes for an image that's centered and links to another page in the same Web site.

The following table lists common HTML tags and explains the roles they play in a Web page document.

Tag	Purpose
`<html>` `</html>`	This opening tag tells the browser that interprets the text to expect HTML and display the Web page accordingly.
`<body>` `</body>`	The `<body>` tag is the second tag in an HTML document and indicates the beginning of the page content. A closing tag appears at the end of the page, before the closing `</html>` tag.

FIGURE B-2

It may seem complicated, but once you understand the parts of an HTML document, you'll be reading and writing them on your own.

This tag indicates an image is inserted.

```
<html>
<head>
<title>Untitled Document</title>
<meta http-equiv="Content-Type" content="text/html;
charset=iso-8859-1">
</head>
<body bgcolor="#FFFFFF" text="#000000">
<div align="center"><a href="contact.htm">
<img src="images/contact.jpg" width="165" height="62" border="0">
</a>
</div>
</body>
</html>
```

This attribute indicates the position of the image.

This attribute says which image it will be and where to find the image file.

Tag	Purpose
`<head>` `</head>`	The `<head>` tag surrounds the identifying information for the page. If you want your page to have a title that appears on the title bar of the browser window, type it between the head tags. For example: `<head>`The Farkle Family Web Page`</head>`
`<h1>` `</h1>`	Not to be confused with a `<head>` tag, a *heading* tag indicates heading-style text. Between the opening heading tag and its closing tag partner, type the text of the heading. For example: `<h1>`Fred Farkle Fuses Form and Function!`</h2>` With heading tags, the number indicates the heading level. `<h1>` is a heading 1 style, `<h2>` for heading 2, and so on. When assigning heading levels, remember that the lower the number, the larger the text will be.
`<p>` `</p>`	This is a paragraph break, and it inserts a blank line. If you want to create vertical space between paragraphs of body text, graphics, or tables on your page, insert a `<p>` tag (don't forget the closing tag). Whenever you press ENTER in a WYSIWYG application, a `<p>` tag is inserted, along with its closing tag mate.
` `	When you don't want a full blank line, but do want to move down to the next line on the page, insert a ` ` tag for a line break. There is no closing break tag.
`<center>` `</center>`	This tag centers the content that falls between the opening and closing `<center>` tag. This can be text or a reference to an image. You can use `<left>` or `<right>` instead of `<center>`.
`<img src= "_____">`	An image source tag indicates the use of a graphic, and tells the browser which graphic file to display. The blank to the right indicates where the graphic file path and name would appear, for example: `<img src="/images/groupphoto.jpg">`
`<a href= "_____"> </a href>`	An href tag starts with an *a* and is used to indicate a hyperlink to another page within your site, to an entirely different Web site, to a file for download, or to an e-mail address. The href tag for a link to Yahoo.com would appear as follows:

Tag	Purpose

```
<a href="http://www.yahoo.com/">Search the Web</a>
```

In this sample, the words "Search the Web" are the text that links to the Yahoo.com Web page.

`<table>`
`</table>`

The `<table>` tag heralds the start of a table. It is followed by `<tr>` and `<td>` tags for rows and columns, respectively. Both the tr and td tags have closing mates `</tr>` and `</td>`. The table tags for a two-column, two-row table would appear as follows:

```
<table width="4">
  <tr>
    <td> </td>
    <td> </td>
  </tr>
  <tr>
    <td> </td>
    <td> </td>
  </tr>
</table>
```

In this sample, the " " indicates a nonbreaking space, and the table's width of 4 indicates the pixel width of the table.

EDITING HTML CODE

Editing an HTML document is just like editing a word processing document. Position your cursor and begin typing if you want to add text, or use the BACKSPACE and DELETE keys if you want to get rid of text. You can also select text with your mouse and replace it by typing something else, or move it by using the Edit | Cut and then Edit | Paste commands. You can copy code (Edit | Copy) if the code should be repeated elsewhere in the document or in another page.

The length of an HTML document is unlimited, and you can just keep typing as long as you need to. You'll want to use the TAB key to indent some tags, and the tags and attributes inside them, as shown in Figure B-3. The indents don't affect the functioning of the HTML code; they just help you see the distinct parts of the document as represented by the code.

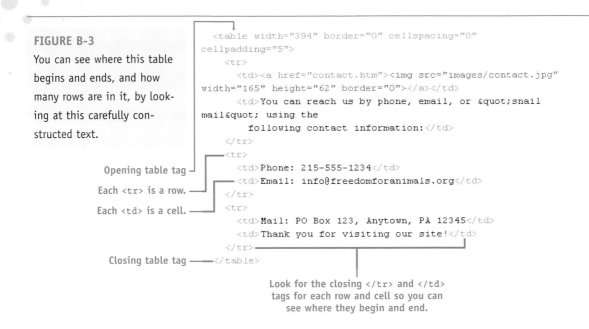

FIGURE B-3

You can see where this table begins and ends, and how many rows are in it, by looking at this carefully constructed text.

Opening table tag

Each <tr> is a row.

Each <td> is a cell.

Closing table tag

Look for the closing </tr> and </td> tags for each row and cell so you can see where they begin and end.

WORKING WITH HTML THROUGH A WYSIWYG APPLICATION

All WYSIWYG Web development applications—such as FrontPage, Dreamweaver, and GoLive—offer a view of the HTML code that's being created as you insert content through the WYSYWIG tools. FrontPage offers a tab that displays the HTML code, so you can switch between WYSIWYG and HTML code views quickly and easily.

Dreamweaver allows you to see both views at once. They call their WYSIWYG view Design view and the HTML view Code view. Using the Design and Code views, you have a split screen that allows you to select something in one half of the window and see its companion content highlighted in the other. As shown in Figure B-4, when you click on a table cell in the Design view pane, the underlying HTML code for that cell is highlighted in the Code view pane.

FIGURE B-4

Learn which code goes with which page elements by seeing both the page and its underlying code at the same time.

The cell's HTML reference in Code view

The selected table cell in Design view

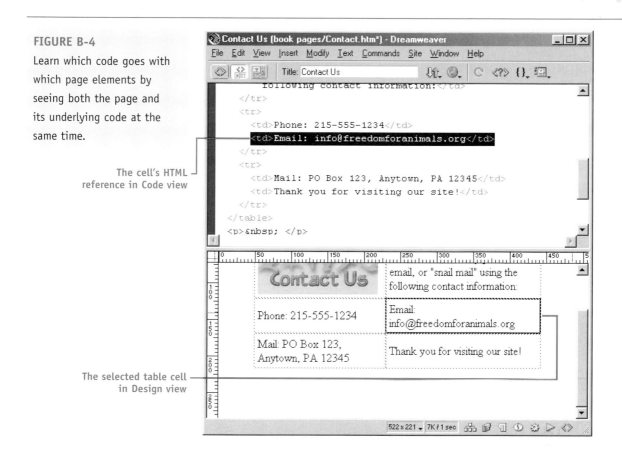

LEARNING THROUGH OBSERVATION AND IMITATION You can learn a lot about HTML by viewing the code that was used to create pages you see on the Web. If you're viewing the page through Internet Explorer, choose View | Source. If you're browsing with Netscape, choose View | Page Source. After either command, a new window opens, displaying the HTML for that page. You can search within the window for specific text (say, a tag you're trying to understand or an attribute that you're not sure how to use). You can also save the file to your local drive, at which point you can edit the code and build a page of your own. Is that stealing? No, because no one can copyright HTML code. Don't borrow anything else from the page, though. Don't save the graphics from their page so you can reuse them, and don't steal their text. You're only borrowing the HTML code—remember to replace any body text with your own, because the original author of the page may have copyrighted their text.

Glossary

Web Design Glossary: A Compendium of Web and Design Terminology

Here's a list of the terms I've used in this book that may be new to you, or that you may not be aware of in terms of their use in the context of the Web in general or Web design specifically. I wanted this book to have a glossary because I've found it to be very useful in books I've read about topics that were new to me. You can use a glossary two ways: you can use it to look up specific terms or words you don't know, or you can browse through it in more of a free-form, exploratory fashion, driven not by the need to define a specific term or word, but to poke around in the lingo of a new area of interest.

As far as the terms and words included in this glossary are concerned, I'm sure I've missed a few, but I tried to define any new terms at the point where I first used them within the text. Between the chapters and this glossary, I hope any big mysteries are cleared up! If you have any difficulty with terminology or concepts discussed in this book, I invite you to e-mail me at laurie@planetlaurie.com, and I'll be happy to do my best to clarify things for you.

alignment   With regard to Web page design, refers to the placement of text and graphics relative to the left and right sides of the page, or to the top and bottom of a table cell.

animated GIF   A GIF file that moves on a Web page when viewed through a Web browser. The movement is achieved through the continuous play of several images. You can also set an animation to occur just once or for a specific number of repetitions.

artifacts   The spots and imperfections that appear on an image after the user has resized an image manually. The process of file compression (saving a file in a lossy format) creates artifacts as well.

attributes   In HTML code, attributes define the properties of tags. For example, a `<table>` tag can include attributes that control the size of the table, background color, border width, and alignment on the page. Attributes are followed by an equals sign, and the attribute value in quotes, as in border="3".

bitmap   Pixel-based graphics in which every tiny dot that makes up the image is mapped and its location and color stored as part of the file.

border   A line around an image, table cell, or frame. Borders are defined in terms of their pixel width and color.

brightness   The amount of white in a color, or the amount of white added to an image to lighten the colors.

browser   Software that allows you to view Web pages, move between pages you've visited, follow links between pages, and print Web page content. Browsers can also be used to view local HTML files before they're posted to the Web.

bytes   The second smallest unit of measurement when it comes to computer capacity and file sizes. The smallest is a bit, and 8 bits make 1 byte. There are approximately 1,000 bytes (1,024 to be exact) in a kilobyte, 1,000,000 bytes (1,048,576 to be exact) in a megabyte, and 1,000,000,000 bytes (1,073,741,824 to be exact) in a gigabyte. When it comes to the Web, small files are best in virtually all situations. Smaller graphic, sound, and movie files load faster, so the site visitor doesn't waste time waiting to view or interact with a Web page.

clipboard   A Windows feature that allows you to cut, copy, and paste content between locations within the same file or between files. With regard to the Web, the clipboard is used to cut and copy text from a document to a Web page or between Web pages. When a page is viewed through a browser, you can copy its content to the clipboard and paste it into another file for reuse. This should not be done with copyrighted material, unless you're referencing the source of the material and have cleared its use with the copyright holder.

CMYK   A color model based on the concept that colors are all made up of varying levels of cyan, magenta, yellow, and black. You can view a color's CMYK levels through an application such as Adobe Photoshop, and by adjusting CMYK levels, create new colors.

complementary colors   Colors that look good together based on their locations on the color wheel. Complementary colors are opposites on the wheel—the colors directly across from each other work well when used together in any design, be it for print work or the Web.

contrast   The amount of difference between two values. With regard to images, contrast normally refers to the amount of light and dark. By adjusting the contrast of an image, you can reduce the brightness of colors (if you're using an overexposed photo, for example) or brighten dark colors if there wasn't enough light in the room when a picture was taken.

domain   The name of a Web site. In the Web address www.planetlaurie.com, "planetlaurie" is the portion of the name that is exclusively yours, the www indicates that the domain is on the World Wide Web, and the .com extension indicates the type of site it is—originally, .com sites were commercial, .org sites were nonprofit organizations, .net sites were internet-related sites, and .edu sites were schools. Now only the use of .edu is restricted (as are .gov and .mil, and you can guess what they're used for), and the extension on a site isn't necessarily an indication of the type of information you'll find there.

download   To copy something "down" from the Web or Internet. When downloading a file from a Web server, a copy is made available, and that copy is what is copied to the user's local drive. This makes the source file (on the server) available to anyone else who tries to download it at the same time.

e-mail   A term that comes from the longer, more cumbersome term "electronic mail." It refers to messages sent to an e-mail server, addressed to a person's e-mail address. When designing a Web page, you can include links to e-mail addresses, so that page visitors can click the link and open an e-mail message window, preaddressed to the recipient of your choice.

font   A typeface. Fonts come in three varieties: serif, sans serif, and artistic. Serif fonts have flourishes on the ends of letters (like wings, the term "serif" coming from the Latin "seraphim"), and sans serif fonts don't. Artistic fonts are ornate and complex. Due to the fact that not all of your visitors may have an extensive array of fonts installed on their computers, it's best to keep to a handful of simple fonts—Arial, Times New Roman, Helvetica, and Verdana—so you know that the font you use will be the font visitors see, with no substitutions imposed by their browsers.

frames   A structural device that sections a browser window into two or more panels displaying separate Web page documents. Each frame can have a separate background color or image, and can operate independently from the other frames on the page—one frame remaining static and another containing scrollable content, for example.

freeware   Software that is available for free. The software's designers/programmers will often accept a donation for the use of their software, but it isn't required. Not to be confused with shareware, which can usually be downloaded for free, but must be purchased in order to use it legally.

FTP   File Transfer Protocol. FTP software is used to connect to FTP sites, where files are stored. By uploading your Web page files to an FTP location (normally named ftp.*yourdomainname*.com), you are putting your pages on the Web, making them visible to people who visit your site.

GIF   A graphic file format favored for Web use. The acronym GIF stands for Graphic Interchange Format. The GIF format is best used for line art, simple shapes, and images with large areas of solid color, rather than complex drawings or photographs. GIF files support 256 colors only.

graphic   A picture, such as a scanned or otherwise digitally captured photograph, drawing, piece of clip art, or collection of computer-generated shapes and/or lines.

HTML   Hypertext Markup Language. HTML is the language in which Web pages are written. Even if you use a program such as Dreamweaver or FrontPage to design your pages, the actions you take through the software to fill the page with text, graphics, color, and other elements are converted to HTML instructions in the form of tags and their attributes.

HTTP   Hypertext Transfer Protocol, which appears as http:// in a Web address. The use of the abbreviation calls a set of data transfer standards into play, making sure that all Web pages, despite their physical location and the location of the person visiting them, are transmitted in the same way.

hue   A specific color location on the color wheel or in a color spectrum.

hyperlink   Text or graphics on a Web page that are linked to another page or file. Hyperlinked text is usually underlined, and its color is determined by your browser's settings for link text. Web designers can set the link colors for individual pages—setting colors for active and visited links—but browsers can be set to ignore the link colors set in the page and use the browser defaults.

image   Another term for *graphic*. Some people refer to "graphic images," but that's redundant—sort of like saying "text characters."

indent   Refers to the horizontal movement of text. Text can be moved to the right, creating a greater distance between the left margin and the text, or moved to the left, creating a greater distance between the right margin and the text. In HTML, a `<blockquote>` tag creates a left and right indent for selected text, moving it in from both the left and right sides.

interlaced   An interlaced graphic appears slowly on a Web page as the page loads. At first, the image appears choppy and blurry, and as the image is loaded, it becomes clearer and crisper. The term *interlaced* refers to GIF files. The term *progressive* is often used interchangeably with interlaced, but progressive refers to JPG images that load slowly. If an image is neither progressive nor interlaced, it won't appear on the page at all until it is fully loaded.

ISP   Internet service provider. Your ISP is the organization that gives you a number for your modem to dial to connect to the Internet. Most ISPs also provide you with at least one e-mail address, and many provide free space for a personal home page.

JavaScript   A scripting language that can be added to HTML documents to expand the capabilities of Web pages. Web page elements such as mouse-over or rollover effects and the validation of submitted user forms are executed through JavaScript.

JPG   This graphic file format (also known as JPEG) is an acronym for the people who created it—the Joint Photographic Experts Group. JPG is one of three Web-preferred graphic file formats (the other two are GIF and PNG), and is best for photographs and complex images. JPG files can contain millions of colors, yet generate very small files, which is very good for Web use, as anything you can do to reduce load times for site visitors is valuable.

layers   Used to provide structure to Web pages, layers are free-floating boxes into which text and graphics can be inserted. Layers can overlap and can be placed anywhere on the page, allowing for a more flexible arrangement than can be achieved with tables or frames. Only the latest versions of browser software recognize layers, however, so use them with caution if many members of your assumed audience will be using older browsers (pre-4.0).

nesting   Placing something inside something else. In the case of Web page content, tables can be nested (placing a table inside another table's cell), and frames can also be nested.

pixel   Stands for "picture element," and is the smallest element your monitor can display. Images consist of thousands of pixels, each being a dot of color. When the dots are viewed together (and at a distance), the image is created by the viewer's eye.

plug-in   A program you must have on your computer in order to view or interact with certain Web page elements and files, such as movies and certain sound files.

PNG   Portable Network Graphics. This Web-friendly graphic file format has been approved by the World Wide Web Consortium (W3C) and is gaining popularity among designers. Newer browsers support the format, which is a good thing for designers—the format is great for both photos and line art.

points   The system by which text size is measured for print work and word processing. Fonts on the Web are measured in pixels, but many Web design software programs do the points-to-pixels conversion for you so you can stick with a sizing system with which you're already familiar.

PPI   Pixels per inch. Refers to the resolution of an image. Obviously, the more pixels per inch, the more detail an image will have.

primary colors   The three colors you can't create by mixing other colors: blue, red, and yellow. When you mix primary colors, you get secondary colors.

progressive   Like *interlaced* (which refers to GIF files that compose slowly), progressive JPG images appear choppy or blurry at first, slowly becoming clearer and crisper as the image is completely loaded through the visitor's browser. If an image is not progressive, it won't appear until the entire image file is loaded.

RGB   Red, green, blue. This color model is based on the idea that all colors are made up of various levels of these three colors. Web browsers recognize RGB colors.

rollover   An image on a Web page that changes when the visitor mouses over the image. A rollover image consists of two images: one that appears when the page loads, and a second image that is swapped for the first if someone points to the first image.

saturation The intensity of a color. A deep, bright, royal blue has a higher saturation, for example, than a more muted shade of slate or denim blue.

search engine A tool that allows a Web user to search for Web sites that meet certain criteria. A search engine is in use at a site such as http://www.google.com/, which invites Web "surfers" to enter keywords by which to search for particular Web pages. Search engines are also used to query online databases.

secondary colors The colors you create by mixing two primary colors. Red and blue make purple, blue and yellow make green, and red and yellow make orange. When secondary colors are mixed, tertiary colors are created.

shareware Software you can download for free, but after testing, you must pay for in order to use legally. Some shareware has a timer built in that disables the software after a certain number of days or uses has elapsed, and others continue to work even if the user doesn't pay the manufacturer. It is both illegal and unethical to use shareware without paying for it after the stated evaluation period has expired.

storyboard To map out, on paper or the computer screen, the layout of a Web site, showing the hierarchy of and relationship between pages. Individual pages can also be storyboarded, whereby the page's content is sketched out to assist the designer in coming up with the most effective composition for the page.

table A grid of rows and columns into which text and graphics are inserted. Tables can be nested, placing an entire table inside another table's individual cell. Tables are one of the most effective and popular structural devices for Web page design.

tags In HTML, tags are the words enclosed in pairs of greater-than and less-than symbols (such as `<table>`) that tell the browser what is included in a Web page, where to place it, and how to display it.

tertiary colors The colors created by mixing secondary colors.

tiling Repeating an image over and over, filling the background of a Web page.

tween When building an animated GIF in Adobe ImageReady (for example), you can create two frames—one being the way the animation should look when it starts, the other the way the animation should look when it finishes. By asking the software to "tween" the images, all the frames that take the image from its first frame to its last are created automatically.

upload   To copy files from a local computer to a Web server. The term can also be used for copying files from a local computer to a network server, not related to or accessible via the Internet.

URL   Uniform Resource Locator. Another way to say "Web address." The URL for my Web site is www.planetlaurie.com.

watermark   An image placed behind the text layer of a document. You can place a logo or other simple image behind your Web page content by reducing the opacity of an image and selecting it as your page background image. What makes a watermark different from any other background image is the faded quality of the image—the watermark should be just a whisper of the image at its full intensity.

WAV   A common sound file format. WAV files are popular for use on the Web because they require no plug-in, making them universally playable by anyone visiting a Web site, as long as their computer has sound capability.

Web server   A computer that houses Web pages and makes them available to anyone connected to the Internet and using Web browser software.

webmaster   The person responsible for maintaining a Web site. A webmaster's job consists of uploading pages to the Web, maintaining pages and testing their functionality, and troubleshooting Web sites.

Web-safe colors   The 216 colors that browsers can recognize and display.

WYSIWYG   What You See Is What You Get. Pronounced "wizzy-wig," WYSIWYG is a term that came into being with the development of graphical interfaces and operating systems. These graphical environments allow users to see documents onscreen as they would appear when printed, taking much of the guesswork out of document layout and design. The advent of Windows made this a much more popular term, as Windows and personal computers became more "user-friendly" when software became picture-oriented, providing a WYSIWYG environment in which to work. When it comes to the Web, WYSIWYG Web design software allows the designer to design Web pages by inserting text and graphics and viewing them onscreen as they'll appear when seen online.

Index

INTERNATIONAL CONTACT INFORMATION

AUSTRALIA
McGraw-Hill Book Company Australia Pty. Ltd.
TEL +61-2-9417-9899
FAX +61-2-9417-5687
http://www.mcgraw-hill.com.au
books-it_sydney@mcgraw-hill.com

CANADA
McGraw-Hill Ryerson Ltd.
TEL +905-430-5000
FAX +905-430-5020
http://www.mcgrawhill.ca

**GREECE, MIDDLE EAST,
NORTHERN AFRICA**
McGraw-Hill Hellas
TEL +30-1-656-0990-3-4
FAX +30-1-654-5525

MEXICO (Also serving Latin America)
McGraw-Hill Interamericana Editores S.A. de C.V.
TEL +525-117-1583
FAX +525-117-1589
http://www.mcgraw-hill.com.mx
fernando_castellanos@mcgraw-hill.com

SINGAPORE (Serving Asia)
McGraw-Hill Book Company
TEL +65-863-1580
FAX +65-862-3354
http://www.mcgraw-hill.com.sg
mghasia@mcgraw-hill.com

SOUTH AFRICA
McGraw-Hill South Africa
TEL +27-11-622-7512
FAX +27-11-622-9045
robyn_swanepoel@mcgraw-hill.com

**UNITED KINGDOM & EUROPE
(Excluding Southern Europe)**
McGraw-Hill Publishing Company
TEL +44-1-628-502500
FAX +44-1-628-770224
http://www.mcgraw-hill.co.uk
computing_neurope@mcgraw-hill.com

ALL OTHER INQUIRIES Contact:
Osborne/McGraw-Hill
TEL +1-510-549-6600
FAX +1-510-883-7600
http://www.osborne.com
omg_international@mcgraw-hill.com

LEARN WEB DESIGN FASTER!

MORE VIDEO LESSONS FROM LAURIE ULRICH AND BRAINSVILLE.COM

Dear Friend,

Thank you for buying this book. I hope that you found it useful and enjoyed the CD-ROM full of video lessons.

There were too many great Web design topics to cover on one CD, so I created the **Web Design CD Extra**, a second CD covering key areas like these:

Graphics and Design Tools
Photoshop, Flash, and Dreamweaver help speed development and produce better-looking images faster

Web Site Critiques
Frank opinions about other people's mistakes--plus simple principles for sharp-looking sites

HTML Basics
Learn the language of the web to make your sites work the way you want

Structuring Pages
See how tables and frames let you control text and image placement

Creative Page Balancing
Eye-pleasing colors, layouts, and designs to keep your site visitors coming back

...And more! The complete contents are listed at www.Brainsville.com.

The lessons on the **Web Design CD Extra** use the same easy-to-follow video presentation style as the CD you already have. I'm right there on your screen, talking to you about Web design in the same practical, understandable way.

The **Web Design CD Extra** is an essential tool for learning Web design. Check it out at www.Brainsville.com.

Best Wishes,

Laurie Ulrich

```
Name: Laurie Ulrich
Project: Web Design CD Extra
```

ORDER THE WEB DESIGN CD EXTRA AT
Brainsville.com™
The better way to learn™